GOD IN THE WASTELAND

God in the Wasteland

*The Reality of Truth
in a World of Fading Dreams*

David F. Wells

William B. Eerdmans Publishing Company
Grand Rapids, Michigan

Inter-Varsity Press
Leicester, England

© 1994 Wm. B. Eerdmans Publishing Co.
255 Jefferson Ave. S.E., Grand Rapids, Michigan 49503

First published jointly 1994 in the United States by Wm. Eerdmans Publishing Co.
and in the U. K. by Inter-Varsity Press
38 De Montfort Street, Leicester LE1 7GP, England
Paperback edition 1995

Printed in the United States of America

09 08 07 06 05 04   11 10 9 8 7 6 5

Library of Congress Cataloging-in-Publication Data

Wells, David F.
God in the wasteland: the reality of truth in a world
of fading dreams / David F. Wells
p.   cm.
Includes bibliographical references and index.
ISBN 8028-4179-1
1. Evangelicalism — United States — History — 20th century.
2. Christiantity and culture.   3. Theology — 20th century.   I. Title.
BR1642.U5W44   1994
230'.046 — dc20   94-18850
                                                        CIP

British Library Cataloguing in Publication Data

A catalogue record for this book is available from the British Library

Inter-Varsity Press ISBN 0-85110-164-5

*Inter-Varsity Press is the book-publishing division of the Universities and Colleges Christian Fel-
lowship (formerly the Inter-Varsity Fellowship), a student movement linking Christian Unions in
universities and colleges throughout the United Kingdom and the Republic of Ireland, and a member
movement of the International Fellowship of Evangelical Students. For information about local
and national activities write to UCCF, 38 de Montfort Street, Leicester LE1 7GP.*

Contents

To
Jonathan and JoAnna,
and
David and Lynne,
with much love

Preface

In 1989, I was the recipient of a significant grant from the Pew Charitable Trusts that enabled me to write *No Place for Truth; or, Whatever Happened to Evangelical Theology?* This book produced only half the picture I wanted to present, however. It offers an explanation of the cultural factors that have diminished the place and importance of theology in the church, but it offers no suggestions for a remedy of the problem. I am grateful, therefore, for the opportunity afforded me through a sabbatical to begin developing the other half of the picture in this book. Here I outline the first step that I believe needs to be taken to reverse the situation I described in the first book.

My absence from Gordon-Conwell Theological Seminary during this time has meant that some of my colleagues have had to assume some of my responsibilities, and I am grateful to them for their help and the generous spirit with which they have provided it.

Chapter 8 of this book reports on and utilizes important research that was done for me by Rodger Rice, director of the Social Research Center at Calvin College. In an effort to measure the saliency of belief among seminarians, we asked seven seminaries for their assistance in producing a representative sampling of evangelical students. I wish to express my deep appreciation to the presidents of these seminaries for their willing cooperation as well as to those who worked so hard to make sure that the surveys were carried out effectively: Leslie Andrews (Asbury Theological Seminary), Kathleen Ericson (Bethel Theological Seminary), Keith Tanis (Calvin Theological Seminary), Lynda Bradley (Denver Conservative Baptist Seminary), Sandee Masuda-Hunt (Fuller Theological Seminary), Margaret Manning (Gordon-Conwell Theological Seminary), and Dennis Gaines (Talbot School of Theology). It has been a pleasure to work with Rodger Rice on this project, and I am much in debt to him for his considerable sociological expertise.

The report that resulted from this survey was, unfortunately, too long to be used *in toto*. Moreover, it was also written in a form that had to be adapted a little to meet the needs of the intended audience of this book. I felt, however, that the results were so significant (this may be the most extensive and searching analysis ever made of the views of evangelical seminarians) that I have included the statistical tables in an appendix. This will at least make this work available for those who may wish to use it or build on it without burdening those for whom the material is of less interest.

While the work was being done on this survey, I was able to obtain from James Hunter the raw data from a survey he made of seminarians in 1982. This proved most valuable to us because it enabled us to run a series of comparisons. I am most grateful to him for his willingness to make this material available to us.

I sent out much of the material in this book to various friends and colleagues for evaluation. Naturally, they are to be exonerated from all blame for what follows, but I do wish to thank Greg Beale, Jack Davis, David Gordon, Os Guinness, Scott Hafemann, Walter Kaiser, and John Seel for their careful and conscientious responses. I am also grateful to Margaret Manning, my student assistant, who helped me in checking parts of the manuscript.

The very day that the manuscript of this book was being sent off to the publisher, I received a copy of Colin Gunton's *The One, the Three, and the Many: God, Creation and the Culture of Modernity,* which I had ordered. It was, of course, too late to profit from his book, which contains the Bampton Lectures of 1992. He traverses much the same territory as I have here, though he does so from a more philosophical angle. Nevertheless, we appear to share many views, and I regret that I was unable to read his work before the completion of my own.

Finally, I wish to express my appreciation for those who are still serious readers in America. Without them, I and many others would be silenced. The time and attention they give to their reading flies in the face of the habits that modernity inculcates so insiduously. And so, I wish to salute their stubborn resistance to modernity! Against all the odds, may their number increase, and may the church, in consequence, once again become a place where life is given its most serious and searching analysis.

PROLOGUE

CHAPTER 1

An Accident in History

Modern man is afflicted with a permanent identity crisis, a condition conducive to considerable nervousness.

Peter Berger

The modern world artfully simplifies, sometimes inadvertently. I was reminded of this yesterday when I unexpectedly encountered the theme of this book in bold, simple letters, right before my eyes.

I was driving down a quiet lane not far from my house. The beauty of the setting was striking. The tall, leafy trees reached over the road, forming a natural cathedral. So thick and luscious was this summer finery that only the thinnest slivers of light were able to pierce through the overhead canopy. A few horses were out romping in a field the grassy mounds of which, bright with sunshine, eventually sloped down to a river. The quietness and magnificence of this pastoral scene was broken only by some crows in irritated contention over the remnants of a small animal that had, in the night, fallen prey to a passing motorist.

Without warning, a white pickup truck suddenly pulled out into the road ahead of me. I had to brake hard to avoid a collision. Now, Boston drivers never take an affront like that lightly, because they have learned from long experience that these infringements on decency and order are never inadvertent. In other places they may be accidental — perhaps they often are — but in Boston they are all calculated insults. The only question that remains is what to do about them.

As this old truck jerked into motion ahead of me, I noticed the

3

two messages on its rear bumper. The one on the left declared for
McGuire, a local politician, in bold letters, and the one on the right
declared for Jesus in equally bold letters. But there were additional
letters, much smaller, above and below both these names. I was more
than a little interested to know exactly what message this kind of driver
would sport, so I accelerated to get within reading distance of the
truck. My intention, I assure you, was completely innocent. But this
driver, no doubt hardened by the routine combat of manners and
vehicles that passes for traffic in and around Boston, looked alarmed,
and, perhaps suspecting some form of retaliation, spurted forward. A
dark cloud of smoke belched from the truck, signaling the driver's
move to make a getaway. Not to be outdone, I accelerated with him.
He pushed on even faster, a sense of imminent retribution no doubt
inspiring his flight. By now we were both well above the speed limit
— by no means without risk on this lane, since the local gendarmes
are notorious for being entirely without compassion. I could see his
darting glances in the rear view mirror as I matched each forward
lurch of his truck with a spurt of my own, acceleration for acceleration.
All I wanted to do was read his bumper stickers, but he was having
none of it. He escaped.

As he sped off, I was left to ponder this strange way, now so
ubiquitous in America, of making a stand for the truth on one's
bumper. I would not want you to consider me a reactionary on this
issue. Let me say at the outset that I understand the argument in favor
the bumper sticker. We live in an age that is thoroughly conversant
with the language of commerce in which our advertisers have tutored
us. It is an age in which we pass the mysteries of life from one to
another in short, pithy slogans. So why not promote Jesus along with
McGuire? I have no doubt that there are good intentions behind the
action. It is a way of telling others, of bringing home to them a thought
that might connect with something else they know, perhaps jog some
internal configuration of yearnings and desires and suggest a way
home to the eternal or a way out of the morass at City Hall. Slapping
on a bumper sticker is a way of standing for the truth.

But it is a peculiarly modern way, is it not? The great issues of
life are compressed into a word or slogan and offered up as a commodity to any takers on the highways and byways of America. It is
assumed that the consumers following the bumper are in a state of
suspended dissatisfaction and that the message will answer their need.
The whole exchange takes place in the impersonal language of the
marketplace. No names need even be exchanged. It is commerce aimed

at need, the transaction hopefully circumventing serious thought and critical reflection entirely. In this particular case, Jesus and McGuire sat side by side on the same shelf, products suited for particular circumstances and needs. Those who needed McGuire were encouraged to purchase him with a vote; those who needed Jesus were informed that he was also available, too, and perhaps on equally convenient terms.

It might be said that this book is about Jesus and McGuire, or, as those in the trade put it, about Christ and culture. McGuire is everywhere in our modern world. He is the symbol not only of political choice but of our commerce in goods and services, the daily business of meeting needs.[1] Personal needs, psychological aches, the imponderable senses that move like tides in and out of the self each day, the eerie sense that all our sound and fury may indeed signify nothing, the alarms that ring in the night when our dreams throw down their apprehensions, the realization that slowly comes to us that our daily routines, so innocent in their appearance, are actually executioners that in time will crack the body and return it to the earth — for all of these needs we are now offered balms, elixirs, and remedies at a price. Medical, chemical, and professional products of all kinds are hawked everywhere, in the newspapers, on the airwaves, in the streets, door to door, on car bumpers. Yet the confusion that they sow for us is not my primary focus here; I am more concerned about the immediate by-product of this confusion, which is the difficulty that is introduced when the name of Jesus goes on the bumper alongside that of McGuire. To get at this issue, we have to look at the larger framework in which it appears, the context of our modern world. This world is the result of revolutionary changes that have taken place over the last century or more. These changes are not the work of conventional revolutionaries, however. What has happened is an accident.

---

1. In what follows, McGuire is more than just a political commodity; he is a construct of the circumstances of modernity more generally. For a brilliant, if acerbic, depiction of the fluid, narcissistic, consumer-oriented culture that negotiates with the likes of McGuire, a culture disconnected from place, community, and family, see the following three volumes by Christopher Lasch: *Haven in a Heartless World: The Family Besieged* (New York: Basic Books, 1979); *The Culture of Narcissism: American Life in an Age of Diminishing Expectations* (New York: W. W. Norton, 1978); and *The Minimal Self: Psychic Survival in Troubled Times* (New York: W. W. Norton, 1978).

The Accidental Revolution

Revolutions usually happen when change has so roiled a society that little of the past remains in place. They happen when change is too rapid, deep, and broad to be absorbed and processed. Then the old ways are simply swept away; old conventions, structures, beliefs, values, and players all become obsolete.

Revolutions aim to unseat those in power. Those who exercise political power, those who have found warm and secure resting places in the status quo, those who preserve society in order to consume the lion's share of its bounty — these are the ones who feel the hot breath of the aggrieved.[2] Injustice — economic, racial, or social — is always the rallying cry of the revolutionaries as they storm the Bastille. When they triumph, those who were once excluded from power can bask in it, while those upon whom power had conferred its sacramental blessing are left out in the cold, stripped of their standing and usefulness. It was so when, earlier this century, the Bolsheviks were dislodged in Russia, when Mao and his armies marched to power in China, when communist regimes fell in Europe in the late 1980s, and it is so with disconcerting frequency in Africa today. It is thus that our world replaces its civilizations and political orders.

At least this is the way revolution has typically come. But today something quite different is afoot in the West. There is no question that Western culture is now being upended. What is interesting about this, however, is the relative ease with which this revolution has occurred. It has not been savage. It has held out blessings indiscriminately to all. It has been a sly, unobtrusive transformation. Nevertheless, every aspect of Western society, every nook and cranny, is now awash with change. And this change has not merely been technological in nature, as innovative products and techniques continue to alter the fabric and the rhythms of our lives. Nor has it simply been political and economic, important as these factors may have been. No, this change has in the profoundest sense been *spiritual*. It is not just the outer fabric of our life that has been assaulted by change but its inner sanctum as well. Change has intruded on the core of our being, the place where values are wrought, appetites emerge, expectations arise, and meaning is constructed. Our world has changed, and so have we.

2. See Jean-François Revel, *Without Marx or Jesus: The New American Revolution Has Begun,* trans. J. F. Bernard (Garden City, N.Y.: Doubleday, 1970), pp. 11-12.

Unlike all of its predecessors, this accidental revolution is not being driven either by a self-conscious ideology or by self-conscious revolutionaries. Our guerrillas are, in fact, very ordinary people, most of whom would be aghast if they could see themselves for what they are: provocateurs and agents of revolutionary change. Indeed, even the most average of Americans — the consumers of Tide and Tylenol, Listerine and Lysol, Coca-Cola and Kleenex, Lemon Pledge and Metropolitan Life — are in the center of this secular transfiguration.[3] They think and act in ways that look safe, predictable, and quite harmless. They are not wild-eyed and incendiary, and they do not spew out the kind of vituperation that is typical of revolutionaries. They produce little anguish, little protest, virtually no disdain. No, they are uniquely mild-mannered revolutionaries, but for all of that they have swept overboard the values that previous generations cherished. Old beliefs and conventions have ended up on many modern trash heaps, but we are neither perturbed nor vengeful. We are, in fact, quite innocent about what we are doing. We are without anger.

World Cliche Culture

This story has of course been told many times and from many angles. I offered my own account in the prologue to the volume on which I am seeking to build in this book.[4] In that account, I distinguished between modernization and modernity, two forces that together are driving the revolutionary transformation of our world. The former is producing changes in the outer fabric of our life; the latter is altering the values and meanings that emerge from within the context of the modernized world — values and meanings that in the modern context seem altogether normal and natural.

The process of modernization is driven by four main realities: capitalism, technology, urbanization, and telecommunications.

1. Capitalism emerged as a defining force in Europe following the collapse of the old medieval synthesis, but it did not effect evident changes until the beginning of the nineteenth century, when industrial-

3. While there is no such thing as an average American, there are identifiable patterns of attitude and consumption that are characteristic of those in the middle range economically; see Michael J. Weiss, *The Clustering of America* (New York: Harper & Row, 1988), p. 81.

4. See *No Place for Truth; or, Whatever Happened to Evangelical Theology* (Grand Rapids: William B. Eerdmans, 1993), pp. 53-91. The themes explored in that volume are the basis of the viewpoint I am developing here.

ization got under way, and it did not reach its full intensity until technology became both ubiquitous in society and indispensable to the functioning of capitalism. At the same time, however, capitalism has developed a profound dependence on the sorts of freedom typically provided by democratic societies. But in societies that have afforded rights of free association, unrestricted travel, and a belief in the propriety of the capitalist economy, capitalism has successfully reorganized the social structure for the purposes of manufacturing, production, and consumption. It has concentrated populations into cities and produced massive systems of finance, banking, law, communications, and transportation. In short, it has changed the shape of our world, how we relate to it, where we live, how we experience our work, and the values and expectations that we bring with us in order to be adaptable to and successful in this public sphere.

2. Technology is, of course, essential to modern capitalism. Its importance lies not simply in the fact that it facilitates the production of knowledge, makes possible medical and engineering breakthroughs, and is now indispensable to all modes of production. Equally important is the fact that it also rationalizes all of life. People who live in technologically dominated societies are prone to think naturalistically and to subject all of life to a calculus of benefits — to assume that whatever is most efficient is most ethical.

3. Modernization has also been driven by the stunning growth of urbanization, which has now spread beyond the West to become a worldwide phenomenon. In Western countries, 94 percent of the population now lives in cities of 50,000 or more. Cities create their own psychological environments because they draw into their precincts and into close contact with one another people with very different worldviews. During the twentieth century, this trend has been amplified in America by mass migrations of peoples from Asia and Central and South America. They have brought with them their own ethnic identities, cultural habits, languages, religions, and values — all of which have been brought into close proximity to one another in our cities. The new multicultural environment has produced a secular ecumenism and a powerful demand for pluralism, for mutual tolerance, for private space in which to hold one's beliefs, live one's own lifestyle, do what one wants to do. Thus far, the Constitution seems to be securing this much for each person, within the boundaries of the law, but it seems to be producing an encompassing relativism as well.

4. Finally, modern telecommunications has made us all citizens

of the whole world. Television is perhaps less a window on the world than a surrogate eye that preselects what images of the world we will be exposed to. Still, we have become witnesses of an extraordinary range of events that daily shape and shake the world. Television gives to us a psychological transcendence of space, both physical and cultural, linking us to other people around the world. The bonds that television creates, unlike those that once prevailed in the small towns of America, are entirely synthetic — even if it doesn't seem that way. The communion that television provides — the communion of common voyeurs — can seem as real as that of a local neighborhood. So it is that Americans have felt outraged by the treatment of blacks in South Africa, felt a strange camaraderie when their armed forces joined the Western allies in attacking Iraq, felt pain over the brutal dismemberment of the former Yugoslavia. And television also produces mass communal reactions to material that is bound to any specific context, to wholly homogenized information, to the fads and fashions and disconnected sound bites of mass culture. It spins out information in such abundance as to rob most of it of any value.

I have spoken of the emergence of this global cliche culture as the birthmark of Our Time. Until modernity was ushered into our world, cultures were always local. They were, by definition, sets of meanings and morals, beliefs and habits that arose in specific contexts of history and religion, a people's social organization and place in the world. Thus we have traditionally spoken of Indian culture as being discernibly different from European culture, or African from Hispanic. But today, modernization is producing comparable ways of thinking, wanting, and being in countries that are very different in terms of their histories, religion, and organization. Today, what is modern can be found, and found in about the same way, in both Tokyo and Canberra, New Delhi and New England, Paris and Cape Town. To stretch this far, to span the globe in this way, modernity must necessarily be culturally thin. It must be able to be present everywhere while denying ownership to anyone in particular. It can be exclusive to no one, neither the Japanese nor the Europeans, neither the Australians nor the Americans. It is everywhere but it can be localized nowhere in particular. And its thinness reduces life to cliches — the same cliches everywhere, served up with the same fast food, the same music, the same blue jeans and T-shirts, the same movies, the same consumer impulses, the same news. It is a generic culture, this culture of the television age, of asphalt, advertising, uniformity, and waste. And those who feed on it, those who live by it, become generic people who also are thin, who stretch far and wide and belong nowhere in particular. They are, in the deepest sense, the "homeless" of our modern world.[5]

The sheer ubiquity of this public environment is what makes the naturalistic, materialistic, secular assumptions of everyday modern life seem so axiomatic, so completely beyond reproach. Few question the propriety of disengaging the public and private spheres of our lives as the new pluralism demands. We shuttle easily from the private world of family, friends, and perhaps neighborhood to the public world of professional and impersonal relationships, in which we know other people only in terms of their functions — the doctor, the plumber, the accountant. The anonymity of the public sphere facilitates the acceptance of new values by diminishing their significance. What difference does it make what the plumber's religion is, or politics, or sexual preference, so long as the pipes are fixed properly? What difference does it make whether the strangers around us are good or bad so long as they serve us professionally? Wherever anonymity increases, accountability diminishes.

The public sphere, dominated as it is by the omnipresence of bureaucracy, systems of manufacturing, the machinery of capitalism, and the audible confetti spewing out of countless radios and televisions, makes it virtually impossible to think that in *this* world God has any meaningful place. He may have a place somewhere, but not here, not in the public square! Perhaps he belongs within a person's soul, submerged there within their private intuitions, but there is no place for him in the structures of our commerce and communications. The truth is that the public dimension of our chrome and plastic world, our cities with their high rises and high rents, admits to no interest in the divine presence, seeks no grace, and asks for no forgiveness. It looks to pluralism as the way out of this awkward dilemma. Let the citizens take care of their relationships to God as private individuals, each in his or her own way, if this is what they wish to do, but let the rest of the world remain free of ranting about God, the supernatural, and moral absolutes.

The conquest of modernity can be gauged in a number of ways, but one of the most interesting is the shift in the way we view life at the point of its termination. An analysis of obituaries published in the *Salem (Massachusetts) Evening News* between 1786 and 1990, for ex-

---

5. See Peter Berger, Brigitte Berger, and Hansfried Kellner, *The Homeless Mind: Modernization and Modern Consciousness* (New York: Random House, 1979).

ample, highlights all of the marks of the transition into the modern world that I have been describing. Three of these stand out in particular.

1. At the beginning of the nineteenth century, most obituaries made some mention of the character of the deceased; by the end of the century this was rarely the case.[6] By contrast, a person's occupation was seldom an important detail in obituaries at the beginning of nineteenth century, but by 1990 it had become the key means by which a person was identified.[7] This substitution of function for character is consistent both with the rise of anonymity in our large, complex, and specialized world and with a new sense that it is inappropriate to define a person on the basis of character in a public context that offers no consensus concerning (and, if it comes to that, is not much interested in) what constitutes good character.

2. At the beginning of the nineteenth century, obituaries were largely written in religious language, much of it specifically Christian.[8] By the beginning of the twentieth century, the use of such language had vanished entirely. This is consistent, of course, with the secularization of our public life. Not insignificantly, the frequency of the mention of pain and suffering in these obituaries declined in tandem with the loss of religious language. Perhaps the decline of a common Christian world-view diminished our capacity to deal with death and suffering.

3. Obituaries published at the beginning of the nineteenth century typically made some reference to the individual's involvement in community life. Between 1810 and 1830 the number of these references declined sharply, and by 1900 they had vanished completely.[9] It

6. In 1786, 80 percent of the obituaries made reference to character. By 1810, this figure had fallen to 71 percent; by 1830, to 45 percent; by 1900, to 10 percent. After that, no such references are found. These figures, along with those in the following three notes, are taken from an unpublished paper by Eric Nelson entitled "Changes in the Public Portrayal of Death" (1991) and are cited here with his permission.

7. In 1786, only 15 percent of the obituaries mentioned the person's occupation. By 1900, this figure had grown to 70 percent. It then declined for a time, but by 1990 it had rebounded and increased to 80 percent.

8. In 1786, 79 percent of the obituaries used religious language in speaking of the person's death. By 1810, only 70 percent did; by 1830, only 20 percent; and by 1900, such references had vanished completely.

9. In 1786, 65 percent of the obituaries spoke of the connection the person had had with the community and often of the person's contributions. By 1810, this figure had fallen to 57 percent; by 1830, to 11 percent; and by 1900, this form of measuring and identifying the deceased had fallen into disuse entirely.

is just one of many indications of the fact that our culture has come to place increasingly less value on ties to community.

Costs and Benefits

It is surely one of the great anomalies of our modern world that the connection between welfare and well-being, between the outward circumstances of prosperity and the inward sense of satisfaction, has come unstuck. It was clear even before the end of the nineteenth century that the transformation of the world through modernization into the sleek thing that it has become would not be realized without some inward cost. In fact, the arrival of the modern world has involved a complete rearrangement of the benefits and costs of living.

The benefits of a modernized world are obvious and innumerable. Modernization has liberated us from the provincialism of small towns, opened the world to us, linked us to anyone, virtually anywhere in the world. With our technological achievements we have made our world more comfortable, in some ways safer, certainly more productive. In this century alone we have come close to doubling our life expectancy. We have enlarged our knowledge of the world, secured freedoms once only dreamed of, expanded rights, opened the doors of education, lifted hopes, and mightily multiplied our prosperity.

But in order to enjoy these manifold benefits, we have had to pay some stiff costs. Modernization has also blighted our lives by cutting our connections to place and community, elevating our level of anxiety, and greatly diminishing our satisfaction with our jobs. It has spawned pervasive fear and discontent. It has contributed to the breakdown of the family, robbed our children of their innocence, diluted our ethical values, and blinded us to the reality of God.[10] It has made us shallow. It has made us empty.

By the end of the nineteenth century, some of these concealed costs had already been paid. The sunny, triumphant optimism that had accompanied America's growth began to dim. Writers of the period began to note the signs of anxiety — what William James called "over-tension and jerkiness" — that were rapidly becoming a defining American characteristic. Some blamed it on the weather, but James offered little encouragement to that theory. No, the problem lay inter-

---

10. For an interesting assessment of costs and benefits of modernization, see Donald B. Kraybill, *The Riddle of Amish Culture* (Baltimore: The Johns Hopkins University Press, 1989), pp. 250-60.

nally, he said, in the undue sense of urgency and haste that was driving Americans. As an antidote he proposed belief in the "Gospel of Relaxation."[11] There is doubtless something to be said for this gospel, at least as a mechanism for survival amid the multiple and competing demands that the modern world places upon us, but it is altogether inadequate as an answer to the difficulties that modernization has heaped upon us. And this has become increasingly evident throughout the twentieth century.

Between 1945 and 1973, the average family income in America increased by two-thirds in constant dollars, unemployment dropped from a high in the Depression of one in three to less than one in ten by 1993, and the American Way of Life rapidly became a byword in many parts of the world. But study after study conducted during this period suggested that although newly prosperous Americans had the money and the leisure time to own and do a multitude of things that had been mere dreams for many of their parents, they were increasingly less satisfied with their lives. City streets became less and less hospitable at night, drugs became more and more prevalent, inner cities began to rot, and a whole generation of baby-boomers became painfully alienated both from their parents and their society. As "economic welfare increased in this country during the postwar period," Angus Campbell has said, "psychological well-being declined."[12] Those who thought that affluence could be made to compensate for or offset the drain on the human spirit that modernization has exacted were sorely disappointed. While we now bask in relative plenty, the very means of amassing that plenty — the reorganization of our world by the processes of modernization — has diminished our soul.

Flight from the Center

We will miss entirely the importance of the new arrangement of costs and benefits if we view them simply as factors on one side of a scale or the other. So many of both the benefits and the costs are related to

11. See Richard Weiss, *The American Myth of Success: From Horatio Alger to Norman Vincent Peale* (New York: Basic Books, 1969), pp. 167-68. Jackson Lears has explored this nineteenth-century restiveness and disaffection under the rubric of antimodernism in *No Place of Grace: Antimodernism and the Transformation of American Culture, 1880-1920* (New York: Pantheon Books, 1981).

12. Campbell, *The Sense of Wellbeing in America: Recent Patterns and Trends* (New York: McGraw-Hill, 1981), p. 6.

the central issue with which Our Time must now reckon: the loss of its center. The world is now filled with so many competing interests, so many rival values, so many gods, religions, and worldviews, so much activity, so many responsibilities, and so many choices that the older symphony of meaning has given way to the random tumult of the marketplace, to a perpetual assault on all of the senses. At its starkest, it is the transition from Mozart to Guns n' Roses, from Aquinas to infomercials, from Milton to gangsta rap. We may now have everything, but none of it means anything anymore. The most we seem able to do is to take daily inventories of personal needs and then try to match up people, products, and opportunities with them. The irony is that this psychological hedonism, in which self is the arbiter of life, is self-destructive. Not only are we betrayed; we betray *ourselves*. Meanwhile, we also pay the price of destroying all interest in the Transcendent, the sole source of genuine meaning in life. God, the supernatural, moral absolutes — these have become strangers in our modern, secularized world. We are like Yeats's falcon, increasingly oblivious to the voice of the falconer. The center no longer holds. All is flung to the periphery, where its meaning is lost.

The transition from a world in which God and his truth were accorded a central and often public place to one in which they have neither did not happen overnight, of course. It came in fits and starts, amid confusion and sometimes conflict. A longer view indicates that it came in two basic stages, however. In the first, God began to disappear from public view, and the whole noisy human enterprise took his place. In the second, the whole human enterprise was itself displaced and the organizing center of life was assumed by the extraordinarily pervasive and impersonal forces that modernization has unleashed on the world. We have thus become the pawns of the world we have created, moved about by the forces of modernity, our inventions themselves displacing their inventors in an ironic recapitulation of the first dislocation in which God's creatures replaced their Creator and exiled him from his own world. As it turns out, we too have lost our center through this transition. We have become T. S. Eliot's "hollow men," without weight, for whom appearance and image must suffice. Image and appearance assume the functions that character and morality once had. It is now considered better to look good than to be good. The facade is more important than the substance — and, that being the case, the substance has largely disappeared. In the center there is now only an emptiness. This is what accounts for the anxious search for self that is now afoot: only the hungry think about food all the time, not the well fed, and only those in whom the self is disappearing will define all of life in terms of its recovery, its actualization.[13]

Thus it is that we have come into the modern world. We have left behind a predominantly agricultural and rural life and exchanged it for an urban and mechanized culture. Our world is now arranged around large cities, centers for the production of the goods and services that our capitalism requires, marketplaces of information and technology. Most Enlightenment ideas fit snugly into this new culture — except for the Enlightenment dogma about inevitable progress, which is now sinking in the quicksands of modern self-doubt. We have ended up with much more, but we ourselves have ended up being much less. We have become spiritual vagrants in the modern wasteland, wanderers with no home to return to. The inner terrain of our lives — including the soil in which our Christian faith grows — is constantly shifting. What are the implications of this? Could it be that our faith is as modern as it is Christian because of the psychological soil in which it is rooted? How could it be any otherwise?

These questions won't seem all that threatening to most of us because, in our innocence, we see no alternative to being modern. After all, what alternatives are there? The Amish may look quaint and admirable from a distance, but most of us dismiss as quixotic and doomed their efforts to hold the modern world at arm's length. No, our faith must go with us as we walk the labyrinthine paths of modern life. It must go with us as we traverse the world each night with the help of television cameras that linger tearless over the worn and spent bodies of the starving of Africa, the broken and bleeding bodies of the war-ravaged in Eastern Europe, the abused and drug-ridden bodies of our own streets. It must reside with us on our sofas and our highways as we receive the daily pounding of advertisements, two million of them by the time we turn sixty-five, the bright starlets and muscled men who have sold their ability to seduce to the highest bidder. It must span the yawning chasm between our public and private worlds, between the home in which we struggle to effect some measure of control and the corporation in which we are controlled, between the arena of personal relations and the arena of professional relations, between the circle of friends and family in which we count for something and wilderness of Big Bureaucracy in which we do not. We must ask of it flexibility — enough flexibility to stretch across these and the countless

13. For an extended development of this theme, see my *No Place for Truth*, pp. 137-86.

other worlds of meaning, each with its discrete language and symbols, that make up modern life.

It seldom crosses our minds that what we are asking may be entirely impossible, or, if not impossible, so difficult that only the most sagacious and iron-willed could hope to keep straight the way. That, at least, would be a natural enough conclusion to draw after surveying the convolutions within the Protestant world during the twentieth century. There have been many moments of success, but there has also been a persistent entanglement in the culture that has produced much weakness. This century has demonstrated with a kind of ruthless insistence that the effort to be both modern and Christian produces deep and perhaps insoluble problems. I believe that our efforts to be both modern and Christian, to relate McGuire to Jesus, accounts for much of what has happened in evangelicalism in the years since the end of World War II, and it is to this topic that I now want to turn.

CHAPTER 2

An Accident of Faith

We are to consider that the end for which God pours out his Spirit is to make men holy, and not to make them politicians.

Jonathan Edwards

Twentieth-century American culture has been remarkably unfaithful in the ways in which it has dispensed its favors on religion. Like a beneficent but petulant monarch, it has given only to take back, blessed only to pour out its displeasure. And those in the religious community who plot their course by the ways in which the winds blow have frequently found themselves having to do embarrassing pirouettes to avoid the cold winds of disapproval after having basked in the warm winds of approbation.

Forty years ago, had someone ventured the thought that Protestantism was in the throes of being turned inside out, that the liberal establishment would find itself in growing disfavor, and that contenders for the White House would one day feel obliged to court the vote of religious conservatives, that person would have been considered a crackpot. But it happened. Since the 1960s, the American Protestant establishment that had been formed out of the older mainline denominational structures and suffused by the older liberal theology had to make way for another establishment with looser denominational bonds, a more conservative theology, a more dispersed organization, and a much less formal operation.

Public notice of this change came in many ways and places, a point recognized by *Newsweek* when it dubbed 1976 the "Year of the

17

Evangelical." It was a change that produced disbelief in the irreligious media, heartburn in the old-line denominations, and the beginnings of some power-mongering among evangelicals. As so often happens, however, the perception was quite out of accord with reality. People thought they saw an invincible religious army composed of the one-third of the American adult population who claimed to have experienced spiritual rebirth poised to sweep before it all its cultural and religious opponents.[1] But the perception was a mirage. The sea that looked to be a mile wide turned out to be only an inch deep. A 1993 survey that measured religious commitment in terms of such modest tests as church attendance, personal prayer, and some formal beliefs found that only 25 percent of the Americans who claim to be born again are in fact religiously committed. When this refinement is factored in, the invincible army is reduced to a relatively small band of only 8 percent of the population — and at that a band that turns out to be seriously hobbled by its entanglements with modern culture.

Perhaps, then, it was simply a shrewd judgment on the part of President Clinton in 1993 to reappoint the National Council of Churches as the official voice of Protestantism after its years in the official wilderness. The golden years of the past two decades, when evangelicals basked in the sunshine, are now over. In truth, the sun never shone that brightly anyway, but to the extent that it did, it showed that evangelicals could be as easily seduced and corrupted by the warmth as the liberal Protestants had been. Thus it was that culture gave and the culture has taken away.

1. The one-third figure is reported by George H. Gallup in *Religion in America 1990* (Princeton: Princeton Religion Research Center, 1990), p. 4. But this figure predictably conceals as much as it reveals. Closer analysis of the survey results shows that a larger percentage of blacks than whites identify themselves as "born again" (57 percent of blacks claim this experience as compared with 31 percent of whites), a larger percentage is above 50 years in age than below 30 (39 percent as compared with 30 percent), more are located in the South (49 percent) than in other regions, more are poor (the highest percentage of those claiming the experience, 40 percent, earns $15,000 or less annually), and more are poorly educated (45 percent of those claiming the experience have not graduated from high school). Nor do we have any assurance that the respondents were identifying the same experience or any idea of how it might be articulated theologically. The question posed by Gallup elicited self-understanding but not by itself a clear measure of theological understanding, still less of the degree of commitment.

From the Inside Out

It is not important, or even possible, to date the exact moment when the changing of the religious guard originally occurred. It is at least clear, though, that the old guard had begun to crumble long before it became a matter of public notice in the press during the 1980s. By the same token, the new evangelical guard was substantially in place long before *Newsweek* announced it in 1976. In fact, the change can probably be dated back as far as World War II, although the parting of the ways was not accomplished overnight. By 1945 it was already clear that the older establishment, which had been suffering from the debilitation of old age and the consequences of a defective theology since the 1930s, had about run its course. It lingered in place, claiming to speak for all Protestants, until the 1960s, when it was overshadowed by ascendant evangelicalism. Now the recent White House recognition has allowed it to emerge once again, weakened in its structures but a formal force nonetheless.

For a long time after the constitutional separation of church and state was formalized, Protestant churches in America continued to function as if they were still established. They retained a cultural rather than legal establishment, largely because of the absence of ethnic and denominational diversity and the persistence of widely shared Judeo-Christian values in society. With respect to the denominations, it is interesting to note that until the year 1700 there were only seven denominations in the colonies — Anglicans, Baptists, Lutherans, Presbyterians, the Dutch Reformed, Congregationalists, and Roman Catholics. By 1750, however, the Reformed stream was differentiating into German, Dutch, and French components. By 1820, these Protestant denominations had been joined by the Unitarians and Universalists. The growth in denominations (or at least discrete groups) since then has accelerated at a ferocious pace, the count ranging from about 200 to 700.[2] While the exact number varies depending on who is doing the counting, the overall trend is hard to miss. But even in the midst of this diversity, the original Protestant denominations, together with the Methodists and Disciples of Christ, have typically presumed to

2. *Yearbook of American and Canadian Churches*, ed. Kenneth B. Bedell (Nashville: Abingdon Press, 1993), pp. 248-55; Frank S. Mead, *Handbook of the Denominations in the United States* (Nashville: Abingdon Press, 1990); Arthur Piepkorn, *Profiles in Belief*, 3 vols. (New York: Harper & Row, 1977-79). For a good treatment of the historical development of the denominations, see Edwin Scott Gaustad, *Historical Atlas of Religion in America* (New York: Harper & Row, 1976).

speak for all Protestants, if not for all Americans. By 1920, these denominations constituted only 60 percent of the total Protestant body, but they provided 90 percent of its leadership, and later they made up half the constituencies of the Federal and National Council of Churches.[3]

The Protestant liberalism represented by these churches unabashedly sought a synthesis between Christian faith and modern culture. The liberals held that culture was flawed but that it was not estranged from the life of God. Because God is to be found immanently within all human beings, they said, the meaning and morality by which America should live is to be found in religious consciousness. This is the means by which God mediates his presence to America. Advocates of the Social Gospel such as Washington Gladden, Walter Rauschenbusch, and Richard Ely went on to respond to the social distress of their day caused by the massively expanding industrial society and ended up recasting the whole meaning of Christianity in ethical terms, reducing the kingdom of God to mere human progress. Those who deigned to speak of the millennium used the term in reference not to some far off dawn but to what was unfolding in modern culture.[4] Christianity was all about the progress of the human race, they maintained — its innate goodness and the inviolability of reason — all of which may have seemed eminently sensible in the early 1920s but was far less tenable after the Great Depression of the 1930s.

The Second World War provided a prolonged disruption in normal life, and America quite unexpectedly emerged from it into a bright new era. Not only was it now a dominant world power politically and economically, but the extraordinary prosperity of the 1950s produced a culture that once again seemed benign. It lent its hollow optimism to the earlier, faint-hearted liberalism. The brief reprieve of the 1950s was followed by the rather brutal 1960s, however, and the inexorable unraveling of the older liberalism has been documented since then in each succeeding *Yearbook of the American Churches*.[5] The upshot of these years is that the liberal alliance between Christ and culture that seemed

3. William R. Hutchison, "Protestantism as Established," in *Between the Times: The Travail of the Protestant Establishment in America, 1900-1960*, ed. William R. Hutchison (Cambridge: Cambridge University Press, 1989), p. 5.

4. See William R. Hutchison, *The Modernist Impulse in American Protestantism* (Cambridge: Harvard University Press, 1976).

5. For a brief but useful overview, see Edwin Scott Gaustad, "*Did* the Fundamentalists Win?" in *Religion in America: Spirituality in a Secular Age*, ed. Mary Douglas and Stephen Tipton (Boston: Beacon Press, 1983), pp. 169-78.

plausible enough in times of tranquillity and relative comfort fell apart in harsher times — first during the Depression years and then again during the 1960s.

Of course the passing of the old liberal religious establishment is more complex than I have so far suggested. For one thing, the task of representing and embodying the aspirations of a Protestant culture has become increasingly difficult for the old-line churches through no fault of their own. The religious complexion of America changed drastically during the nineteenth and early twentieth centuries as waves of immigrants flooded in. As the relative number of Protestants dwindled, they lost their claim to a cultural monopoly, their power began to erode, and their identity became blurred. Robert Handy has argued that when this process reached its peak during the 1920s, it produced a "second disestablishment." He suggests that the later drive to construct large, bureaucratic agencies for the ecumenical movement, such as the National Council of Churches, was as much a reaction to this lost standing as anything else.

Old-line Protestantism initially tried to attribute its declining fortunes to pluralism, secularism, demographic changes, the impact of higher education, the effects of growing urbanization, the public sense of alienation from organized religion, the conflict between the growing political conservatism of the laity and the liberalism of the clergy, and a multitude of other such factors. There was undoubtedly some validity in these explanations, but the graph lines of decline in the old-line denominations were so consistent with one another, and the lines of growth among the more conservative churches so startling by comparison, that the explanations seemed to point to only a small aspect of the truth at most.[6]

6. Since 1960, attendance at worship — be it Catholic, Protestant, or Jewish — has remained relatively static. The number of those who attend weekly has ranged from a low of 40 percent to a high of 49 percent, but the distribution of attendance, at least among Protestants, has shifted dramatically, as have other measures of commitment such as church membership, financial support, religious knowledge, and practices of personal piety. In the decade between 1955 and 1965, the old-line denominations all grew numerically. The United Presbyterians, for example, grew 11 percent; the United Methodists, 10.5 percent; Presbyterians (U.S.), 17.2 percent; the Lutheran Church in America, 22.4 percent; the Episcopalians, 20.2 percent; and the American Baptists, 1.6 percent. In subquent years, however, they all declined, and in the decade from 1973 to 1983, the declines were precipitous. The United Presbyterians (U.S.A.) lost 12.4 percent; the United Methodists, 10.1 percent; Presbyterians (U.S.), 7.6 percent; the Lutheran Church in America, 5.0 percent; the Episcopalians, 16.7 percent; and the American Baptists, 4.2 percent. Moreover, this decline has not yet abated, and it contrasts sharply with

Wade Clark Roof was doubtless also correct when he argued that the mainline churches lost members because they lost their plausibility. They were no longer able, he said, "to fashion a meaningful and compelling faith congruent with modern culture."[7] Caught between a traditional Christian worldview and the emerging secular consensus within a modernized culture, these churches were unable to put together a faith that was both modern and Christian. The more modern they felt themselves compelled to be, the less Christian were they able to remain. It was a predicament from which they could find no way to extricate themselves.

A 1993 study seems to have uncovered a more crucial factor than any mentioned thus far, however, at least with reference to the Presbyterian Church (U.S.A.). One of many fresh studies, it suggests that the best predictor of whether baby boomers will stay in the church or leave is the relative presence of orthodox belief. Among the subjects of the study, those who believed in the uniqueness of Christ's salvation were almost invariably in the church, and those who did not had dropped out. Furthermore, the study found that the presence of Christian orthodoxy alone was sufficient "to impel people to commit their time and other resources to a distinctively Christian regime of witness

---

extraordinary growth among the more conservative churches during the same period, producing what Martin Marty has called a "seismic change" in the Protestant world. From 1965 to 1975, the Southern Baptists grew 18.2 percent; the Assemblies of God, 37.3 percent; the Church of the Nazarene, 8.4 percent; and the Seventh-Day Adventists, 36.0 percent. During the decade from 1973 to 1983, the Southern Baptists added 15.0 percent; the Assemblies of God, 71 percent; and the Church of the Nazarene, 22.0 percent. See George Gallup and Jim Castelli, *The People's Religion: American Faith in the 1990s* (New York: Macmillan, 1989), p. 17; and *Understanding Church Growth and Decline, 1950-1978*, ed. Dean R. Hoge and David A. Roozen (New York: Pilgrim Press, 1979). By 1961, the old-line denominations, with only 38 percent of the total Protestant body, had ceased to be the mainline.

This decline was long in the making. One of the many signs of the ebbing vitality of the mainline denominations can be seen in their periodicals. In 1931, the Protestant denominations produced 542 magazines and periodicals. Of the 143 denominations at that time, those in the mainline, the "seven sisters," constituted only a very small percentage of all the Protestant bodies, but they produced 272 of these magazines and periodicals. Thirty years later, this number had dwindled to 75, of which the Methodists alone were responsible for 30. In these years, then, the mainline denominations saw their output of magazines fall from almost half of the total Protestant production to only 15 percent. See Dennis Voskuil, "Reaching Out: Protestantism and the Media," in *Between the Times*, p. 75.

7. Roof, *Community and Commitment: Religious Plausibility in a Liberal Church* (New York: Elsevier, 1978), p. 7.

and obedience in the company of other believers." The study also suggests that lay liberalism may have the virtue of personal honesty, but it lacks the ability "to inspire the kind of conviction that creates strong religious communities."[8]

It is therefore not surprising that as the older establishment became soft, losing numbers steadily every year after 1964, it suffered what Edwin Gaustad has called its "Second Disillusionment" — namely, "the realization that no one was any longer watching the nameless city set upon the no-longer-existing hill."[9] The power to interpret American life, to direct its morals, to explain its destiny, and to talk about meaning in transcendent ways had slipped between the fingers of the older liberalism and, by implication, from the hands of the old-line denominations.

From the Outside In

When the National Association of Evangelicals for United Action (N.A.E.) was formed in 1942 almost precisely on the model of the Federal Council of Churches in the older establishment, *The Christian Century* seemed to read the writing on the wall. An editorial belittled the new association as simply a vehicle for expressing the sectarianism that had "long been the scandal of Protestant Christianity."[10] Those present at its inauguration were dismissed as "several hundred representatives of the sects which hitherto have refused to cooperate with their fellow Protestants on anything."[11] The charge by the founders of the N.A.E. that the Federal Council poorly represented the twenty-three million Protestants within its fold and disregarded the twenty-four million outside of its fold was airily dismissed. This new development, the *Century* asserted, had nothing to do with doctrine and everything to do with power. "What the organizers of this new movement seek is . . . not representation within a united Protestantism but control of one segment of a divided Protestantism."[12]

8. Benton Johnson, Dean R. Hoge, and Donald A. Luidens, "Mainline Churches: The Real Reason for Decline," *First Things* 31 (March 1993): 15-16.

9. Gaustad, "The Pulpit and the Pews," in *Between the Times*, p. 40.

10. "Sectarianism Receives New Lease of Life," *Christian Century*, 19 May 1943, p. 596.

11. "Set up Rival to Federal Council," *Christian Century*, 19 May 1943, p. 614.

12. "Sectarianism Receives New Lease of Life," p. 596. For an earlier reaction to the "new evangelicalism," see Mark Silk's essay "The Rise of the New Evangel-

Power was what the Federal Council of Churches had wielded. Power is what any establishment is about. It is what the editor at the *Century* feared might be flowing away to the evangelicals who were regrouping in the early 1940s. They were, at that time, driven by a sense of being outsiders, of having been shut out of the circles of churchly influence, of not having counted. When *Christianity Today* was launched in 1956, its first editorial spoke of evangelicals as having been "neglected, slighted, misrepresented," and it promised that now a clear voice would be heard advocating historic Christian faith in place of the tired liberalism that had failed both the individual and society.[13]

There was some awareness of the parting of the ways that was taking place, but probably no one fully understood the momentous character of the changes that were afoot. In a short period of time, *The Christian Century* found how radically its constituency was shrinking and how quickly the constituency of *Christianity Today* was growing. By 1979, Gallup discovered that *Christianity Today* was read by vastly more ministers than was *The Christian Century*. And the National Association of Evangelicals, at least through the 1970s, managed to gather more momentum than the National Council of Churches had lost.

The 1960s, then, represent the end of the liberal era, although liberal ideas still have their advocates in the churches today and especially in academia. But while this decade pulled the covers off the emptiness of the liberal Protestant establishment, it ironically seems also to have propelled evangelicalism into the same religious void. Before the 1960s, evangelicalism was a cultural outsider; after, it rapidly became a part of the inside. Before, it defined itself theologically; after, it increasingly has not. Before, its leaders were seldom managers and bureaucrats; after, they usually were. To use Dean M. Kelley's categories, before the 1960s evangelicalism was "strong"; after, it was "weak."[14] And in all of these ways, *Christianity Today* has accurately

---

icalism: Shock and Adjustment," in *Between the Times*, pp. 278-99. Silk shows that in the 1950s and 1960s, when Billy Graham was at his height and such thinkers as E. J. Carnell and Carl F. H. Henry were beginning to make their mark, there was both consternation and uncertainty in the liberal Protestant establishment about how to meet the challenge. Although some sought a rapprochement with the evangelicals during the period from World War II to the Vietnam War, evangelicalism for the most part "provided the establishment with a foil against which to define its concerns" (p. 299).

13. "Why *Christianity Today*?" *Christianity Today*, 15 October 1956, p. 20.

14. See Kelley, *Why Conservative Churches Are Growing* (Macon: Mercer University Press, 1986), pp. 56-77.

reflected what was transpiring. It is the mirror in whose pages are reflected the modernized, contemporary evangelical soul.[15]

In 1975, when I co-edited *The Evangelicals: Who They Are, What They Believe, and Where They Are Changing*, these changes were not yet fully apparent. Thus it was that we sought in that book to identify the common ground on which evangelicals stood as that of theological confession, specifically the confession about the functioning authority of Scripture and Christ's substitutionary atonement on the cross. We could have added much more, but we maintained that evangelicalism could not confess less than the Reformers' principles of *sola Scriptura* and *sola gratia* and remain true to itself.

This contention accorded with what had generally been true from the end of the Second World War until the 1970s. Evangelicals had found their center, their unity and definition, in a core of biblical-theological confession. It was for this reason that, in both Britain and America, the early postwar years were marked by a clear, tough-minded strategy to develop the tools and knowledge for such a confession. Out of those early years came a powerful stream of biblical commentaries, dictionaries, and books on doctrinally shaped Christian belief. By the end of the 1970s, however, this kind of evangelicalism was losing its momentum. As the theological boundaries in evangelicalism expanded, as the theological core began to disintegrate, the ground for unity had to shift from a common confession of theological unity to a common acceptance of diversity. In the process, evangelicalism was transformed into little more than a fraternity of organizations.[16]

From another angle, the key to what transpired may well be a group of changes that Robert Wuthnow has charted. He has argued that the postwar period produced two quite different forms of civil religion.[17] During this period, denominational allegiances diminished as Protestants began to realign themselves around either of two poles, one conservative and the other liberal or progressive. The organizing principle in each camp was less theological than cultural. Those in the

15. For an analysis of the changes at *Christianity Today*, see my *No Place for Truth; or, Whatever Happened to Evangelical Theology* (Grand Rapids: William B. Eerdmans, 1993), pp. 207-11.

16. For a more detailed review of these changes, see my essay "On Being Evangelical: Some Theological Differences and Similarities," in *Evangelicalism: Comparative Studies of Popular Protestantism in North America, the British Isles, and Beyond, 1700-1990*, ed. Mark A. Noll, David W. Bebbington, and George A. Ralwyk (New York: Oxford University Press, 1993), pp. 389-410.

17. See Wuthnow, *The Restructuring of American Religion: Society and Faith since World War II* (Princeton: Princeton University Press, 1988), pp. 241-67.

liberal camp — regardless of whether they were Baptists, Presbyterians, or Methodists — were drawn to an agenda defined by America's place in the modern world. They were most interested in issues such as the disproportionate distribution of wealth in the world, environmental degradation, nuclear proliferation, and cultural pluralism. Those on the conservative side — regardless of whether they were Baptists, Presbyterians, or Methodists — were drawn to an agenda defined by their vision of America as a Christian nation. They were most interested in issues such as the place of God in national life, the Judeo-Christian heritage, prayer in schools, abortion, and family values. In their own way, however, each camp was pursuing a form of civil religion.

This may be the key to understanding the transformation of evangelicalism in the 1970s, a period marked by fading theological interest, larger and more numerous concessions to modernity, and a growing inability to think incisively or to act boldly precisely when incisive thought and bold action have most been needed. Evangelicalism consented to become a form of civil religion in the mistaken belief that if it could win the war on such personal issues as family values, abortion, and prayer in the schools, it would thereby be able to hold the rest of society in check, ethically speaking.

The problem with all civil religion, whether of the right or the left, is that it tends to be civil in the sense that it is inoffensive. It has no edges because it is driven not by a passion for God's truth but by the politics of the day, whatever those politics might be. Without God's truth, without his Word as its center, a civil religion also forfeits his grace and his judgment — and without these, it has no means to survive in the modern world.

If a convergence has in fact taken place between modernity and evangelicalism, it is not because modernity has become more theological but because evangelicalism has become modern. It has become an informal religious establishment that derives its power not from its theology but from its culture. It may be that this sort of thing occurs in every secularized age, but evangelicals have not evidenced any awareness of that fact. On the whole they seem convinced that their religion rather than their culture has given them the power they believe they wield. But this is an illusion. Whatever power they may have is culturally derived and hence borrowed. And borrowed power can be withdrawn as easily as it has been conferred.

The older confessional interest has markedly declined in evangelicalism, and it is now driven by trends that are indisputably modern.

It is here that the therapeutic culture, which treats badness simply as disease, is often given its most fulsome treatment. It is here that consumerism, with all of the appetites for purchase, ownership, and power that go with it, has become indistinguishable from the practice of evangelical faith in many of its far-flung enterprises. It is here that religious life is orchestrated and regimented by managers pursuing private careers that could, with hardly a hitch in the rhythm, be carried on in most secular corporations in America. It is here that entertainment and worship are not merely interspersed but often indistinguishable. And it is here, where life should be receiving its most serious and sustained analysis, that tons of literature and countless hours of television and radio programming are being produced that contain nothing more than the sorts of empty cliches and hollow comforts that are available everywhere else in the modernized world. At the very moment when the modern world is mangling those whom it blesses, disordering their inner lives even as it smothers them in plenty, and rubbing its own nerves raw in its bumbling efforts to address its most painful and destructive problems — at this very moment, evangelicalism has bought cultural acceptability by emptying itself of serious thought, serious theology, serious worship, and serious practice in the larger culture. And most evangelicals appear to be completely oblivious to this sellout or at least unconvinced that the deal was a bad one.

Modernity has been hard at work reducing evangelical faith to something that is largely private and internal. Belief has shrunk from being a contemporary confession of God's truth in the church and beyond to being simply a part of personal identity and psychological makeup. Many evangelicals quietly assume, perhaps even without much thought, that it would be uncouth and uncivil to push this private dimension too noticeably or noisily on others or into the public square. The right of each individual to his or her own private thoughts and beliefs is held to be both axiomatic and inviolable. So it is that the particularities of evangelical faith — the things that make it *different* — are dissolved. Modern culture grants me absolute freedom to believe whatever I want to believe — so long as I keep those beliefs from infringing on the consciousness or behavior of anyone else, especially on points of controversy. So it is, as John Cuddihy has suggested, that civil religion is always a religion of civility: the edges of faith are rounded off, the angles softened.[18]

18. See Cuddihy, *No Offense: Civil Religion and Protestant Taste* (New York: Seabury Press, 1978), pp. 1-30.

The legacy of Protestant orthodoxy has been surgically altered to fit modern standards of pleasantness and light. If the spirit of Puritanism was best represented graphically by a preacher in an elevated pulpit, the arm raised in vigorous punctuation upon the truth of God, that of modern evangelicalism is probably best represented today by the ubiquitous happy face, a bright smile beckoning smiles in return. There is an indefatigable sociability to this religion of civility, a perpetual friendliness, a harmlessness in the name of God. It finds dissent uncongenial, if not abhorrent. It wishes not to appear disagreeable. It veers away from intruding upon the world any truth that might be discomfiting. All too often its passions — if any remain — are kept carefully concealed. Thus it is that evangelicalism, no less than the earlier liberalism, pays its social dues. Liberalism never had a view of the transcendence of God, and evangelicalism rarely has a *functioning* view of the transcendence of God. Neither has had a place to stand outside the culture, therefore, and so each has been left to echo that culture, one on the high end and the other on the popular end.

This brings us to the central issue I am seeking to deal with in this book: the relationship between Christ and culture. Is modernity one issue among many with which Christian faith must be engaged, or is it *the* issue that is encountered in every aspect of the modern world? Contemporary evangelicalism has, for the most part, assumed that modernity is simply one issue among many that may require some thought from time to time, that it is not a pervasive reality intruding on virtually every aspect of the inner life of faith. It is quite natural that evangelicals should adopt this view, because they typically think of culture as neutral and no more a carrier of implicit or explicit values than are the clothes that they wear. From time to time, modernity may raise its head, like atheism and humanism, and then the faithful must rise to denounce the danger, but for the most part modern culture seems a safe place in which to practice faith.

I sought to challenge this assumption in my book *No Place for Truth; or, Whatever Happened to Evangelical Theology* by showing the manifold ways in which modernity has twisted evangelical faith. If my analysis is correct, modernity is not simply *an* issue; it is *the* issue, because it envelops all our worlds — commerce, entertainment, social organization, government, technology — and because its grasp is lethal. There is no part of culture that can gain any distance from it and hence no part of culture that is neutral or safe. All of culture is touched by the values and appetites, the horizons and hopes that modernity excites.

If this is the case, then modernity is to contemporary Christians what the medieval synthesis was to the sixteenth-century Reformers: it is *the* issue. If in the Middle Ages Catholicism was at the center of the culture, posing an overwhelming challenge to the Reformers, modernity is in the center of our culture, and the challenge it poses is even more serious. We have to contend with the modern mind, with its complete lack of interest in truth — especially the truth of God. And none of the other questions that now engage the church will find any lasting resolution until this is understood and confronted. The church's diminished standing in society, the irrelevance of its concerns to those who work on the ramparts of secularized society, the church's profound confusion about its mission in life, the fragmentation of denominations and, in some cases, their dramatic decline, the stunning growth of parachurch movements, the triumph of the therapeutic and the managerial in evangelicalism, uncertainty in the seminaries — none of these issues will be satisfactorily addressed until the church is ready to face up to the question of modernity.

Modernity presents an interlocking system of values that has invaded and settled within the psyche of every person. Modernity is simply unprecedented in its power to remake human appetites, thinking processes, and values. It is, to put it in biblical terms, the worldliness of Our Time. For worldliness is that system of values and beliefs, behaviors and expectations, in any given culture that have at their center the fallen human being and that relegate to their periphery any thought about God. Worldliness is what makes sin look normal in any age and righteousness seem odd. Modernity is worldliness, and it has concealed its values so adroitly in the abundance, the comfort, and the wizardry of our age that even those who call themselves the people of God seldom recognize them for what they are.

Where, then, do we begin the reconstitution of evangelical faith? I begin by reserving my deepest suspicions for those who want answers to the difficulties I have mentioned. The desire for answers is innocent enough, but the spirit in which they are demanded frequently is not.

Too often the quest for answers is driven by impatience, by a refusal to do the hard work in taking the measure of the problem first. Answers assembled apart from such work tend to treat symptoms rather than the disease; they are often little more than management techniques, mere Band-Aids. Those whose instincts are most in tune with modernity will be most inclined to rush to these sorts of solutions, because it is precisely these sorts of techniques that the modern world most prizes. The modern mind will be quick to conclude that evangelical faith is faltering because it is not *efficient* enough, for example, or because it is not *appealing* enough, because it has not adapted itself adequately to the inner needs of those in the modern world. It is thus that many are stepping forward as managers or psychologists in Christ's name, and for the good of the church, to address the world.

It is one of the remarkable features of contemporary church life that so many are attempting to heal the church by tinkering with its structures, its services, its public face. This is clear evidence that modernity has successfully palmed off one of its great deceits on us, convincing us that God himself is secondary to organization and image, that the church's health lies in its flow charts, its convenience, and its offerings rather than in its inner life, its spiritual authenticity, the toughness of its moral intentions, its understanding of what it means to have God's Word in this world. Those who do not see this are out of touch with the deep realities of life, mistaking changes on the surface for changes in the deep waters that flow beneath. An inspired group of marketers might find a way of reviving a flagging business by modifying its image and offerings, but the matters of the heart, the matters of God, are not susceptible to such cosmetic alteration. The world's business and God's business are two different things.

The fundamental problem in the evangelical world today is not inadequate technique, insufficient organization, or antiquated music, and those who want to squander the church's resources bandaging these scratches will do nothing to stanch the flow of blood that is spilling from its true wounds. The fundamental problem in the evangelical world today is that God rests too inconsequentially upon the church. His truth is too distant, his grace is too ordinary, his judgment is too benign, his gospel is too easy, and his Christ is too common.

In this book, therefore, I begin in the land of McGuire, with an examination of the "world" and its correlation with what we today speak of as modernity. I do so because the New Testament is clear that love of God and love of the world are in competition with each other, and we have to understand this competition in order to pinpoint how our love for God has dimmed as our love for the world has grown. In Chapter 4, "Clerics Anonymous," I give an example of the general principles I have just discussed, the upshot of which has been an attempt to advance management of the church, to employ new techniques in marketing its wares as a way of shoring up its weaknesses. I argue that such strategies have the fingerprints of modernity all over them.

The heart of this book, however, lies in the three chapters that follow. In Chapter 5, "The Weightlessness of God," I try to explain the peculiar character of religion in the modern context — namely, that God is believed but he is not of much consequence to those who believe. Although much can be said about this by way of remedy, in the two chapters which follow, "The Outside God" and "God on the Inside," I have attempted to understand how modernity rearranges the reality of God such that he comes to rest inconsequentially upon the church. In the first of these chapters, I speak of his transcendence, and in the second I speak of his immanence and of the church's need to rediscover the one and to turn from its abuse of the other. Only then will God begin to have weight again. In Chapter 8 I put my own thesis to the test by examining empirically the coming generation of church leadership. What are they like and how do they function? In Chapter 9 I ponder some of the changes that the church needs to effect in order to regain its spiritual authenticity.

It is thus that I am taking the first step in making good on the promise I made in *No Place for Truth* to follow that critique with a more constructive proposal. My work here amounts to far less than a complete answer to the issues I raised earlier, however. It is only a first step, and a very modest one, in which I have sought to develop in part the *perspective* within which we now need to think about the reconstitution of evangelical faith. I can already see the need for additional study in a number of areas. We need to take a closer look, for example, at the ways in which modernity has infused into the church an anthropology that is at odds with biblical faith and that is intent on rewriting that faith in its own image. And we need to outline the specific steps that will have to be taken to reverse the evangelical church's unhappy entanglements with culture, to recover authentic Christian practice, and to resurrect bold Christian witness.

So this book is only a tentative first step. But at least I have started in the right place — with God. The church is called by him, constituted by him, empowered by him, and cleansed by him. It is therefore with God that we must begin thinking about the church's reformation today.

STRANGERS AND ALIENS

CHAPTER 3

The Alternative to God

*If we imagine the world as a world of generally righteous men with
— at any given moment — only one especially wicked nation in it,
we shall never envisage the seriousness of that situation with which
Christianity sets out to deal.*

Herbert Butterfield

It is ironic that there are those in the church who view culture as mostly
neutral and mostly harmless, even though they have a compelling
Christian reason to think otherwise, while there are those in society
who recognize that culture is laden with values, many of which are
injurious to human well-being, even though they have no compelling
religious or ideological reason to come to this conclusion. Surely a
parable could be constructed out of this strange situation, one that
might end with the words "the sons of this world are wiser in their
generation than the sons of light" (Luke 16:8). The church may choose
to disregard many of today's cultural critics who are raising the alarms
about the drift of Western culture and its internal rottenness — indeed,
it is presently doing so — but it does not have the luxury of disregard-
ing what Scripture says about our world. And today, what Scripture
says about the "world" and what these critics are seeing in contemporary culture are sometimes remarkably close.

The "world" is the biblical way of speaking of the cultural ethos,
the social arrangements, the habits of life that follow upon the corrupting of human nature. It is, of course, true that human nature
retains the divine image after the fall, just as the physical creation

retains its goodness despite the fall, but the disordering of life following the fall is both individual and collective, with the latter giving
plausibility to the former and the former fueling the latter. In the
current Western context, the plausibility of unbelief arises very significantly from modernity.[1] In many ways, modernity is the contemporary realization of what the biblical authors had in mind when they
spoke of the *world* — a reality that is by no means innocent, neutral,
or harmless.

In this chapter, I first wish to explore the meaning of the "world"
in its biblical setting, noting along the way some of the contemporary
realizations of the Bible's more generic descriptions. Second, I want
to explore the peculiar vulnerability of the American church to the
worldliness that is transmitted to us through modernity. This discussion
actually illumines a curious paradox involving the way in which biblical
other-worldliness provides the leverage for Christian this-worldly per-
tinence. It is only those who are "not of this world" in their inner being
who have the reason and acquire the fortitude to resist the charms and
allurements of the world and who, for that reason, are able to be
culturally pertinent. Those who are cognitively and morally dislocated
from worldly culture are the ones who are driven to change it; those
who are comfortable and at home with it, who may in the process
acquire a sheen of success and of acceptability, are often so beholden
to it as to find dislocation from the source of their blessings most
uncongenial.[2]

1. For an extended definition and discussion of the concept of modernity to
which I am referring here, including a description of its "carriers" and an enumera-
tion of some of its consequences, see my book *No Place for Truth; or, Whatever
Happened to Evangelical Theology* (Grand Rapids: William B. Eerdmans, 1993), pp.
53-94.

2. I am aware that this assertion runs counter to a popular view of religious
types. It has been argued that people whose lives are on the whole pleasant tend
to find ultimate meaning in a god who is immanently present within life, whereas
those whose lives are on the whole more painful and dark tend to find ultimate
meaning in a wholly transcendent god. Those who follow this logic typically identify
Christianity as a faith fixed on the transcendent and therefore mistakenly conclude
that it has no interest in the world. See, e.g., James Woelfel, "Indwelling and Exile:
Two Types of Religious and Secular World Orientation," *American Journal of Theology
and Philosophy* 8 (September 1987): 93-108; Patrick Burke, *The Fragile Universe: An
Essay in the Philosophy of Religions* (New York: Barnes & Noble, 1979), pp. 13-38;
and Edward Norman, *Christianity and the World Order* (New York: Oxford University
Press, 1979), p. 50.

The Scarecrow World

In the World . . .

In the New Testament, the term *world* (Gk. *kosmos*) has three basic meanings: (1) the earth, the created order; (2) the nations, the human community; (3) the ways of fallen humanity, alienated from God and his truth. It is this third sense of the term that I have suggested is largely equivalent to "modernity" in contemporary Western culture. It is worthy of note that this sense of the term as it appears in the New Testament signifies not a sociological reality but a theological reality. This may explain why worldliness is so frequently being missed, or misjudged, in the evangelical church today: it takes theological sense, theological judgment to recognize it, and that is precisely what has disappeared from the church. That is why, as we shall see in Chapter 4, the propriety of marketing Christian faith, or adapting it to the culture, or inadvertently hitching it up to cultural trends is seldom questioned; that is why this kind of enterprise is usually discussed simply under the rubric of methodology, as if theological principles and issues of truth were not at stake.

We can pass over the first two senses of *kosmos* quite rapidly here — not because they are unimportant but simply because they are not the focus of our discussion.

First, the word is used of the earth itself. God, we are told, "made the world and everything in it" (Acts 17:24). Christ was chosen "before the foundation of the world" (1 Pet. 1:20), and Hebrews speaks of what Christ said when he "came into the world" (Heb. 10:5). Paul says that there are "many different languages in the world" (1 Cor. 14:10). The meaning is straightforward: the reference is to our physical habitat, the earth.

Were we to pursue this further now, we would quickly discover that the language of creation is richly explicated in Scripture, giving to Christian faith what Emil Brunner believed to be its most distinctive doctrine. This language is used both of the first act by which God brought the universe into existence and of his continuing relationship to it whereby he sustains and upholds what he made and now directs its life to the conclusion he purposed for it in eternity. It was by the Son that God "created the world," and it is the Son who is now "upholding the universe by his word of power" (Heb. 1:2-3). Thus it is that creation bespeaks the power (Isa. 40:26-28), greatness (Ps. 90:2), wisdom (Isa. 40:12-14), goodness (Acts 14:17), and wrath of

God (Rom. 1:18-20). All of this is implicit in this first sense of the term.[3]

Second, *kosmos* is used of the nations of the earth, the human fraternity. It was into this "world" that sin came through Adam (Rom. 5:12), and it is this world — the entire human family — that will stand before God in judgment (Rom. 3:6; 1 Cor. 11:32). Jesus foresaw the gospel being preached "in the whole world" (Mark 14:9), by which he probably meant among peoples of all kinds and in all times. Certainly, it is to all people groups that the church is commanded to go, teaching and baptizing in Christ's name (Mark 16:15; Matt. 28:19-20). Paul later said that the faith of those in Rome was being "proclaimed in all the world" (Rom. 1:8), and he also said of himself and his coworkers that "we have behaved in the world . . . with holiness and godly sincerity" (2 Cor. 1:12). The "world" here is the human race or the inhabited earth. Modern organizations with a global reach, such as the World Health Organization, use the word in the same way.

Biblically speaking, it is entirely inappropriate for the church to become "other-worldly" with respect to these first two meanings of *kosmos,* though it needs to be noted immediately that the biblical understanding of creation, and of a biblical engagement with it, has fallen on extremely hard times in recent years. Not only has it been attacked by the Barthians and dismissed as irrelevant by the pietists, but it has been rendered unbelievable to many people by modernity. Secularism has marginalized God, removing him from effective engagement with society, and modern life has churned up so much chaos and pain that it has rendered the doctrine of providence, of God's sovereign control over all of life, unbelievable. At a single stroke, the creation in its origin, its present life, and its destiny are wrenched apart from its Creator by unbelief and sent to seek its own life and explanation within itself. The disappearance of these themes from the center of Christian reflection and their absence from the contemporary pulpit is neither a small nor an innocent matter.

3. On the biblical understanding of creation, see Paul K. Jewett, *God, Creation, and Revelation: A Neo-Evangelical Theology* (Grand Rapids: William B. Eerdmans, 1991), pp. 438-505; and Gustav Aulén, *The Faith of the Christian Church,* trans. Eric H. Wahlstrom and G. Everett Arden (Philadelphia: Muhlenberg Press, 1948), pp. 181-206. The contribution of Gustav Wingren in redeeming the doctrine of creation for Christian thinking has been signal. For a brief treatment, see his essay "The Doctrine of Creation: Not an Appendix but the First Article," *Word and World* 4 (Fall 1984): 353-71; for longer explorations, see his books *Creation and Law,* trans. Ross Mackenzie (London: Oliver & Boyd, 1961); and *Creation and Gospel: The New Situation in European Theology* (Lewiston, N.Y.: Edwin Mellen Press, 1979).

The church is clearly called to be thoroughly engaged with creation and with human life.[4] The creation is the source of our physical well-being; in it lie the principles of aesthetic practice for those who are called to be subcreators in word and image, their work the mirror of their Creator's. As God's image-bearers, we are called to be stewards of creation, conserving its resources and modeling the presence of God in it. The human fraternity is the arena in which we are called to exemplify our faithful dependence on God in work, to bring to bear on its life the moral values of both the creative and redemptive orders, to learn and practice the Christian virtues in family, church, and community, to preach the gospel, and to show care and compassion to the afflicted. In these and many other ways, Christian truth makes our engagement with the "world" in these first two senses inescapable.

But it is the third sense of *kosmos* that is of special interest here because of the predicament in which the evangelical church today finds itself. It is in connection with the third sense that we hear a biblical demand for other-worldliness. But we need theological understanding to make sense of this demand.

. . . but Not of It

As I have already indicated, the third basic sense of *kosmos* refers to fallen humanity en masse, the collective expression of every society's refusal to bow before God, to receive his truth, to obey his commandments, or to believe in his Christ. Further, the "world" is what fallen humanity uses as a substitute for God and his truth. The "world" in this sense is the life of unredeemed humanity, what Rudolf Bultmann refers to as "the sphere of all men's thinking, planning and desiring, in their cares and wishes, their pleasures and pursuits, their pride and arrogance."[5] It encompasses the cognitive horizons of the fallen, their appetites, the way that they order their life, their priorities, their behavior, what they really *want*, and what they will do to get it. It encompasses the set of social arrangements, the public context in which fallen life is lived out. It is the sole preoccupation of those who are fallen — those one-dimensional earth-dwellers for whom there are no

4. Whatever else Richard Mouw has in mind in his use of language such as "holy worldliness," this kind of biblically prescribed engagement with creation is undoubtedly at the heart of his concern. See his *Called to Holy Worldliness* (Philadelphia: Fortress Press, 1980).

5. Bultmann, *Essays: Philosophical and Theological*, trans. James C. G. Greig (New York: Macmillan, 1955), p. 77.

considerations in life more important than eating, drinking, possessing, and being merry. This world is fading, but that is no impediment to those who seek their fulfillment in it rather than in God. So it is, as Flannery O'Connor observed, that if you are a Christian, you "have to cherish the world at the same time that you struggle to endure it"[6] — cherish the first two senses of *kosmos* while you struggle to endure the third sense.

This "world," then, is the way in which our collective life in society (and the culture that goes with it) is organized around the self in substitution for God. It is life characterized by self-righteousness, self-centeredness, self-satisfaction, self-aggrandizement, and self-promotion, with a corresponding distaste for the self-denial proper to union with Christ. As comfortable as this self-centered reordering of moral and spiritual reality may seem, however, it is inevitably attended by "worldly grief" (2 Cor. 7:10), because, having displaced God from the center of our personal universe, we have made it impossible to care for ourselves as we should. The triumph of the self is always Pyrrhic; it amounts to a paradoxical abandonment of the true self, a ruin that begins to cast its shadows over the human spirit long before the day in which God's judgment is heard.

Sometimes Scripture uses the term *world* to signify this whole way of life; sometimes it uses the term in reference to how these general assumptions come to expression through individual people. In the latter instances, however, the individuals are representatives of all those who are unredeemed and at enmity with God. It is important to note that worldliness has this *collective* sense about it: there is public approbation for the private desires and appetites that are hostile to God and to his truth (Rom. 3:19; 2 Cor. 5:19). The "world" is a godless curia demanding that its teaching be obeyed, rewarding those who acquiesce, exacting sanctions on those who do not, and generally making belief and trust in Christ difficult. Christ himself was alienated from the "world." He was not of this world (John 17:14; 18:36), refused to pray for it (John 17:9), opposed its ruler (John 12:31; 14:30), and is now its judge (John 9:39; 16:7-11).

There is a clear line, then, between those who belong to Christ and those who do not, a line separating two very different ways of viewing self and world. If we stay with John, we can easily see how sharply he differentiates these two spiritual realms. Those who belong

---

6. O'Connor, *The Habit of Being*, ed. Sally Fitzgerald (New York: Vintage Books, 1980), p. 90.

to the church have been born of God (1 John 3:1-3); those who belong to the world have not (1 John 4:4-6). The church belongs to Christ (1 John 3:7-10); the world belongs to Satan (1 John 5:19), its "prince" (John 12:31; 14:30; 16:11). All that is of Christ endures forever; all that is of the world is transient, fading (1 John 2:17), and under God's judgment (1 John 4:17). Love for God, therefore, is utterly incompatible with love of the world (1 John 2:15).

Thus there is a profound sense in which the church has to be "otherworldly." It carries within itself a discernibly different view of life from what passes as normal and normative in society.[7] The church is defined by a knowledge that creates — or should create — an unbridgeable chasm between its own moral and spiritual values and those of the society. Christians are called to be exiles from the world (1 Pet. 1:1; Heb. 11:13), however personally painful that exile may be. They are supposed to be aliens to the world's darkness (1 Pet. 2:11) as they seek another city, "whose builder and maker is God" (Heb. 11:10).

This is no easy antagonism to maintain, as Peter Berger has pointed out.[8] The keener the alienation, the more important it is to find the means of mutual support among the like-minded, for creeping doubt is always a threat to believers. If the unique knowledge they have of life is so vital, so indispensable, how is it that those outside the body of Christ seem to do so well? (Cf. Ps. 73.) The deeper the chasm, the greater will be the need for the believer to develop the "character of a desert saint" in order to preserve the vital moral and cognitive differences and to avoid accommodation.

Bultmann has suggested that John shaped this antithesis between the character of God and the nature of life in four ways, contrasting light and darkness, truth and falsehood, freedom and bondage, and life and death.[9] These categories are not mutually exclusive, of course; in fact, they overlap in significant ways.

The imagery of light and darkness is used in the Old Testament in several different contexts, but in the New Testament it is usually used in relation to Christ. John uses it in two distinct ways. In some passages, light stands for God's truth revealed in his Word, written or

---

7. For pioneering work on the significance of knowledge that deviates from what is socially normative, see Max Weber, *The Sociology of Religion*, trans. Ephraim Fischoff (Boston: Beacon Press, 1963).

8. See Berger, *A Rumor of Angels: Modern Society and the Rediscovery of the Supernatural* (Garden City, N.Y.: Doubleday, 1969), pp. 9-26.

9. See Bultmann, *The Theology of the New Testament*, 2 vols., trans. Kendrick Grobel (New York: Scribner's, 1951-55), 2:15-17.

living; in such contexts, to be in darkness is to be ignorant of this truth (John 1:4, 5, 9; 8:12; 12:35-36, 46). Elsewhere, however, light stands for moral purity, and darkness, by contrast, for moral corruption (John 3:19-21). The connection between these two senses is important, for it implied a connection, a bond between truth and morality. God's truth has an inextricable moral dimension to it. Those who choose not to believe it are not merely mistaken, have not merely made an intellectual error: they have done something *wrong*. That is why the apostles treated heresy as both a departure from true belief and a moral offense. At the same time, what is morally right is inextricably bound to what is intellectually true, and we are duty bound to reflect that truth in our actions. John insisted that it was not enough to see; those who have received the light are obliged to walk in the light.

This light, in the person of Christ, came into the "world" and was neither understood (John 1:5) nor recognized (John 1:10) because of the darkness. So what is this darkness? It is not the shadow of some other presence falling over life; rather, it is something inherent to and pervasively present throughout human nature. It is the darkness of fallen human nature, a predisposition to embrace falsehood (cf. John 18:37) and to love corruption (John 3:19). It is the the love of sin that John equates with blindness (John 9:41). It would be a serious mistake to underestimate the power and pervasiveness of this corrupting darkness. When Paul spoke of it, he borrowed a devastating series of images from the Old Testament. Among those who are captive to the darkness, "none is righteous, no, not one, no one understands, no one seeks for God. . . . No one does good, not even one," and "there is no fear of God before their eyes" (Rom. 3:10-12, 18).

From other standpoints, the distinction between light and darkness can be seen as the distinction between truth and error, between freedom and bondage, between life and death. Truth is not simply knowledge untainted by life's biases and conventions: it is the reality of God himself (John 7:17; 8:47; 1 John 3:10). It has the power to dislodge people from the safe and comfortable conventions of the world where these are mistaken or unethical, to wrench people free from their sin (John 8:32-34). To be in the truth is to be in God, to be free, to have life. To be separated from the truth is to be mired in darkness, falsehood, and corruption with the stink of death hanging over everything.

Am I then describing a dualism? If so, it is clearly not the sort of dualism we find in Buddhism and Hinduism, between a world of reality and a world of experience that is mostly mere illusion and futility from which the enlightened seek escape. Nor is it the dualism of Greek philosophy (especially Plotinus), between the physical and the spiritual, between the body and the soul. Nor is it the dualism of Zoroastrianism and various Christian cults, between warring legions of the morally "good" and the morally "bad." No, this is a moral "dualism" of an entirely different order. It neither views the physical world and the body as inherently evil nor all spirituality in human experience as innocent and uncorrupted. Rather, it holds that good and evil are coextensive throughout all of creation, locked in a battle the outcome of which is already known but the outworkings of which are still painfully slow in their development. It is a dualism between "this present age" and "the age to come," and the New Testament tells us that the latter has intruded on the former (Rom. 12:2; 1 Cor. 1:20; 3:18; 2 Cor. 4:4; Gal. 1:4; Eph. 2:2; Tit. 2:12). That is to say, the "dualism" is *eschatological* and it must work itself out in ways that are trenchantly moral and intellectual. This has profound implications for the relationship between Christian faith and culture.

The frequently reiterated distinction between "this age" and "the age to come" was hardly original to the authors of the Gospels and Epistles, but its use in the New Testament does constitute a radical reordering of the older Jewish distinction between the ages around the incarnation, resurrection, ascension, and return of Christ, through whom the "age to come" has been inaugurated and is now, even at the present time, intruding on "the present age." The key point here is that the New Testament writers no longer speak of "this age" ending when "the age to come" began. Rather, they indicate that "this age," with all its corruption and rebellion against God, exists coextensively even within those in whom "the age to come" has already begun through their union with Christ.[10] From the apostolic perspective, all of history is centered in this intrusion, in the coming of the reign of God, the finale to which will be the return of Christ and the triumph of his kingdom over all that has asserted itself against the centrality and rule of God. Here again we see the correspondence between "this age" and the "world." To say that the whole "world" is under the control of Satan (1 John 5:19; cf. Gal. 4:3; Rom. 8:38; 16:20; 1 Cor. 2:6; 15:24) is equivalent to saying that he is "the god of this age" (2 Cor. 4:4; cf. Rom. 3:6; 1 Cor. 1:20; 3:19; 2 Cor. 7:10). And if it is the case that by spiritual resurrection we are transferred from "this age" to the

10. See Geerhardus Vos, *The Pauline Eschatology* (Grand Rapids: Baker Book House, 1979), pp. 1-41.

"age to come" through Christ, it is also the case that by the same divine work we are torn loose from this "world" in order that we might know and serve him.[11]

The Human Center

What is the difference between what we read about the "world" in the New Testament and what we read about in *Time* or *Newsweek?* Some would say that there is no really no comparison, that it's a matter of apples and oranges. The New Testament authors are describing a concept or providing a category, whereas the newsmagazines are giving summaries of the week's events. True, Scripture offers descriptions of many abstract virtues such as wisdom, kindness, and righteousness and many abstract vices such as arrogance, unbelief, and hardness of heart — but it also obligates readers to translate these virtues and vices into the reality of their own lives wherever they live. So again I will ask, What is the difference between John and *Time,* Paul and *Newsweek,* when the "world" is in view?

The difference is that the biblical authors see everything from a theocentric viewpoint, and secular writers see everything from an anthropocentric viewpoint. That means that the biblical perspective must be seen as theological knowledge in its strictest sense: it is knowledge in relation to God, knowledge as defined by his character, acts, and will, knowledge that derives from him, knowledge that is no less authentic than the One who guarantees it. The biblical writers compel us to read the world from this perspective, to see it in relation to the moral character of God and the ways in which he has disclosed his saving intentions in human history. Secular writers, by contrast, force us to read the world from within a framework in which God's moral will and saving intentions, his truth and his Christ, are never the criteria of meaning or importance.

To say that the secular viewpoint is anthropocentric is, in some ways, only to state the obvious. All our knowledge is in a sense necessarily anthropocentric inasmuch as it is the sum of what *human beings* know. It is the past as we have reconstructed it, matter as we have analyzed it, space as we have peered into it, society as we have organized it, justice as we have delivered it, and the human body as we understand it. There is a built-in liability in all of this, because the

11. Cf. Robert A. Guelich, "Spiritual Warfare: Jesus, Paul, and Peretti," *Pneuma* 13 (Spring 1991): 33-64.

assemblage of human knowledge is a work in progress, and as such it is susceptible to revision. Given this limitation, to characterize our knowledge as anthropocentric is not necessarily to damn it.

But this characterization is less felicitous if it conveys the sense that our knowledge is anthropocentric *as opposed to theocentric,* if it connotes not merely the knowledge that human beings have amassed but the way in which *sinners* see things. In this sense, it corresponds not to the New Testament's first two meanings of *kosmos* but to the third. In a theocentric vision, all of life is understood from within the perspective that God himself has provided for its understanding; in a solely anthropocentric vision, all of life is evaluated from within the perspective that fallen human nature provides. Our choice of center, our choice of which vantage point we will choose to read the world from — whether it is that of God or the corrupted self, "this age" or "the age to come" — has momentous consequences.

There are, then, two opposing ways of thinking about the world that can be found in the West today. The one belongs to those who have narrowed their perception solely to what is natural; the other belongs to those whose understanding of the natural is framed by the supernatural. The one takes in no more than what the senses can glean; the other allows this accumulation of information to be informed by the reality of the transcendent. The one indiscriminately celebrates diversity; the other seeks to understand life's diversity in the light of its unity. The one can go no further than intuition; the other pierces through to truth. The one presumes that everything changes and that change is the only constant; the other measures the things that change by the standard of things that are changeless. The one looks only to the shifting contents of human consciousness, which differ from one individual to the next; the other holds the individual consciousness up for comparison to the larger realms of meaning in which are rooted those things that are common to all human nature. The one acknowledges no ultimate certainties; the other places the highest value on ultimate certainties. All of these differences arise from the simple fact that the one perspective receives its meaning from God and the other does not.[12]

12. For a useful overview of these issues, see Ronald Nash, *Faith and Reason: Searching for a Rational Faith* (Grand Rapids: Academie Books, 1988). More specifically, see Alvin Plantinga's essay "Reason and Belief in God," in *Faith and Rationality: Reason and Belief in God,* ed. Alvin Plantinga and Nicholas Wolterstorff (Notre Dame, Ind.: University of Notre Dame Press, 1983), pp. 16-93; and Nicholas Wolterstorff, *On Universals: An Essay in Ontology* (Chicago: University of Chicago Press, 1970).

In a Post-Modern Framework

This set of choices is bleak and unqualified today because the Enlightenment project collapsed in the 1960s. The assumption among the Enlightenment's proponents that meaning and morality could be discovered
simply within the bounds of natural reason and without reference to God
has, even in our very secular age, become ever more empty. Their naive
faith in inevitable progress has been torpedoed by the brutality and the
manifold frustrations of the twentieth century. And their belief that
knowledge is always good, that knowledge is salvific, is mocked by our
deep fears regarding scientific and technological accomplishments,
many of which can as easily be used to thwart human well-being as to
promote it.[13] By the end of the 1960s, modernity had lost its Enlightenment soul. Thus it was that post-modernity began to emerge in the
1970s.[14]

Norman Cantor has argued that three developments in particular
have given birth to the growing sense of nihilism in art, architecture,
literature, dance, theater, and rock music.[15] First, biotechnology, which
built on the discovery in 1953 of the structure of DNA, has succeeded
in driving home the idea that human life is defined by impersonal
genetic codes rather than personal choices. This perception has greatly

13. See Diogenes Allen, *Christian Belief in a Postmodern World: The Full Wealth
of Conviction* (Louisville: Westminster/John Knox, 1989), pp. 1-19.

14. The literature on post-modernity is now massive, so I will recommend
only a few representative titles. For overviews of the emergence of post-modernity
out of the rubble of modernity, see Norman F. Cantor, *Twentieth Century Culture:
Modernism to Deconstruction* (New York: Peter Lang, 1988); Anthony Giddens, *The
Consequences of Modernity* (Stanford: University of Stanford Press, 1990); and David
Harvey, *The Condition of Postmodernity: An Inquiry into the Conditions of Social Change*
(Oxford: Basil Blackwell, 1989). For analyses of post-modern thought as critique
of modernity, see Herbert Blau, *The Eye of the Prey: Subversions of the Postmodern*
(Bloomington, Ind.: Indiana University Press, 1987). For assessments of how the
post-modern perspective has shaped various aspects of contemporary life, see
Kenneth Gergen, *The Saturated Self: Dilemmas of Identity in Contemporary Life* (New
York: Basic Books, 1990); Jean-François Lyotard, *The Postmodern Condition: A Report
on Knowledge,* trans. Geoff Bennington and Brian Massumi (Minneapolis: University
of Minnesota Press, 1985); Andreas Huyssen, *After the Great Divide: Modernism, Mass
Culture, Postmodernism* (Bloomington, Ind.: Indiana University Press, 1987); Charles
Jencks, *The Language of Post-Modern Architecture* (London: Academy Editions, 1981);
Anne Kaplan, *Rocking around the Clock: Music Television, Post-Modernism, and Consumer
Culture* (New York: Methuen, 1987); and Edith Wyschogrod, *Saints and Postmodern-
ism: Revisioning Moral Philosophy* (Chicago: University of Chicago Press, 1990).

15. See Cantor, *Twentieth Century Culture,* pp. 337-40. For brief essays on
various areas of post-modern endeavor, see Hugh J. Silverman, *Postmodernism:
Philosophy and the Arts* (New York: Routledge, 1990).

diminished the sense of human significance. Second, astounding advances in computer science and technology have reproduced or surpassed many of the tasks that were once thought to be defining marks of human uniqueness. Third, new communications technology has not only brought news, sports, and entertainment from around the world into American living rooms each day but has also given vast new power to multinational corporations and forced the last pockets of Marxism into desperate disarray. Like computer technology, the new communications technology has expanded human capability and increased human efficiency, but it has diminished human stature. We have been dwarfed by our own inventions and in many ways have become irrelevant to their workings. For these and many other reasons, we have come to feel small, empty, unspecial, meaningless.

This rather forlorn turn in our self-perception has coincided with a sense of betrayal on the part of many of the Enlightenment's children. The autonomous, unaided reason of the Enlightenment has not produced the promised emancipation in our social and political life. Quite the reverse. It has produced the ponderous bureaucratic societies of the West, massive in their structures and weight, unfeeling in their workings, and not infrequently unfriendly to human well-being. Postmodern thinkers are the vanguard of a profound reaction to the failure of the Enlightenment project, giving expression to a deeply held suspicion that modernity is in fact the enemy of human life.

The Enlightenment worked its dark magic by seizing such Christian motifs as salvation, providence, and eschatology and rewriting them in humanistic terms, offering their substance in this-worldly ways. It replaced the Christian virtues with the humanistic virtues of truth, freedom, and justice, promoting them as the means to social and political salvation in the here and now. It is this promise of a salvation on humanistic terms that is now being recognized as completely fallacious, and in the ensuing despair the post-modernists are now attacking *all* "metanarratives," all beliefs in overarching meaning, all beliefs rooted in a transcendent order, all values. It is thus that modernity has brought forth its own intellectual conquerors in the post-moderns. They are eviscerating its hopes while having to leave its structures — urbanization, capitalism, technology, telecommunications — in place. In effect, they are producing a version of modernity bereft of its beliefs, sunk in despair. On the one hand, post-modern authors have made the Christian critique of modernity easier, but on the other hand their virulent attack not merely on Enlightenment meaning but on *all* meaning has made Christian faith less plausible in the modern world.

Under the post-modern onslaught, all boundaries and distinctions rapidly fall. Some of the losses associated with the collapse of traditional distinctions have been trivial, but others have been earth-shaking, and there seems to be no way to distinguish between the two in the post-modern context. People no longer know where the lines fall. Linda Hamilton pumps iron and straps on automatic weapons in the *Terminator* movies while, with the help of plastic surgeons and makeup artists, Michael Jackson continues to look more like his sister. Our computers are starting to talk to us while our neighbors are becoming more distant and anonymous. An advertisement for a car speaks of it as having a mind, a heart, and a conscience while the new eugenics seems to be saying that human beings — especially those at the peripheries of life, the unborn and the aged — do not have hearts or minds worth worrying about.

No one in mass culture has more effectively perceived and capitalized on this collapse of boundaries than the pop star Madonna. She has in fact made a career out of crossing one line after another. She is the quintessential virgin whore, by turns sophisticated and vulgar, vulnerable and bulletproof, seductive and demure. She is, in many ways, a perfect personification of the post-modern reality: sensation without substance, motion without purpose, a self-created persona undergoing perpetual change for its own sake. In her world, everything is fluid and open. All boundaries and taboos are gone. Everything is possible. In the absence of the "metanarratives," there are no structures of meaning that transcend personal preferences. In this territory, distinctions between right and wrong, good and bad, decent and indecent have not merely collapsed but become irrelevant.

The imprint of post-modernity on popular culture is also very evident in the way that MTV does its business. It is first of all evident in the structure of the rock videos that constitute most of its programming. In a significant departure from traditional filmmaking, the videos typically jettison any sort of meaningful narrative in favor of a collage of discordant and often surreal images. The artistic goal of rock videos is not reasoned discourse but a visceral response, an emotional reaction that is ultimately plugged into the consumer culture. "It evokes a kind of hypnotic trance," writes E. Ann Kaplan, "in which the spectator is suspended in a state of unsatisfied desire but forever under the illusion of *imminent* satisfaction through some kind of purchase."[16] The desires most commonly targeted for satisfaction are those

16. Kaplan, *Rocking around the Clock*, p. 12.

of love, sex, freedom, and violence. Of course, rock videos don't do a very good job of satisfying these desires, but they do manage to strike an important chord in their principal audience. The fact is that the private narratives of most MTV viewers are radically fractured, too; their own histories are often little more than sets of fleeting and disconnected experiences. MTV effectively recapitulates the way they are processing these experiences; it is, on a subterranean level, a case of art imitating life.

And, in keeping with the post-modern impulse, what content the rock videos do have is typically flat and shallow, empty of any moral structure. The distinction between good and evil has been replaced by the distinction between having and not having. MTV is preeminently consumer-driven programming. It markets not merely an endless stream of consumer goods but also images, styles, behavior, and promises. It markets *satisfaction*. It feeds basic hungers — for sensations, power, a sense of inner wholeness — through the vicarious satisfaction of the rock stars. When Eddie Van Halen gets his, I get mine by proxy. MTV is built out of the new generation's veneration of the older generation's acquisitiveness. It's the same old lyrics — "to have is to be" — set to new music.

The more virulent forms of post-modern, this-worldly anthropocentrism are easy enough to see in the caricature environment of the mass media, but there are quieter evidences of it elsewhere that may well constitute a greater danger precisely because they seem altogether harmless. Our society operates on the basis of any number of unconsciously held beliefs and assumptions that deeply affect our view of the world.[17]

To cite just one area of contemporary life, the capitalistic order that is now entrenched in the West has produced a whole array of latent assumptions about life. It not only showers its blessings on all but it has also produced what sociologists call a "rationalization" of life that is thoroughly this-worldly in its outlook. Capitalism is the way in which economic means and ends are linked in the most efficient way, a way that requires freedom of movement and private ownership of property and that produces markets wherever the law of supply and

---

17. For a discussion of the latent dimension of knowledge in a society, see Michel Foucault, *The Archeology of Knowledge* (London: Tavistock, 1972). Foucault argues that in the absence of ethical values, a society's basic assumptions can be, and usually are, exploited in the search for power. On Foucault himself, see the excellent biography by James Miller, *The Passion of Michael Foucault* (New York: Simon & Schuster, 1993).

demand operates. This law is held to be inviolable — not because it is rooted in an ultimate system of ethics but simply because it has proved to be most efficient. Thus we have arrived at a self-enclosed and this-worldly system, the ethos of which is produced entirely by competition on the one side and anonymity and bureaucratic structures on the other. It is what Max Weber called an "iron cage."

To participate in the productive order of capitalism is not worldly per se, but to think about life solely from within its "iron cage," to evaluate life solely in terms of products and services, to assume that everything in life is amenable to capitalistic techniques, to grant efficiency the value of an ultimate criterion — to do this is to become so anthropocentric, so "this-worldly" in spirit as to be worldly in the biblical sense. Moreover, those who slide into worldliness this way are not likely to be conscious of the fact that they are doing so; the ways in which capitalism works are so much second nature to them that they will barely ever think about it. And since capitalism has been so extraordinarily successful, a person who prizes efficiency as an ultimate criterion will scarcely have any grounds on which to question its techniques. Indeed, they will be inclined to suppose that these same techniques might profitably be applied in spheres of life beyond the economic. I will argue in Chapter 4 that it is just this sort of hope that animates those who are busy marketing the church while remaining entirely unaware of how thoroughly worldly the enterprise has actually become. A fascination with the reward of instant and measurable success seems to stand in the way of serious analysis of what is actually taking place.

The anthropocentric perspective inclines post-modern sinners to miss, if not deliberately to obscure, a significant part of reality. The narrow cognitive bearings of such individuals distorts their moral perception. They have, as John puts its, fallen into a fatal bondage to the world; they have come to *love* the darkness. For those who are dazzled by the darkness and hence inclined to dismiss his discussion of "world" as arbitrary counsel, the word with which he closes his first epistle is especially apropos: "Little children, keep yourselves from idols" (1 John 5:21).

Godlets and Godding

John's concluding admonition, it should be noted, is addressed to Christians. Among their pagan contemporaries, the worship of gods and goddesses was commonplace, but apparently that was not what

John had in mind in this admonition. The original prohibitions against such idol worship (Exod. 20:3) and against the use of images to worship Yahweh (Exod. 20:4-6) were made because Yahweh alone is true and because, although he is immanent in the creation, he also transcends it — which is to say that he cannot be captured in any *thing*.[18] To represent the character and being of God through a thing is, inevitably, to represent God as less and other than he is.

By New Testament times, the rubric of idolatry had been broadened to include such things as immorality and covetousness (Eph. 5:5; Col. 3:5), and we will probably be correct in viewing the final admonition in John's first epistle as a similar application of Old Testament teaching. Certainly he was warning of the danger that "false and counterfeit ideas of God" might be accepted as true, as C. H. Dodd says, and it may be that, like the author of the Corinthian correspondence, he was speaking to people who, under pressure "to be open, tolerant and accommodate other faiths," unwittingly replaced faith in the God of Old Testament revelation with faith in something small and twisted.[19] "It is no longer plausible," Dodd says with reference to the contemporary world, "either to hold that a man's theology — that is, his thought about God — does not matter; or to pretend that there is no great difference between Christian faith and any sort of religiosity that might appeal to this man or that" for, when all is said and done, our modern idols, when judged by their

18. On the mechanisms of idolatry in the life of Israel, see Owen Barfield, *Saving the Appearances: A Study in Idolatry* (New York: Harcourt Brace Jovanovich, 1965), pp. 107-15. Moshe Halbertal and Avishai Margalit have also noted, however, that the notion of idolatry is not exclusively biblical. Pagan philosophers also attacked folk religion along these lines, suggesting that it was "a religion molded by imaginative, manipulative, entertainer-poets who lacked any concern for truth" (*Idolatry*, trans. Naomi Goldblum [Cambridge: Harvard University Press, 1992], p. 112). Later, proponents of the Enlightenment used the language of idolatry to attack the religious authority from which they were seeking release. More recently still, critics have characterized various racist, classist, and nationalist ideologies as modern forms of idolatry because of their capacity to exercise such compelling power (*Idolatry*, pp. 114-15).

19. On the textual, literary, and theological issues related to idolatry in the Corinthian texts, see Wendel Willis, "An Apostolic Apologia: The Form and Function of 1 Corinthians 9," *Journal for the Study of the New Testament* 24 (1985): 33-48; Wayne A. Meeks, "And Rose Up to Play: Midrash and Paraenesis in 1 Corinthians 10:1-22," *Journal for the Study of the New Testament* 16 (1982): 64-78; and Harold S. Songer, "Problems Arising from the Worship of Idols: I Corinthians 8:1–11:1," *Review and Expositor* 80 (Summer 1983): 363-75. On the apostolic decree, see additionally C. K. Barrett, "The Apostolic Decree of Acts 15:29," *Australian Biblical Review* 35 (1987): 50-59.

effects, have shown themselves to be no "better than the abominations of the heathen."[20]

So, what is idolatry more precisely, and what is its connection with the "world"? Richard Keyes argues that true idols are internal spiritual configurations.[21] The heart — no less the modern heart — is an idol factory. Idolatry, ancient and modern alike, consists in trusting some substitute for God to serve some uniquely divine function. These substitutes need not be supernatural; money, power, expertise, the location of the planets on the astrological charts, and a belief in Progress are among the most popular idols of Our Time. We have used both our psychological and physical selves idolatrously — although, as the post-modern condition empties out the self, rendering it ever thinner and less substantial, we have increasingly begun to turn more to our bodies than our psyches.[22] One quite predictable turn in this regard is a revival of the worship of sexuality. For example, Carter Heyward, an Episcopalian theology professor, speaks of sexual experience as "sexual godding." In an epigrammatic chapter heading, she cites a theological student's testimony that one "of my most profound experiences of Goddess is with my lover — while we are having sex and especially at the moment of peaking, I feel a deep sense of her love and presence with me."[23] This is deified experience. It is a substitute for the genuine article.[24]

20. Dodd, *The Johannine Epistles* (New York: Harper & Row, 1946), pp. 141-42.

21. Keyes, "The Idol Factory," in *No God but God*, ed. Os Guinness and John Seel (Chicago: Moody Press, 1993), pp. 29-48.

22. Nancy Brewka Clark has proposed that for many the contemporary interest in physical exercise is not simply a way of achieving or retaining health but is a kind of secular religion. As "churches empty, health clubs flourish; as traditional fervor wanes, attention to the body waxes. In other words, as the baby boomers approach middle age, a yearning toward perpetual youth flares up and denial of the biological takes the form of aerobics" ("Faith in the Flesh: An Essay on Secular Society's Preoccupation with Life [Somewhat] Eternal," *Lynn Magazine*, October 1985, p. 18). Fitness is the new path to (comparative) immortality. The pain of the workout is the new penance; the monk's hair shirt has been replaced by the modern's sweatshirt. For a listing of more intellectual contemporary idols, see Herbert Schlossberg, *Idols for Destruction: Christian Faith and Its Confrontation with American Society* (Nashville: Thomas Nelson, 1983).

23. Heyward, *Touching Our Strength: The Erotic as Power and the Love of God* (San Francisco: HarperCollins, 1989), p. 88. This is, of course, simply a recrudescence of ancient pagan ideas in modern conceptuality. Jean S. Bolen appears to espouse a similar worldview using the rhetoric of Jungian psychology in *Goddesses in Everywoman: A New Psychology for Women* (San Francisco: Harper & Row, 1985).

24. In New Age circles, some are suggesting that the Christian era has been but an interlude between two phases of paganism. We are now experiencing the

Why do people choose the substitute over God himself? Probably the most important reason is that it obviates accountability to God. We can meet idols on our own terms because they are our own creations. They are safe, predictable, and controllable; they are, in Jeremiah's colorful language, the "scarecrows in a cucumber field" (10:5). They are portable and completely under the user's control. They offer nothing like the threat of a God who thunders from Sinai and whose providence in this world so often appears to us to be incomprehensible and dangerous. People who "remain in the center of their lives and loyalties, autonomous architects of their own futures," Keyes argues, thereby avoid coming face to face with God and his truth.[25] They need face only themselves. That is the appeal of idolatry.

But the fruit of replacing God with the self — whatever form it takes — and the corresponding loss of accountability to God can become very bitter. G. K. Beale has argued that the prophet Isaiah's indictment of Israel for its idolatry exemplifies the whole Old Testament case against God's people for their faithlessness. The irony is that those who worship idols become as dead as the idols they worship, and those who inflame themselves in worship of them are consumed by the fires of divine judgment. Imagining themselves to have perceived great spiritual reality, they are in fact incurably blind.[26] And so it is in every age. Having displaced God, sinners can no longer gauge the depths of their sin, even if they do experience a tormented conscience. In the ensuing spiritual disintegration, typically "the consciousness of guilt is suppressed and driven below consciousness," says Emil Brunner, and "there it assumes the strangest forms." The wrath of God, for

---

reemergence in modern culture of an intuitive, feminine principle after a long period dominated by male, rationalistic, linear thinking, they say. The divine is now being reintegrated in the creation after a long period of its separation. Classical theism is giving way to pantheism. Shirley MacLaine sees no distinction between God and her self. The New Age visionaries maintain that the changing relations between the sexes are opening up whole new realms of meaning. They have identified a Purpose, but it is purpose grounded in the destruction of distinctions between good and evil, Creator and creation, men and women. It is a form of idolatry as bold as any denounced by any biblical prophet. For more on this, see Peter Jones, *The Gnostic Empire Strikes Back* (Phillipsburg, Pa.: Presbyterian & Reformed, 1992); Theodore Roszak, *Unfinished Animal: The Aquarian Frontier and the Evolution of Consciousness* (London: Faber, 1976); and Lawrence Osborn, *Angels of Light: The Challenge of the New Age* (London: Darton, Longman & Todd, 1992).

25. Keyes, "The Idol Factory," p. 33.

26. See Beale, "Isaiah 6:9-13: A Retributive Taunt against Idolatry," *Vetus Testamentum* 41 (1991): 257-78.

example, "is expressed in the figures of the Furies and of the avenging deities."[27] These Furies emerge in obsessions that may be deeply evil and are always destructive.[28]

By this point it should be clear that worldliness is not simply an innocent cultural escapade, still less a matter merely of inconsequential breaches in behavior or the breaking of trivial rules of the church or the expected practices of piety. Worldliness is a *religious* matter. The world, as the New Testament authors speak of it, is an alternative to God. It offers itself as an alternative center of allegiance. It provides counterfeit meaning. It is the means used by Satan in his warfare with God. To be part of that "world" is to be part of the Satanic hostility to God. That is why worldliness is so often idolatrous and why the biblical sanctions against it are so stringent. "Do you not know," asks James, "that friendship with the world is enmity with God? Therefore whoever wishes to be a friend of the world makes himself an enemy of God" (James 4:4).

27. Brunner, *The Christian Doctrine of Creation and Redemption,* Dogmatics series, vol. 2, trans. Olive Wyon (Philadelphia: Westminster Press, 1952), p. 119. In Niebuhrian fashion, John Macquarrie suggests that human existence is typically disordered in one of two patterns. Some individuals defy the limits of human existence and asssume God-like qualities of transcendence, producing political tyrany, prideful domination, and utopianism of one kind or another. Some individuals accept a subhuman role, abdicating their responsibility to make sound decisions, think rationality, and act ethically. It is this pair of competing drives to be God-like and to be animal-like, says Macquarries, that produces the "massive and manifold disorder of human existence" (*Principles of Christian Theology* [New York: Scribner's, 1977], pp. 69-70). Cf. Reinhold Niebuhr, *The Nature and Destiny of Man,* 2 vols. (New York: Scribner's, 1964), 1:1-25. Whatever patterns this disorder may produce, it is rooted in human rebellion. See James Orr, *The Christian View of God and Man as Centring in the Incarnation* (New York: Scribner's, 1897), pp. 166-99.

28. M. Scott Peck has sketched out this inner mechanism in those whom he calls evil — the people of the lie. He includes in this category not only those who have committed heinous crimes but also those who repetitively and consistently act unethically. How can they do this? Doesn't a sense of guilt ever deter them from their evil? Peck's studies indicate that they feel no guilt. They think of themselves as perfect; they absolutely refuse "to tolerate the sense of their own sinfulness" (*People of the Lie* [New York: Simon & Schuster, 1983], p. 71). Since they experience no inward reproach, they refuse to accept reproach from anyone else. And often this refusal is expressed through the mechanism of projection. "Since the evil, deep down, feel themselves to be faultless, it is inevitable that when they are in conflict with the world they will invariably perceive the conflict to be the world's fault. Since they must deny their own badness, they must perceive others as bad. They *project* their own evil onto the world" (pp. 73-74). Which is to say that when the lines of accountability before God are severed, his wrath moves inward, producing psychological furies that are subsequently unleashed on the world.

Today, evangelicalism reverberates with worldliness. In first impressions, this worldliness does not appear ugly at all. Quite the opposite. It maintains a warm and friendly countenance, parading itself as successful entrepreneurship, organizational wizardry, and a package of slick public relations insights that are essential to the facilitation of evangelical business.

Now, there is nothing wrong with entrepreneurship or organizational wizardry or public relations or television images and glossy magazines per se. The problem lies in the current evangelical inability to see how these things carry within them values that are hostile to Christian faith. The problem, furthermore, lies in the unwillingness of evangelicals to forsake the immediate and overwhelming benefits of modernity, even when corrupted values are part and parcel of those benefits. What is plainly missing, then, is *discernment,* and this has much to do with the dislocation of biblical truth from the life of the church today and much to do with the dying of its theological soul.

Discernment is a spiritual capacity. It is the insight that comes with Christian wisdom. It is the ability to see "through" life, to see it for what it really is. Some people are more naturally sagacious than others, some more critically astute than others, and God may enhance this sort of gift by his grace, but it is not this natural ability that I am referring to here. The heart of the ability to discern right from wrong in the actual circumstances of life is the rich flowering that God intends from the interactions of the truth of his Word, reflection on it, and the moral character that grows out of it.[29] It is this culture of wisdom with which the Bible, in both Testaments, is much concerned and in which the evangelical world appears to have lost interest.

The alternative wisdom that modernity now proposes clearly has its fascinations, not to mention its rewards. Western society accepts it as normal and in its brassy moments loudly insists that it is normative. It is popular because it works. But, in many ways, it is offering the church a counterfeit reality with the power to destroy what the church is. It is certainly robbing the church of its insight into the real meaning of life, a foundationally moral insight, because it is robbing the church of its ability to take its bearings from God, who is centrally holy.

Indeed, wherever there is worldliness in the church today, it has made its inroads because of insufficient belief in the Transcendent and a surfeit of belief in the modern world. The problem of worldliness, of modernity happily ensconcing itself in the church, is a problem of

29. See my *No Place for Truth,* pp. 97-109.

misplaced belief. It is a problem of mistaken loyalties, of misjudgment about how relevance is really to be assessed and how success is to be defined. Christian faith made relevant to the "world," in this third and final sense, will be Christian faith no longer relevant to God, to his Christ, to his truth.

If the stakes are so high, why has this departure been so notoriously difficult to recognize? Why do we find it so difficult to discern how to be in the world but not of it? I believe it is because the evangelical world has abandoned theology and is now running on the high octane fuel of modernity. It cannot see as alien the values that it has already taken to heart. But there is another dimension of this problem that calls for some further exploration — the way in which characteristics that are unique to American life also contribute to this difficulty, making worldliness unusually hard to unseat in the church.

Manufactured in America

I have argued elsewhere that the uniqueness of the American character lies in the way in which it manages to mix individualism and conformity.[30] Neither of these traits by itself is uniquely American. It is the way they are combined in America that is unique. In other countries — Britain, for example — the impulses toward individualism and conformity tend to offset or balance each other, but in America each impulse typically comes to full expression in its own right, related to but not diminished by the other. The two impulses are naturally contradictory, but American culture has tended to resolve the tension between them by diverting the stream of individualism into private life and the stream of conformity into public life. Thus it is that in the public sphere Americans are uncomfortable with the unconventional and yearn for consensus, whereas in the private sphere they prize the personal vision, the strength and willingness to live by one's own lights regardless of what others think and what the conventions dictate.

This combination of traits has created soil uncommonly fertile to worldliness and uncommonly inhospitable to the church. To change the image, the modern cultural context is like a pair of powerful pincers locked on the church, in some cases squeezing its identity as the people of *God* beyond recognition.

How exactly does worldliness infiltrate the church through these

30. See my *No Place for Truth*, pp. 137-217.

deep and seemingly natural inclinations toward individualism and conformity? On the one side, modern individualism has been reduced to little more than a technique for adjusting a personal image to what seems valued, admired, and desired in society. This adaptation to cultural norms and expectations is precisely the mechanism by which worldliness takes root. On the other side, the need to conform — the sense of being ill at ease when one is at odds with the public perception of what is normal and normative — makes it extremely difficult for the church to preserve its distinctive identity, to be different. This combination of a desire to be like admired people and a discomfort in being unlike them goes a long way toward explaining how it is that the church has found it so hard to recognize worldliness and even harder to dislodge it. Indeed, without a powerful theological vision as its antithesis, these cultural currents are impossible to resist.

There was a time when individualists lived by the internal gyroscope of character. They thought for themselves, did what they believed to be right even if they received no approbation from others, judging that it was better, as David Riesman put it, to be right than to be president. The new individualists are quite different. They have unhooked the self from meaningful connections to the past, community, work, and family, thereby emptying it of its substance. To fill the resulting vacuum, they have sought surrogate connections in the larger society. They have replaced character with a desire to be like others, to have what they see as pleasing, to be what they admire. Paul declared that we need to be redeemed from "the course of this world" (Eph. 2:2), but the new individualists are actually seeking to use the course of this world to redeem themselves. And the same strategy is also arising out of the contrary impulse toward conformity.

The undercurrents of conformity in America are not merely a matter of the triumph of statistics, the accumulation of consensus through the flattening of class distinctions and the leveling effects of mass culture. There is at work here a positive veneration of the center — what Ann Douglas calls the "exaltation of the average."[31] For the conforming American, democracy is not simply a political system but an entire worldview dictating, among other things, that culture and truth belong to the people and in a sense are determined by the people. Our custodians of culture and truth are constrained to operate within the bounds of popular consensus. They can lead only so far as the

31. Douglas, *The Feminization of American Culture* (New York: Alfred A. Knopf, 1977), p. 4.

people are willing to follow, which is to say that their leadership is essentially tied to public opinion. This situation may constitute something of a civic virtue, but it is liable to produce much mischief when it is transplanted into the church. In fact, it more or less guarantees that the church will be unable to reform itself if and when culture intrudes on the pew.

Nevertheless, conformity is as much triumphant in modern evangelicalism as it is in American culture. In both spheres the power of the pollsters is extraordinary. Their ability to gauge the "norm" of belief and practice in a society that worships that norm has effectively conferred on them the power to prescribe what *should be* believed and practiced. Because of our deep need to conform, we have in effect allowed pollsters to become our teachers and ethicists, our philosophers and theologians, the arbiters of what the church must model if it is to be accepted and to succeed. The pollsters provide only one of the many channels along which worldly values are mediated to the church, but we have granted them a special, virtually unassailable authority. Unlike the other channels of mass culture (e.g., television, the movies, rock music) that reflect our image back at us, that embody and pass along the values that we hold in common, the offerings of the pollsters carry the imprimatur of science, the validity of hard numbers and margins of error fixed to the decimal point.

There was a time when American evangelicals prized and cultivated biblically chaste Christian thought and an incisive analysis of the culture from a perspective apart from it. But the past few decades have seen an erosion of the old distinctions, a gradual descent into the "self" movement, a psychologizing of faith, and an adaptation of Christian belief to a therapeutic culture. Distracted by the blandishments of modern culture, we have lost our focus on transcendent biblical truth. We have been beguiled by the efficiency of our culture's technique, the sheer effectiveness of its strategies, and we have begun to play by these rules. We now blithely speak of marketing the gospel like any other commodity, oblivious to the fact that such rhetoric betrays a vast intrusion of worldliness into the church.[32]

It was once one of the hallmarks of evangelicalism that it offered

32. For my analysis of how this trend has worked out in the career of *Christianity Today* during the past forty years, see *No Place for Truth*, pp. 207-11. More broadly, see Carl F. H. Henry, "The Church in the World or the World in the Church? A Review Article," *Journal of the Evangelical Theological Society* 34 (September 1991): 381-83.

a pronounced cultural critique, but now it is as attentive as any other aspect of that culture to the pronouncements of the pollster. Today any evangelical who demurs from the cultural consensus will almost certainly be viewed as a rebel, perhaps even a subversive, and almost certainly as irrelevant and out of it. All of this may be deeply alarming, but it is not more alarming than the prospect of falling in with the world, of capitulating to a system of values and set of assumptions that kills the love for God required by the first and great commandment upon which all Christian faith must be based.

It is, of course, true that all human beings are made in the image of God and are spiritually descended from the same Adam, so sin has essentially the same character in all people, whether ancient or modern, black or white, Eastern or Western, male or female, educated or uneducated. At the same time, ethnic and cultural differences do create differences in the specific contours of worldliness from one to another. Every culture makes some sins easier to indulge in and others more difficult, throws a cloak of legitimacy over some but not others. It is especially important for the church, in its own cultural location, to be able to discern generically how sin is made to look normal and normative and how righteousness is made to look strange. If it is unable to make this discernment, it will cloud the difference between sin and righteousness, its message will become confused and distorted, its practice will be compromised, and the honor of God will be besmirched. It is precisely this, I believe, that has happened in America. It is because worldliness has the capacity to destroy the very center of Christian faith — its understanding of the being and character, the acts and truth of God with all of the consequences that this has for Christian faithfulness — that we are now seeing such a drastic transformation of evangelical faith.

It is important, however, that the abstract notion of the "world" be given some concrete form, lest we oppose it in theory while inadvertently embracing it in day-to-day living. To that end, in Chapter 4 I want to take a close look at the growing enterprise of marketing Christian faith — an enterprise that promises so much success but comes packaged with values that are quite destructive to Christian faith. What successes have been achieved in this regard have come at a high cost — the triumph of worldliness in the church — and hence I believe that they are doomed to be short-lived and, in the end, culturally irrelevant.

CHAPTER 4

Clerics Anonymous

Jesus Christ was a marketing specialist.

George Barna

The word of God is not for sale; and therefore it has no need of shrewd salesmen. The word of God is not seeking patrons; therefore it refuses price cutting and bargaining; therefore it has no need of middlemen. The word of God does not compete with other commodities which are being offered to men on the bargain counter of life. It does not care to be sold at any price. It only desires to be its own genuine self, without being compelled to suffer alterations and modifications. . . . It will, however, not stoop to overcome resistance with bargain counter methods. Promoters' success are sham victories; their crowded churches and the breathlessness of their audiences have nothing in common with the word of God.

Karl Barth

The Church is looking for better methods; God is looking for better men.

E. M. Bounds

It may be a coincidence that at the very moment when shopping malls have become the nerve centers of our domestic commerce, mega-churches have emerged to become the most visible symbols of innova-

60

tion among evangelical churches.[1] There are those who think that this development was inevitable, however, because, in their different ways, both malls and megachurches are perfectly in tune with modernity.

Malls are monuments to consumption — but so are megachurches. Both places celebrate the coupling of the appetites of consumption with religion. The religion of the mall has been condensed into the secular creed that to have is to be; in the megachurch, the psychological need to consume is expressed as a form of spiritual hunger, a need to be connected with others. But in neither place are the tendrils of human connectedness very substantial. That, of course, is also one of the marks of the modern world.

Much has been written on the theme of the consumer mentality, because it is very much at the heart of the twentieth-century Western experience. We are nothing if not consumers — consumers of things, words, images, sex, power, relationships, experiences, and ethnicity. We are all suspended in a state of unsatisfied desire, perpetually expecting that immediate satisfaction is at hand, trying to work out the key to obtaining it. There is scarcely any available resource that has not been pressed into use to provide satisfaction, emancipation, or self-actualization; there is scarcely any part of life over which we, as a society, do not seek control in the interests of ease, security, and having plenty. Those are the hallmarks of consumption: a hunger for satisfaction on the part of those who consume and a hunger for control on the part of those who dominate the processes of production.

The primacy of the consumer mentality has loosed two connected revolutions on the modern world — the therapeutic and the managerial. The former assumes that all human badness is but disease, that there is nothing in human experience that is not amenable to healing if only the right technique is used, and that the techniques we need for our selfrecovery are all made available to us within the marketplace. The latter assumes, as all secular practice does, that efficient control through spreadsheets, flow charts, and bureaucratic organization will produce the most profit from the least effort — that refined techniques of production and control can provide optimum happiness, both taming and rendering life beneficent. Together, the

---

1. There is no agreement as to what constitutes a megachurch. In Britain, a weekly attendance of 300 is considered substantial enough. In America, analysts typically set the bar somewhere in a range from 1,000 to 3,000. I have in mind the figure 2,000. For a brief account of the emergence of these churches, see Lyle E. Schaller, "Megachurch!" *Christianity Today*, 5 March 1990, pp. 20-24.

therapeutic and managerial revolutions presume to offer a kind of secular providence, transferring the control of the world from the hands of God to those of managers and therapists. Given the radical displacement of God associated with the assumptions implicit in these revolutions, it is a little surprising to discover them taking root in the church, but they have managed to do so because they are typically viewed as innocent, as simply the most productive way of doing business, religiously speaking.

In this chapter, I want to focus on one aspect of the consumer culture in the church — the part of it in which marketing is prominent.[2] I will focus on just one exemplar, George Barna. By way of preface to this case study, I will first show that what he is attempting to do has become possible because a profound change occurred in the church over a long period of time, a change that began in the American Revolutionary War era and grew into something truly significant during the nineteenth century, a change that rendered the church as receptive as the general culture to adoption of the techniques of capitalism. Having quickly reviewed this change, I will proceed to a consideration of Barna's specific proposal. All of this is preparatory to an

2. The consumer culture has infiltrated today's evangelical churches in two main areas. First, it has reordered the church's *ethos,* as I will explain in greater length in this chapter. Second, it has reordered the *structure* of evangelicalism in ways that to this point seem to have been largely overlooked. The most obvious sign of the change in the structure of evangelicalism is the explosion of parachurch groups that began in the 1970s. Evangelical organizations dominate the pages of J. Melton Gordon's *Directory of Religious Organizations in the United States* for 1993. In one small segment of the *Directory* — under the letter "F" — for example, 40 percent of the organizations listed are evangelical, substantially more than any other group. Among those listed (excluding overseas missions and conventional presses) are the following, with founding dates enclosed in parentheses: Faith Christian Fellowship International Church (1978); Faith Partners for Missions (1986); Faith Publications (1961); Family of Faith Ministries (1972); Far Eastern Broadcasting Co. (1946); Fellowship of Christian Cowboys (1974); Fellowship of Christian Athletes (1954); Fellowship of Christian Airline Personnel (1972); Fellowship Associates of Medical Evangelism (1970); Fellowship of Christian Peace Officers (1971); Fellowship of Christian Magicians (1953); Fellowship of Christian Firefighters, International (1978); Fellowship of Companies for Christ, International (1980); Fellowship of Artists for Cultural Evangelism (1974); Fellowship of Fire Chaplains (1978); Fellowship of Mission (1969); Focus (1979); Focus on the Family (1977); The Fold (1967); Forum for Scriptural Christianity (1966); Foundation of Praise (1970); Freedom of Fellowship Foundation (1984); Full Gospel Grace Fellowship (1970); Full Gospel Student Fellowship (1969); and Fuller Evangelistic Association (1933). This represents a remarkable transformation and decentralization of the evangelical world since the immediate postwar years.

assessment, in Chapter 5, of the devastating effects that such accom-
modations to modernity have had on our understanding and experience of God, for the love of the world and the love of God are in
unrelenting competition with each other.

The Religious Economy

It may strike some readers as gauche to suggest that the failure and
success of church bodies can be understood by the market model, that
there are religious economies just as there are commercial economies.
But that is what Roger Finke and Rodney Stark have proposed, and
their theory offers an interesting framework for understanding past
cycles of growth and decline. Still, it should be noted immediately that
although Barna also advocates this analogy, Finke and Stark have a far
more developed and sophisticated understanding of what constitutes
market forces, because they see a market as embracing far more than
simply consumer need.

Finke and Stark maintain that four factors are essential to both
economies: (1) organization (or church polity); (2) sales representatives
(or clergy); (3) product (or religious doctrine and life); and (4) marketing techniques (or evangelism and church growth).[3] In other words,
supply and demand explain the workings of both economies. They
use this thesis to explain the changes that have occurred in the religious
landscape, citing as an example the way in which American Protestantism was transformed after the Revolution.

In 1776, America's three most dominant denominations, claiming
55 percent of all the nation's church members, were the Congregationalists, the Episcopalians, and the Presbyterians. By 1850, however,
these three bodies had only 19.1 percent of the "market" share, even
though the number of those belonging to churches in America had
doubled during the same period from 17 percent to 34 percent. By
1850, Congregationalists, who constituted 20.4 percent of the total in
1776, constituted only 4 percent. Episcopalians had fallen in this same
time from 15.7 percent to only 3.5 percent, and Presbyterians declined
from 19.0 percent to 11.6 percent. By contrast, Baptists, who in 1776
amounted to 16.9 percent of the "market" share, had increased to 20.5
percent. The Methodists had grown from only 2.5 percent of the total

---

3. See Finke and Stark, *The Churching of America: Winners and Losers in Our
Religious Economy* (New Brunswick, N.J.: Rutgers University Press, 1992), p. 17.

in 1776 to 34.2 percent of the total in 1850, from 65 churches to 13,302.[4]

How is all of this to be understood? Finke and Stark think that their market model provides the explanation. Baptists and Methodists were democratic in their organization at the local level, which was an enormous advantage in the years following the Revolution. Moreover, their ministers had the common touch, perhaps because they were mostly uneducated.[5] Furthermore, their message was down-to-earth and practical, and their method was carefully worked out and effective. Perhaps it would be best to say that this "market" was a very complex amalgam of forces, ideas, and a new national disposition, which the Baptists and Methodists were able to exploit, however unconsciously, in a way that the Congregationalists, Episcopalians, and Presbyterians were not.

The sweeping changes in the ecclesiastical topography that followed the Revolution were, in fact, as much the result of a conquest of class as of theology. Nathan Hatch has argued that in the decades following the Revolution, Christians of all kinds yoked "strenuous demands for revivals, in the name of George Whitefield, with calls for the expansion of popular sovereignty, in the name of the Revolution," and the result was a transformation of their churches in the areas of organization, belief, and practice.[6] "As religious disunity was followed by religious multiplicity," writes Richard Hofstadter, "Americans uprooted church establishments and embraced religious liberty."[7]

These populist religious movements — including the Methodists, the Baptists, the Mormons, the Disciples of Christ, and even the Universalists — drew on the same sort of energy as the populist political movements of the day.[8] Both types of movement produced leaders

4. Finke and Stark, *The Churching of America*, p. 55.

5. It has been estimated that in 1823 only 100 of 2,000 Baptist clergy had the equivalent of a college education. In 1844, among the Methodist circuit riders, only 50 among 4,282 had gone beyond grade-school level.

6. Hatch, *The Democratization of American Christianity* (New Haven: Yale University Press, 1989), p. 7. Hatch's view has been challenged on some particulars by Jon Butler. Specifically, Butler argues that the revivals enlarged the role of the clergy more than that of the laity. This was the case only in selective areas, however; it was seldom true of the Methodists and even less true of the Baptists. See Butler, *Awash in a Sea of Faith: Christianizing the American People* (Cambridge: Harvard University Press, 1990).

7. Hofstadter, *Anti-Intellectualism in American Life* (New York: Vintage Books, 1963), p. 81.

8. On political populism, see Christopher Lasch, *The True and Only Heaven: Progress and Its Critics* (New York: W. W. Norton, 1990), pp. 168-225.

who were able to appeal to the masses, able to attract followers with a vision of common ideals and efficient means of communication, and able to sustain participation in the movement by the commoners that democracy required.[9] The young nation offered an environment in which ordinary, often untrained people found the freedom to act on their own impulses, unhampered by the doctrines of the past, whether Christian or political, and to find in the bonding within their movements a defense against contrary viewpoints.

In this lies the strength and vulnerability of modern evangelicalism, which has been significantly affected by these earlier movements. Its strength has always been its identification with people. Hatch notes that while others in America were giving their attention to building impressive religious institutions, and while many of the graduates of Harvard, Yale, and Princeton in the early part of the nineteenth century continued to reflect in their ministries the older world of privilege, deference, and learning, the Baptists, Methodists, and Disciples of Christ were out on the highways and byways winning the soul of America. They profoundly affected the nation. There was, however, a cost to be paid in the upheavals that accompanied these ministries.

This ambitious drive produced some savage anti-clericalism, for example, not solely because of undercurrents of anti-intellectualism but also because the insurgent leaders were "intent on destroying the monopoly of classically educated and university trained clergymen."[10] Their sermons were colloquial, "employing daring pulpit storytelling, no-holds-barred appeals, overt humor, strident attacks, graphic application, and intimate personal experience."[11] The point of it all was to engage the audience. Charles Finney despised sermons that were formally delivered on the grounds that they put content ahead of communication,[12] and, although both he and Dwight L. Moody had their own theologies, they both vigorously opposed "the formal study of divinity."[13] Leonard Sweet has argued that Jacksonian politics "was not so much a defense of the rising common man as a defense of the ability of the common man to rise" despite the stratification in society and, correspondingly, that the new-measures revivalism of Finney and

9. See Hatch, *The Democratization of American Christianity*, p. 58.
10. Hatch, *The Democratization of American Christianity*, p. 162.
11. Hatch, *The Democratization of American Christianity*, p. 57.
12. Nathan O. Hatch, "Evangelicalism as a Democratic Movement," in *Evangelicalism and Modern America*, ed. George Marsden (Grand Rapids: William B. Eerdmans, 1984), p. 74.
13. Hatch, "Evangelicalism as a Democratic Movement," p. 74.

others "was less a faith in the worth and dignity of the common man than a demand that the common man become worthy and dignified."[14] In practice, however, the worth and dignity of the average individual was championed by expressing faith in this person's ability to take religious matters into his or her own hands and to act on instinct and private opinion.

As this psychology took root in the mass movements of Christian faith at the beginning of the nineteenth century, certain predictable characteristics began to emerge. First, in all of these movements, the distinction between clergy and laity and deference toward learned opinion were greatly diminished. Leadership was redefined in the context of the new democratic assumptions that had "sent external religious authority into headlong retreat and elicited from below powerful visions of faith that seemed more authentic and self-evident."[15] In place of the old respect for learning that the clergy had embodied was a new confidence in the capacity of the untrained individual to know intuitively what was right and true. The ability to judge doctrine and even to formulate it was assumed to be part of a common rather than a privileged inheritance, something that naturally belonged to the people. Second, these movements were driven by the hope of emancipation from the past, a hope for a new order of social and religious relations — perhaps the millennium itself.

To those who spoke the new language of freedom, the churches that had been numerically superior at the time of the Revolution — the Anglicans, Presbyterians, and Congregationalists — now looked decidedly suspect. Their clergy had the appearance of a privileged class still clinging to its privilege, their creeds seemed to bear the stink of the corruptions of the past, and their sermons seemed bent on preserving the language of an aristocracy still refusing to adjust itself to the people. With the Revolution came deep yearnings among ordinary Christians for churches emancipated from the past, freed from vested privilege, for leaders who would be like the people and preach in the vernacular, and for worship that would express the sentiments of the masses rather than the interests of the elite. Calvinistic orthodoxy, which seemed to be anchored in the older world of hierarchy and privilege and also to be decidedly undemocratic, was put to flight before Arminianism. In this large-scale triumph of Arminianism over

14. Sweet, "View of Man Inherent in the New Measures Revivalism," *Church History* 45 (June 1976): 221.

15. Hatch, *The Democratization of American Christianity*, p. 34.

Calvinism, William J. McLoughlin says, we see "the theological side of the political shift toward democracy."[16] The church-centered faith that had been favored before the Revolution retreated before itinerant revivalism, reasoned faith retreated before exuberant testimony, and theological confession retreated before the self-evident truths of experience. "As the common man rose in power in the early republic," says Hatch, "the inevitable consequence was the displacement from power of the uncommon man, the man of ideas."[17] Never again, he adds, would America produce people of the caliber of Adams, Jefferson, and Madison in the realm of politics or of Jonathan Edwards in the realm of theology.

What this meant — and what it will continue to mean insofar as evangelicalism remains true to its origins — is that there are at its psychological center two ideas that are also at the heart of the practice of democracy and, as a matter of fact, of capitalism.[18] These ideas are (1) that the audience is sovereign and (2) that ideas find legitimacy and value only within the marketplace. That is to say, evangelicals operate on the assumption that ideas have no intrinsic value, that they receive value when people determine that they are legitimate. The work of doing theology, therefore, ought not to be left to an intellectual elite that considers itself gifted for and called to do such work and that views the discovery of truth as an end in itself. It should instead be taken on by those who can persuade the masses of the usefulness of the ideas. Given the vagaries of modern culture, ideas quickly lose their power to compel if they cannot immediately be translated into technique.[19] Evangelicals have been willing to bestow legitimacy only on ideas that *work*.

All of this suggests to me that we do indeed have to take the notion of a religious market seriously, because it may well explain why some movements succeed and others fail. At the same time, we have to be aware that markets are often extremely complex. In the case of evangelicals, the market involves issues of public psychology, undercurrents of political ideology, nationalism, class warfare, the public

16. McLoughlin, "Pietism and the American Character," in *The American Experience: Approaches to the Study of the United States,* ed. Henning Cohen (Boston: Houghlin Mifflin, 1968), p. 44.

17. Hatch, "Evangelicalism as a Democratic Movement," p. 75.

18. Hatch, "Evangelicalism as a Democratic Movement," pp. 73-76.

19. On the nature and mechanics of rationalization in American society, see George Ritzer, *The McDonaldization of Society: An Investigation into the Changing Character of Contemporary Social Life* (Newbury Park, Cal.: Sage Publications, 1992).

sense of what is religiously appropriate, the moral climate, and definitions of public virtue. Denominations that were adept at identifying and responding to the demands of this complex marketplace flourished; those that could not, or would not, declined. In any event, evangelicalism has shown itself to be a religious tradition with an enormous capacity to adapt to the cultural climate.

In looking at what transpired, however, it is far from clear that all of the forces, ideas, and passions that have been unleashed during the past two centuries of American history to determine the relative success of the nation's religious communions were uniformly good. In many ways, adaptation to this market brought about the end of historic Protestant faith or at least created serious tensions within it. Perhaps we should view the refusal to adapt to some of these torrents of cultural demand as a badge of honor rather than an emblem of disgrace. It may be that it is only our enthusiasm for pragmatism — our assumption that only the consequences of an idea reveal whether it is true or false — that incline us to think that anything that succeeds in the marketplace must, in the nature of the case, be true and virtuous. In fact, I would argue that if Christian assumptions are to be allowed to have their place, we cannot assume that success in a cultural market is necessarily an indication of the presence of truth and virtue. Such success might just as easily be a sign that the church has been willing to prostitute itself by seeking worldly accommodation. This consideration becomes particularly pertinent when we consider how enthusiastically evangelicals have become about marketing the church to the world.

On Growing the Church

Although Donald McGavran had already formulated the main principles of Church Growth theory in the 1930s while serving as a missionary to India, it was not until the 1970s that his ideas moved outside missiological circles and entered the established churches. Important in this development were his book *Understanding Church Growth* (1970) and the formation of the Institute for American Church Growth and a "school" of thinkers at Fuller's School of World Mission including Arthur Glasser, Peter Wagner, Alan Tippett, Charles Kraft, and Paul Hiebert. This fraternity of the like-minded became a potent engine for the dissemination of Church Growth ideas. A survey taken in 1991 reported that 86 percent of the pastors who read *Leadership* magazine had heard of the Church Growth movement and that most were positive toward it. Only 4 percent thought that Church Growth methods should not be used, whereas 86 percent thought that they should be used *because these methods were effective.* Among the respondents, 45 percent indicated that their minds had been changed on this matter, that initial doubt had given way to a more positive attitude.[20] As this approach has moved out from a small, scholarly enclave to the larger evangelical world, however, its character has also changed. All too often, thought has been replaced by mere technique — a characteristic sign of the sort of damaging adaptations to modernity that have occurred. I want to take a closer look at this transition, because I believe it has the capacity to reshape the meaning of evangelical faith.

According to Os Guinness, the Church Growth movement is defined by its focus on "the centrality of the church, the priority of mission, the possibility of growth, the necessity of speaking to outsiders, the acknowledgement of culture and cultures, the insistence on real results, and the wisdom of using the best insights and technologies proffered by the key disciplines of the human sciences."[21] The tools it proposes to use to bring about growth and renewal — psychology, marketing techniques, and the findings of the behavioral sciences — have been questioned, but at least the movement should be applauded for raising the issue of growth as a *church* issue. Numerical growth is something the churches have all too often left to evangelists and parachurch groups with the organization, money, gifts, and desire to reach out to unbelievers. All too often, local churches have acted as though their only task is that of maintaining the faithful. The Church Growth movement has challenged that.

Early on, however, three issues emerged in Church Growth thinking that provoked widespread debate. First, McGavran was not theologically oriented.[22] His thinking was quite pragmatic and results-oriented.

20. James D. Berkley, "Church Growth Comes of Age," *Leadership* 12 (Fall 1991): 108-15.

21. Guinness, "Sounding Out the Idols of Church Growth," in *No God but God,* ed. Os Guinness and John Seel (Chicago: Moody Press, 1992), p. 153.

22. On Donald McGavran, see Arthur F. Glasser, "An Introduction to the Church Growth Perspectives of Donald Anderson McGavran," in *Theological Perspectives on Church Growth,* ed. Harvey Conn (Nutley, N.J.: Presbyterian & Reformed, 1976), pp. 21-42, and "Church Growth at Fuller," *Missiology* 14 (October 1986): 401-20; Alan Tippett, "Portrait of a Missiologist by His Colleague," in *God, Man and Church Growth: A Festschrift in Honor of Donald Anderson McGavran,* ed. Alan R. Tippett (Grand Rapids: William B. Eerdmans, 1973), pp. 19-42; and David Smith, "The Church Growth Principles of Donald McGavran," *Transformation* 2 (April-June 1985): 25-30.

He argued, for example, that the only barriers to conversion were social, such as class and ethnicity — and that they were not theological in nature at all; remove these barriers and conversions should follow as naturally as water running downhill. This unintended advocacy of a form of faith stripped of theological content has made Church Growth technique completely vulnerable to the intrusions of modernity, because it filters out the transcendent features of the Christian faith that constitute its best defense against the relativizing dogmas of modernity. This point is seldom noted even though those uneasy with the movement often pick up on its nonchalance about biblical doctrine. Glenn Huebel complains that in Church Growth circles "doctrine is not a vital ingredient of a growing, flourishing church." Anyone, from the theologically liberal to the theologically conservative, can expand their churches if they adopt Church Growth principles. These are just "pragmatic, organizing principles, many of which are patterned after the business world." Church Growth, he complains, is just "applied sociology."[23]

Second, McGavran's notion that churches should be created to cater to those of the same tribe and language — what he called the "homogeneous unit principle" — was stiffly debated.[24] There are some mission contexts in which this strategy seems to make sense. In multilingual settings, for instance, attempting to deal with multiple translations of the written and spoken word may simply prove to be too cumbersome and unworkable. And certain immigrant enclaves may feel it very important to remain in a distinct ecclesial community as they seek to preserve their language, customs, and memories in the midst of much that is foreign. But an unrestrained extension of this principle can lead to mischief. Should churches seek out only those of the same class, the same cultural tastes, the same income level? Undoubtedly, they will feel more comfortable with people of the same class, tastes, and income, but how can they witness to the gospel's truth that in Christ all barriers have fallen — those of race, education, class, profession, and social status — if they are carefully and deliberately preserving these barriers as a part of their mission strategy?

23. Huebel, "The Church Growth Movement: A Word of Caution," *Concordia Theological Quarterly* 50 (July-October 1986): 175. Note also, along similar lines, Carter Lindberg, "Church Growth and Confessional Integrity," *Concordia Theological Quarterly* 54 (July 1990): 131-54; and Earl V. Comfort, "Is the Pulpit a Factor in Church Growth?" *Bibliotheca Sacra* 140 (January-March 1983): 64-70.

24. See, e.g., C. René Padilla, "The Unity of the Church and the Homogenous Unit Principle," in *Exploring Church Growth,* ed. Wilbert R. Shenk (Grand Rapids: William B. Eerdmans, 1983), pp. 285-302.

Third, some critics charged McGavran with being interested only in the numbers of converts gathered into the churches and not in other kinds of growth — growth in character and understanding, commitment and service, for example — that could not be reduced so easily to numbers.

McGavran's colleagues granted the validity of some of these concerns and sought to address them by altering the basic model for growth. Alan Tippett, for example, argued that the qualitative growth of the church should not be separated from quantitative growth.[25] Charles Kraft sought to correct some of McGavran's overly simplistic views of culture.[26] Arthur Glasser began to reinforce McGavran's thinking where it was especially thin theologically. And Charles Van Engen offered a careful assessment of the whole package of Church Growth in *The Growth of the True Church*.

However, once these theories moved outside scholarly circles — once it was seen that McGavran's ideas could be used to ensure pastoral success — the seriousness of the discussion quickly evaporated. It is probably no accident that these principles began to find wide acceptance in the evangelical world during the 1970s, because, as I have suggested, this was a time when the confessional and theological character of evangelicalism began to fade, leaving the churches wide open to the intrusions of raw pragmatism. As theology moved from the center to the periphery of evangelical faith, technique moved from the periphery to the center. The one gained at the cost of the other. A new and more culturally adapted evangelicalism emerged, the central figures of which were no longer the scholars who had been prominent in the immediate postwar years but rather a host of managers, planners, and bureaucrats — and, not far behind them, marketeers. This new set of leaders view growing a church or,

---

25. Tippett, *Church Growth and the Word of God: The Biblical Basis of the Church Growth Viewpoint* (Grand Rapids: William B. Eerdmans, 1970), pp. 12-14. George Peters likewise distinguishes between the church's inward and outward form in his *Theology of Church Growth* (Grand Rapids: Zondervan, 1981), pp. 188-239, and Eddie Gibbs uses the distinction between the church's modality and sodality to make the same point in *I Believe in Church Growth* (Grand Rapids: William B. Eerdmans, 1981), pp. 344-52. Nevertheless, this aspect of Church Growth thought continues to trouble its critics. See Charles Van Engen, *The Growth of the True Church* (Amsterdam: Rodopi, 1981), pp. 403-53, and David Bosch, "Church Growth and Missiology," *Missionalia* 16 (April 1988): 13-24.

26. See Kraft, "Christian Conversion or Cultural Conversion?" *Practical Anthropology* 10 (1963): 179-86, and *Christianity in Culture: A Study in Dynamic Theologizing in Cross-Cultural Perspective* (Maryknoll, N.Y.: Orbis Books, 1981).

for that matter, any Christian ministry as essentially no different from growing a business. In both cases, it was simply a matter of understanding the market and then applying the right techniques. Church growth has increasingly been reduced to a matter of knowing how to market the church, and George Barna is the epitome of this diminished understanding.

Ecclesiastical Barnacles

The New Vision

Like all Church Growth advocates, Barna is very aware that the world around us is changing, that changes in the inner life and habits of people are producing a new set of appetites and expectations, and that these changes are placing new demands on the churches. He began his career as a Church Growth advocate by publishing a study on the contours of contemporary culture called *Vital Signs* (1984), which he updated in 1990 under the title *The Frog in the Kettle*. He has also produced a quarterly survey of cultural trends called *Christian Marketing Perspective*.

Barna's strategy for revamping the church involves a combination of the techniques of big business and the ethos of the recovery group. He argues that the traditional church must free itself from an addiction to smallness and then avail itself of the same techniques that marketeers use to discover what product will be most likely to sell in a given area.

Big Business

Barna contends that the church is engaged in a war. Aggressive marketeers are vigorously working to place their products in the minds of contemporary consumers. More than that, they want their philosophy to dictate people's appetites and horizons, and they have become highly proficient in accomplishing their goals. It is in this war for the marketing niche that modern people are made and shaped, and in this highly competitive environment, the church has lost out.

Because competition is so fierce, business knows that it must be flexible and quick to adapt its products to existing circumstances. It must constantly assess consumer needs and competition from similar products; it must accept a rapid turnover in the product line as a matter of course. Apple Computer learned this hard fact, he says; why can't the church do the same thing?[27] The answer, quite simply, is that it has not thought of itself in these terms. It has failed "to embrace a marketing orientation in what has become a marketing driven environment."[28]

It is time, says Barna, for the church to adopt a whole new paradigm for understanding itself, a model borrowed from the contemporary business world. Like it or not, the church is not only in a market but is itself a business. It has a "product" to sell — relationships to Jesus and others; its "core product" is the message of salvation, and each local church is a "franchise." The church's pastors, says Barna, will be judged not by their teaching and counseling but by their ability to run the church "smoothly and efficiently" as if it were a business.[29] And, like any secular business, the church must show a "profit," which is to say it must achieve success in penetrating and servicing its market.[30] If the proven truths of marketing are followed, Barna tells us, each church "can be the Chrysler of tomorrow": they can recover from the decrepit condition in which many of them now find themselves and once again begin to flourish.[31]

Needless to say, pastors are typically ill-equipped for such an undertaking. Their seminary training was aimed at producing M.Div.'s, he notes, not M.B.A.'s,[32] and now they may find themselves quite ungifted for the calling into which they have fallen, where their success will be judged by criteria more businesslike than religious. To be successful, Barna argues, a modern pastor is going to need a portfolio of gifts rather different from those that Paul had in mind. Modern pastors need the "gifts" of delegation, confidence, interaction, decision-making, visibility, practicality, accountability, and discernment much more than they need gifts related to teaching and counseling.[33] The modern pastor, in other words, must be an efficient manager or, perhaps more to the point, a capable C.E.O. Barna ushers the manage-

27. Barna, *Marketing the Church: What They Never Taught You about Church Growth* (Colorado Springs: Navpress, 1988), p. 13.

28. Barna, *Marketing the Church*, p. 23.

29. Barna, *Marketing the Church*, p. 14.

30. Barna, *Marketing the Church*, p. 26.

31. Barna, *Marketing the Church*, p. 15.

32. Significantly enough, however, several seminaries are beginning to offer an M.B.A. in Church Management. And, in any event, some D.Min. degrees manage to do much the same thing for pastors that the M.B.A. does for those going into business. See my *No Place for Truth; or, Whatever Happened to Evangelical Theology* (Grand Rapids: William B. Eerdmans, 1993), pp. 227-45.

33. George Barna, *User Friendly Churches: What Successful Churches Have in Common and Why Their Ideas Work,* ed. Ron Durham (Ventura, Cal.: Regal Books, 1991), pp. 143-46.

rial revolution into the inner sanctum of the church's life, insisting that all must now be subject to it. As in most of the processes of modernity, truth and the transcendent are casualties of this intrusion.

The key to Barna's revamping of the church, however, is his understanding of *need*. He argues that the church must define its services in terms of contemporary needs just as any secular business must. The question, of course, is what constitutes a need.

Despite the importance of the concept of need in Barna's proposal, he has not analyzed it with any thoroughness, so one is only left to guess at what he might have in mind. He does repeatedly reaffirm the sovereignty of need, however, asserting that it should determine the shape of the church in exactly the same way it determines what a business will do in designing its products or services. But a business will cater as much to wants as to needs, and Barna gives no indication of distinguishing one from the other. In fact, there is no clear indication that he considers it necessary to distinguish between needs that are spiritually good and needs that are spiritually detrimental.

In a consumer culture, need is often indistinguishable from mere acquisitiveness. A sense of need may be nothing more than habit among those who have long lived off the fat of the land, who have come to view access to plenty as a right. Indeed, it may be that this largely explains the emergence of the megachurches. The expectations of the postwar baby boomers have been shaped by such a therapeutic bounty and surfeit of on-demand entertainment that small, struggling, one-dimensional churches may well appear unattractive and uninviting however real and faithful their worship and service may be. In order to offer a rich array of programs to this new generation — a large selection of Sunday school classes, support groups, and specialized pastoral staff from which to choose, good child care facilities, and engaging (or even entertaining) worship services — churches have to become large. This generation is used to working and living within large bureaucratic structures, so they may well feel more at home in the corporate environs of a megachurch than in the more familial context of a small congregation. That may explain why a new megachurch emerges every two weeks in America.

But this amazing success appears to have been built very largely on the one element most contested in McGavran's theory — the homogenous unit principle. Barna speaks of finding the market niche.[34]

34. Barna, *User Friendly Churches,* p. 107. Cf. Douglas D. Webster, *Selling Jesus: What's Wrong with Church Marketing* (Downers Grove, Ill.: InterVarsity Press, 1992), pp. 58-73.

The niche into which all marketeers now want to fit is, of course, that of the baby boomers. This is the demographic pot of gold at the end of every advertising executive's rainbow. And so the churches that are allowing themselves to be shaped by the sovereignty of social need invariably wind up being most sensitive to the needs of the baby boomers. But can a body that contorts itself in this fashion any longer claim to be the church? Is it truly modeling the biblical affirmation that in Christ there is neither rich nor poor, male nor female, cultured nor uncultured, educated nor uneducated? The insensitive perpetuation of offensive class distinctions and the pandering to the "needs" of affluent baby boomers that are characteristic of the megachurch are no less damaging to the spiritual interests of the church than the small-mindedness to which traditional churches are said to be prone.

Allowing the consumer to be sovereign in this way in fact sanctions a bad habit. It encourages us to indulge in constant internal inventory in the church no less than in the marketplace, to ask ourselves perpetually whether the "products" we are being offered meet our present "felt needs." In this sort of environment, market research has found that there is scarcely any consumer loyalty to particular products and brands anymore. The consumer, like the marketeer, is now making fresh calculations all the time. And so it is that the churches that have adopted the strategy of marketing themselves have effectively installed revolving doors. The pews may be full, but never with the same people from week to week. People keep entering, lured by the church's attractions or just to check out the wares, but then they move on because they feel their needs, real or otherwise, are not being met.

Should the church grant "need," which is often culturally created and driven, such sovereignty? Should the church be so accommodating if it means that other aspects of its ministry are going to be obscured in the process? What is going to happen when churches meet all of the felt needs of their consumers and then realize that they have failed to meet the genuine need for meaning? Meaning is provided by the functioning of truth — specifically biblical truth — in the life of the congregation. In contrast to Barna, who seems to think that the importance of such truth is peripheral at best, Finke and Stark see it as an important factor in the rise and fall of churches. In their model of the religious market, they notice that "as denominations have modernized their doctrines and embraced temporal values, they have gone into decline."[35] In America, they say, true success has come only to

---

35. Finke and Stark, *The Churching of America*, p. 24.

those groups aggressively committed "to vivid otherworldliness."[36] The contemporary marketing of the church, by contrast, seems to be aggressively committed to a vivid this-worldliness operating under the guise of a dedication to the virtue of meeting people's needs.

How far can the process of accommodation go? Barna says that offering to meet people's needs is not a marketing gimmick but a "method of ensuring effective ministry."[37] But he doesn't speak to the issue of whether the church retains a right or obligation to serve as a mold in any context. Is the church simply so much gelatin to be poured into the mold that the modern world offers it? This haziness at the center of Barna's proposal is essential to the integrity of his analogy between the church and the corporation: if the haziness is cleared up, the analogy breaks down.

A business is in the market simply to sell its products; it doesn't ask consumers to surrender themselves to the product. The church, on the other hand, does call for such a surrender. It is not merely marketing a product; it is declaring Christ's sovereignty over all of life and declaring the necessity of obedient submission to him and to the truth of his Word. When the church is properly fulfilling the task it has been assigned, it is demanding far more than any business would ever think of asking prospective customers. Simply put, the church is in the business of truth, not profit. Its message — the message of God's Word — enters the innermost place in a person's life, the place of secrets and anguish, of hope and despair, of guilt and forgiveness, and it demands to be heard and obeyed in a way that not even the most brazen and unprincipled advertisers would think of emulating. Businesses offer goods and services to make life easier or more pleasant; the Bible points the way to Life itself, and the way will not always be easy or pleasant. At most, businesses are accountable only to stockholders and a variety of regulators; the church is accountable to God.

We will take a closer look at why the analogy between the church and the capitalistic marketplace is fallacious, but at this point it will be enough to note that Barna believes that technique alone, the marketeer's technique, is the answer to the church's ostensible problem of stunted growth. If businesses face the prospect of a cold market, they reassess their product and look for ways to repackage it to renew market interest. Barna contends that the church has to do the same thing with its product or it will perish as surely as Eastern Airlines did in the doldrums of the late 1980s.

36. Finke and Stark, *The Churching of America*, p. 26.
37. Barna, *User Friendly Churches*, p. 107.

Workshops of Recovery

During the 1980s, recovery groups began to appear all over our cultural horizon, I suspect because they were able to unite three powerful forces in our society: a national obsession with health, a therapeutic view of reality in which all of life's problems are viewed as treatable ailments, and a desire to make money. Many recovery groups have arisen in response to great tragedies in life, but it must not be forgotten that many have also become big business. Lucrative careers have been launched in the business of recovery, and publishing houses are nourished by commerce with these groups.

By some estimates, over 90 percent of Americans are addicted in some way — to alcohol, drugs, sex, gambling, violence, and even to shopping. In the rhetoric of the recovery groups, these people are *codependent*.[38] The term does something to take the edge off their personal responsibility for their condition. Their addictions are seldom viewed as matters of bad judgment, bad habits, or bad character. Almost invariably the source of the problem is traced to a bad home life or bad social circumstances in relation to which they understand themselves and their roles — they are *co*dependent.

There are grounds for saying that the Church Growth movement is rapidly becoming a religious recovery group for pastoral codependents. The addiction from which relief is being sought, and from which *many* evangelical pastors are now seeking healing, is *smallness*. Smallness is presented by Church Growth advocates as a frame of mind, a condition resulting from an inability think beyond the traditional, an inability to make connections with contemporary people, an inability to update routines, music, plans, expectations, services. Smallness is attributed to hidebound, pinched, and narrow thinking. And it is charged that the traditional church has an addiction to smallness.

It is clearly the case that some churches do retreat into themselves in this way, thereby shirking their responsibility to act as the people of God in the modern world. They are not being true to themselves as

---

38. The term *codependent* has traditionally been used more narrowly to describe individuals — also called "enablers" — who attach themselves to people with afflictions, such as alcoholics, in order to gain some sense of worth through their ability to help. (See Robert C. Roberts, *Taking the Word to Heart: Self and Other in an Age of Therapies* [Grand Rapids: William B. Eerdmans, 1993], pp. 229-35.) Obviously the addict is a key figure in this relationship, however, and is typically as dependent on the enabler as the enabler is on the addict. Colloquial usage of the term has broadened to the point that it is now used in reference to both the addict and the enabler.

people who profess to be owned by God, who are called to live out his truth in thought, word, and deed, to exhibit spiritual authenticity in the midst of modernity's wasteland, to bring a vital and incisive analysis to its patterns of life, to care for those on its fringes as well as those at its heart, where what is great and unique about human life is routinely minimized or destroyed. It must be said, however, that the Church Growth critique does not typically focus on lapses of this sort; it tends to focus instead solely on the issue of growth measured in numbers of new congregants. And in this regard, a little myth-making is now under way.

It is true that since 1976, growth among self-professed born-again Christians has apparently remained flat, at 32 percent of the U.S. population. Barna further maintains that only 5 percent of American churches on a typical Sunday are attended by more than 350 people, and 50 percent of the churches attract fewer than 75. He interprets this as proof that the local church has ceased to be a flourishing enterprise, since by his reckoning these numbers are not adequate to sustain the church's prosperity either financially or spiritually. And here, as Philip D. Kenneson observes, we encounter one of Barna's important presuppositions — namely, that although it is possible to distinguish quality from quantity in the context of the church, it is not possible to secure quality without quantity.[39] He assumes without question that all the rules that pertain in the world of commerce and manufacturing automatically apply in the world of the church and that, indeed, we should proceed to rewrite our ecclesiology on this assumption — an assumption that is in fact highly questionable.

Setting aside the significance of the incidence of the sort of spiritual rebirth that gets reported in surveys, we can at least say with some certainty that historically most churches have come in at the small end of Barna's yardstick. Reliable comparative statistics are not easy to find, but a general picture can be pieced together. A century ago, in 1890, for example, the average Protestant church had only 91.5 members, not all of whom would have been in attendance on any given Sunday;[40] a century before that, in 1776, the average Methodist congregation had 75.7 members. It seems to be the case that our churches today are about the same size as they have always been, on average, and the supposition that we are now experiencing drastic shrinkage needs to

39. See Kenneson, "Selling [Out] the Church in the Marketplace of Desire," *Modern Theology* 9 (October 1993): 322-24.

40. Finke and Stark, *The Churching of America*, p. 24.

be clearly justified before it can be allowed to become the premise for new and radical strategies.

With respect to overall church affiliation, the picture is just the opposite. There was an almost unbroken line of increase from the time of the Puritans, when only 17 percent of the nation belonged to any church, to well into the twentieth century.[41] Only the past fifty years have shown a slight reversal of this trend. Membership in churches and synagogues fell from 73 percent in 1937 to 65 percent in 1988.[42] Church attendance on any given week, however, has remained almost unchanged, with 41 percent attending in 1937 and 42 percent in 1988.[43]

With the growth in population, of course, the number of churches has increased (as have the number of denominations), but the size of local churches appears to have remained about the same. The real exception to this pattern is the comparatively recent emergence of the megachurches. They constitute the anomaly. Barna's efforts to make megachurches the benchmark of normality and then to argue that churches of conventional size are failures is simply unwarranted and wrongheaded. Nevertheless, the perception has set in that our churches are failing because they are not expanding numerically, and in response to this anxiety Church Growth seminars have become commonplace. Pastors everywhere feel obliged or pressured to attend.

I will grant that Barna has not engaged in some of the worst practices of his counterparts in the secular recovery group arena. He doesn't present himself as a guru with all the answers, and he doesn't deliver his techniques for growing the church in the cadences of psychological rhetoric so popular in other recovery groups settings. Nevertheless, his reliance on technique alone to solve the perceived problem is very much characteristics of the recovery group strategy. His prescriptions for churches addicted to smallness sound very similar to the collections of techniques that other recovery groups prescribe for individuals addicted to food, shopping, spouse abuse, drugs, or any of a host of other problems.

Barna's solution to the problem of smallness is to transform traditional churches into User Friendly churches — bodies that freely adapt themselves to meet the felt needs of their targeted clientele. The key to success in this endeavor is to make the transition from life in

---

41. Finke and Stark, *The Churching of America*, p. 26.
42. George Gallup and Jim Castelli, *The People's Religion: American Faith in the 90's* (New York: Macmillan, 1989), p. 38.
43. Gallup and Castelli, *The People's Religion*, p. 41.

the world to life in the church as invisible as possible. Everything is done to eliminate obstructions that typically have stood in the way of unbelievers. For example, pastors make a greater effort to explain what is happening during worship services for the benefit of those in the congregation who may be unfamiliar with the liturgy. Some churches have gone so far as to remove Christian symbols, such as the cross, that outsiders might find alien or intimidating. Others have removed pulpits or otherwise altered the sanctuary or even constructed new buildings to look more like airports or shopping malls than traditional churches. Such efforts range from sensible to silly, but few could be characterized as pernicious. There are two other aspects of Barna's programs that are more problematic, however.

First, Barna's User Friendly churches, like all recovery groups, are driven by a pragmatic optimism. "In the self-help universe," Wendy Kaminer writes, "anything is possible: anyone can be rich, thin, healthy, and spiritually centered with faith, discipline, and the willingness to take direction."[44] And Barna affirms that anything is possible in his universe, too, if a church is willing to take the right steps and apply proven methods of marketing. Any church can grow if it wants to grow. There is no more reason for a church to remain addicted to smallness than there is for people to continue being enslaved to food or liquor when they have made up their minds to break free.

An important part of the recovery process, regardless of the addiction from which recovery is being sought, is to lay claim to one's own power. For those who have been brought low by drugs or alcohol or abuse, this is no easy matter. These addictions typically produce low self-esteem in the victim, a sense that he or she is powerless to change the habit or situation. Hence recovery group leaders often ask their clients to make positive affirmations about themselves as a step toward a cure, to exert mind over matter, mind over the past, mind over relationships — mind over anything anywhere that is painful and negative. Norman Vincent Peale confessed to emptying out his mind twice a day of all painful, negative thoughts and thereby asserting his conquest over himself and his circumstances.

User Friendly churches employ this technique in a couple of ways. Barna urges every church to develop a "vision" and to focus on it repeatedly until it is firm rooted in the congregation's mind. The term *vision* as he uses it in this context involves more than just the sort of clearly

44. Kaminer, *I'm Dysfunctional, You're Dysfunctional: The Recovery Movement and Other Self-Help Fashions* (Reading, Mass.: Addison-Wesley, 1991), p. 46.

understood goals and objectives that every church should have; it involves having a "clear mental image of a preferable future."[45] He contends that the vision is not humanly contrived but that God "conveys his view of that future to a leader" — a specific "customized" vision that will be different for each church and outline the direction in which it should be headed. The purpose in having a vision "is to create the future." It is important to realize, says Barna, that "the future is not something that just happens; it is a reality that is created by those strong enough to exert control over their environment."[46] Thus we see that he combines both the old mind-over-matter philosophy and the new confidence in managerial control. The User Friendly church breaks out of its addiction to smallness by asserting a contrary vision, just as an addict in a recovery group breaks out of addictive habits by verbally defying those habits. That, says Barna, is what changes churches; that is what makes them grow. But despite all the God rhetoric, Barna's strategy is quite clearly anthropocentric, a strategy for co-opting God into a bureaucratic, therapeutic process, and this is surely one of the telltale signs that a profound worldliness has intruded here.

Second, therapeutic models of reality tend to shy away from the concept of sin, or at least to tame it by calling it sickness instead. Many recovery groups perceive and treat clients as innocent and injured children. They view the addiction as a tool the client is using to keep the wounded inner child out of sight or at least out of mind. Even addictive behavior of a violent sort is typically considered a symptom of disease. And Barna's view of the dysfunctional church is really not that different: it simply has a bad attitude about the world, itself, and perhaps God. But this attitude will never be so deeply entrenched or so powerful as to be beyond the power of good technique to set things straight.

Barna's outlook is remarkable for its innocence about sin. What he actually is serving up is the old Pelagianism, the view that sin is not inherited by nature but caught from the environment, as one might catch a germ. And where he believes the church's ailment to be mild, he naturally prescribes only modest remedies — all of which, of course, are a matter of proper technique. In fact, this is a perfect methodology for domesticating sins. Why bother God with matters that a little judicious marketing strategy can clear up? He blithely maintains that the church's health and wholeness are being threatened by bad attitudes rather than

---

45. Barna, *The Power of Vision: How You Can Capture and Apply God's Vision for Your Ministry,* ed. Duncan Kyle (Ventura, Cal.: Regal Books, 1992), p. 28.

46. Barna, *The Power of Vision,* p. 48.

sin, that we should be more concerned with technique than with repentance, and that neighborhood surveys are more crucial than the Word of God for securing the church's spiritual growth.

The fact is that while we may be able to market the church, we cannot market Christ, the gospel, Christian character, or meaning in life. The church can offer handy child care to weary parents, intellectual stimulation to the restless video generation, a feeling of family to the lonely and dispossessed — and, indeed, lots of people come to churches for these reasons. But neither Christ nor his truth can be marketed by appealing to consumer interest, because the premise of all marketing is that the consumer's need is sovereign, that the customer is always right, and this is precisely what the gospel insists cannot be the case.

We all have needs. Some people live with an aching sense of emptiness, a sense that things have gone awry; some are crushed by a burden of guilt, by pain that won't go away; some live in dread of what the future may hold; some long for friendship, a sense of belonging. There are needs like these in every pew in every church. But God does not want us to interpret the *meaning* of these needs ourselves because, being sinners, we resist seeing such needs in terms of our broken and violated relationship with him. Christ's gospel calls sinners to surrender their self-centeredness, to stop granting sovereignty to their own needs and recognize his claim of sovereignty over their lives. This is the reversal, the transposition of loyalties that is entailed in all genuine Christian believing. Barna's program inverts this basic truth; it is the antithesis of the biblical affirmation that the church will grow only through greater fidelity to the radical commands of the gospel — commands that God himself authorized to challenge all of our natural expectations. In order to market the church, Barna must obscure its essential reality. It has to be marketed as an organization rather than an organism, as a place to meet people rather than as the place where one meets God on terms that he establishes, as a commodity for consumption rather than an authority calling for penitence and surrender.

It is not difficult to see how the marketeer's evangelicalism might begin to resemble the old liberalism, the gospel H. Richard Niebuhr once described as consisting in a God without wrath bringing people without sin into a kingdom without judgment through a Christ without a cross.[47] Hawking the church as a product inevitably violates its nature as the gathering of the redeemed for service in God's kingdom and in

47. Niebuhr, *The Kingdom of God in America* (New York: Harper Torchbooks, 1953), pp. 191-92.

his world. What is lost is biblical truth. It is not the truth about Christ, his work, or his presence in the church that is important in the modern selling of the church but something entirely different.

When I suggested that Barna's program is driven by pragmatic optimism, I did so with some small qualms, because pragmatism as such amounts to something of a philosophy, and it is not clear that Barna has a philosophy. What he offers is something more along the lines of a recipe for success. Still, it may be worthwhile to consider this point a bit further, because there is a sense in which Barna's emphasis on technique alone plugs into a long-standing disaffection in the evangelical world with the value of thought.

William James codified modern pragmatism in America as a means for testing the rival truth claims of competing philosophies.[48] If the actual consequences of two philosophies were identical, then James held it could no longer be argued that the philosophies were at odds with one another as understandings of what was true.[49] This program of subjecting philosophical beliefs to the test of daily experience and observing how well they hold up under the scrutiny of empirical reality has the effect of reducing "truth" to an ongoing, experimental matter. It is true, as Richard Rorty asserts, that pragmatism is "a vague, ambiguous, and overworked word,"[50] but in essence it constitutes a "principled aversion" to formulating general principles. It is a philosophy that restricts its purview to the practical and that, in the nature of the case, is always fluid, open, and full of surprises.

James contrasted pragmatism with what he called "rationalism," a term that he idiosyncratically used to connote devotion to a body of timeless, unchanging principles. He himself denied the existence of any such principles. He maintained that "rationalists" were really prag-

---

48. "True ideas are those which we can assimilate, validate, corroborate and verify," said James. "False ideas are those which we cannot" (*The Meaning of Truth: A Sequel to Pragmatism*, vol. 2 of the Works of William James, ed. Frederick Burkhardt et al. [Cambridge: Harvard University Press, 1975], p. 3). On the question of James's understanding of truth, see Patrick Kiaran Dooley, *Pragmatism as Humanism* (Chicago: Nelson-Hall, 1974), pp. 115-61. On his overall philosophy, see the brief but useful account in Frederick Copleston, *History of Philosophy*, vol. 8: *Bentham to Russell* (London: Burnes & Oates, 1966), pp. 330-44.

49. James, *Pragmatism: A New Name for Some Old Ways of Thinking* (Cambridge: Harvard University Press, 1907), p. 201.

50. Rorty, *The Consequences of Pragmatism* (Minneapolis: Minnesota University Press, 1982), p. 160.

matists who were holding their principles on credit until such a time as experience proved them to be correct.

What started out as a way of testing truth claims thus ended up as a form of radical empiricism, the view that philosophy can deal only with what is experienced, since that is all that can be verified. In the twentieth century this general position has spilled out in many philosophical directions, but its essence was well summed up by A. J. Ayer's aphorism that what is not sense is nonsense. It is not hard to discern among the church marketeers a corresponding impatience with eternal principle, a corresponding lack of interest in the value of truth in itself, a corresponding lack of constraint about what might be tried by way of experimentation with the church,[51] a disposition to think that experience is preeminently valuable, an assumption that the external features of the church are more important than the substance because those are the features that draw people in.

It is surely ironic that those who seek to promote the church have adopted strategies that deliberately obscure its essence. The church should be known as a place where God is worshiped, where the Word of God is heard and practiced, and where life is thought about and given its most searching and serious analysis. This, in fact, is what the traditional church has seen as its chief business, however badly it may have been doing this business. But none of this can be marketed, and so it is ignored. The interest turns to how well appointed and organized the church is, what programs it has to offer, how many outings the youth group has organized, how convenient it is to attend, how good the nursery is. The truly important matters are marginalized, and the marginal aspects of the life of the church are made central. Barna shows no interest in the New Testament criteria for those in leadership, such as soundness of character, knowledge of God, understanding of his Word, and an aptness to teach it; he focuses instead on traits valued in modern business, such as self-confidence and managerial skill.

Engineering the Spiritual

The march from the American Revolution to George Barna, from the breach with England to the breach with the traditional church is long enough to make generalizations rather hazardous. But it is at least clear that two major shifts have occurred during this period. The first

---

51. Rorty, *The Consequences of Pragmatism*, p. 163.

was historical. It occurred in the aftermath of the Revolution, and it led to a disposition that has largely reshaped evangelical faith in America over the past century and a half. As moderns we are now disposed to believe that the audience is always sovereign and that ideas are valid only to the extent that they prove their usefulness in the marketplace. This outlook was further developed in the second great transition as modernization took hold during the nineteenth century as the major shaping force in society. Modernization introduced the growing and pervasive presence of capitalism, which has redefined all "markets," even the market for religious ideas, narrowing the focus to an unquestioning supply of consumer demands. And now this approach has been applied to effectuate church growth. The American disposition to think that ideas have no intrinsic value was formalized into pragmatism. The infiltration of capitalism and pragmatism into evangelicalism during this period has produced a form of Christian faith that has so adapted to its context as to be uniquely American and increasingly modern in its psychology and appetites.

The inevitable question is whether this form of cultural adaptation has done any fatal damage to the biblical authenticity of the faith. Understandably, but regrettably, this question has seldom been asked by those who have been most successful in creating churches by marketing means. It would never occur to them to question the use of tools that have proved so powerful and effective.

Marketing *is* successful in America. Our secular marketeers are so slick and proficient that they have persuaded the great majority of the nation to go into deep personal debt, trading away their futures for gratification now. Marketeers know how to create felt need, and they know that, once created, this need is quite irresistible. They know how to induce us to act in ways that may not be in our own best interests at all. It should be no surprise that the proponents of Church Growth have been very successful using some of these same techniques. With the tools of modernity, says Os Guinness, "we modern Christians are literally capable of winning the world while losing our souls."[52] And in America, only fools quarrel with such success.

But the church is paying a high price for all of this success. When success is purchased by setting aside the truth of God, by dabbling in ecclesiastical engineering that is open to all that is new and experimental and closed to what is fixed and eternal, when it involves trans-

---

52. Guinness, *Dining with the Devil: The Megachurch Movement Flirts with Modernity* (Grand Rapids: Baker Book House, 1993), p. 43.

forming spirituality into organization, the pastor into a business executive, and genuine Christian hope into churchly amusement and
fraternity — then it is putting the evangelical soul at grave risk. And
the risk is amplified by the fact that those who are eagerly taking it
are least likely to be aware of the danger in which they are placing
themselves. All the superficial vital signs look so good that it's hard to
believe the patient might be in trouble. The deep and powerful undercurrents of conformity that flow through the American psyche
make identification with the culture, especially the part of it that glitters
with success or that has broad public approbation, almost irresistible.
And so it is that the church in Our Time is rushing headlong toward
worldliness and at the same time fleeing the sort of "vivid otherworldliness" that has produced its greatest moments and achievements
throughout its past.

Worldliness, as we have seen, is that set of practices in a society,
its values and ways of looking at life, that make sin look normal and
righteousness look strange. It is the view of the world that puts the
sinner at its center and relegates God to the periphery. This disposition
takes different forms in different cultures. In our secularized Western
culture, it has produced an environment in which there is no place
for truth, no place for the transcendent summons of God's word of
grace, an environment in which all reality is contracted into the self
and accountability before God has vanished, leaving felt need as its
own justification. It has produced a world of solely horizontal reality
in which human beings have supplanted God and declared themselves
the captains of their fate, the masters of their destiny.

The marketing of the church, then, may well be attended by
considerable success. Indeed, I believe it will be. But, unlike its advocates, I do not believe that this validates the effort, any more than I
believe that the current successes in promoting "safe" sex, or abortion,
or realistic portrayals of violence in the movies validate those efforts.
Success is not an adequate criterion for either truth or wisdom. In fact,
what is now occurring within this process of adaptation to cultural
need is a set of substitutions that might well have a lethal effect on the
practice of historic Christian faith. Technique is being substituted for
truth, marketing action for thought, the satisfaction of the individual
for the health of the church, a therapeutic vision of the world for a
doctrinal vision, the unmanageable by the manageable, organism by
organization, those who can preach the Word of God by those who
can manage an organization, the spiritual by the material. At the center
of these substitutions is an individualism fired by a shallow, self-

centered consumerism. And along with this, and because of it, has come a debilitating loss of truth — the very thing that brought the mainline denominations low — and behind that there lies the loss of awareness of God as objective and transcendent. This, too, is an inescapable part of the move into the market, of adaptation to the ways of the world that modernization has brought about. If we are going to do something about this plight, we need to spend some time in understanding it more clearly. It is to this that we turn in Chapter 5.

CHAPTER 5

The Weightlessness of God

The Sea of Faith
Was once, too, at the full, and round earth's shore
Lay like the folds of a bright girdle furled.
But now I only hear
Its melancholy, long, withdrawing roar,
Retreating, to the breath
Of the night wind, down the vast edges near
And naked shingles of the world.

Matthew Arnold

It is one of the defining marks of Our Time that God is now weightless. I do not mean by this that he is ethereal but rather that he has become unimportant. He rests upon the world so inconsequentially as not to be noticeable. He has lost his saliency for human life. Those who assure the pollsters of their belief in God's existence may nonetheless consider him less interesting than television, his commands less authoritative than their appetites for affluence and influence, his judgment no more awe-inspiring than the evening news, and his truth less compelling than the advertisers' sweet fog of flattery and lies. That is weightlessness.[1] It is a condition we have assigned him after having nudged him out to the periphery of our secularized life. His truth is no longer welcome in our public

1. Cf. Jackson Lears, *No Place of Grace: Antimodernism and the Transformation of American Culture, 1880-1920* (New York: Pantheon Books, 1981), p. 32.

discourse. The engine of modernity rumbles on, and he is but a speck in its path.

Few would deny that this is the case in our modernized society; it is less clear to many that it may also be the case, albeit in less blatant and obvious ways, in the church. Why is this so? One of the reasons is that it is always more difficult to perceive a pattern of which we ourselves are a part. We need the advantage of a little distance to grasp the meaning of complex events. We experience our own time as such a rich and intense confusion that it is not always easy to distinguish vices from virtues. The untrue appears true, the bad passes itself off as good, and often the trivial masquerades as important. This perennial difficulty is only compounded by the effects of modernity. The faster pace of life and the relentless roar of the media only heighten the confusion, and the unprecedented wealth of goods, conveniences, and opportunities with which modernity has showered us constitute a powerful incentive not to look too closely at its liabilities and biases.

Moreover, when God becomes weightless, as I believe he is so often today, we lose the doctrinal signals that might otherwise warn us that some profound change has taken place — the sorts of signals that once warned of the threat of heresy. Too often in Our Time, there is only peace and quiet. The traditional doctrine of God remains entirely intact while its saliency vanishes. The doctrine is believed, defended, affirmed liturgically, and in every other way held to be inviolable — but it no longer has the power to shape and to summon that it has had in previous ages. Among those claiming to be born-again Christians today, for example, only 25 percent could be said to be committed Christians by even modest tests, such as regularity in church attendance and at personal prayer. Presumably most of the remaining 75 percent would not contest the validity of doctrinal beliefs, but neither do they seem to accord these beliefs any power to affect their behavior. Some might dispute their claim to be born again on these grounds, but I don't think that this fully explains the case.

Elsewhere I have discussed this phenomenon of the weightlessness of God using a different figure of speech, speaking of the disappearance of God.[2] God has not disappeared in the sense that he has been abducted or overwhelmed. He is not like a child snatched away while its parents were momentarily distracted. No, God is more like a child that has been abandoned within a family, still accorded a place

2. See *No Place for Truth; or, Whatever Happened to Evangelical Theology* (Grand Rapids: William B. Eerdmans, 1993), pp. 106-14.

in the house, but not in the home. Because the doctrine is professed, perhaps even routinely in creed or confession, it seems as if all is well. But it is like a house that gives no outward signs of decay even though termites have rendered it structurally unsound.

The growing weightlessness of God is an affliction that is neither peculiarly Protestant nor peculiarly Catholic but is the common form in which modernity rearranges all belief in God. It is an illness that has entered the bones of religious liberals and conservatives alike. Weightlessness is a *condition*, a cognitive and psychological disposition. It can sweep through all doctrinal defenses because it is not itself perceived to be a doctrine. It can evade the best ecclesiastical defenses, sidestep the best intentions, and survive the most efficacious spiritual techniques because it is not recognized as a kind of belief. Although this weightlessness is not itself a doctrine, it has the power to hobble all doctrines; although it is not an ecclesiology, it can render all ecclesiologies impotent; although it is not itself a spirituality, all spiritualities are withered by its presence. Weightlessness tells us nothing about God but everything about ourselves, about our condition, about our psychological disposition to exclude God from our reality.

The consequence of all this is that what was once transcendent in the doctrine of God has either faded or been relocated to the category of the immanent, and then this diminished God has been further reinterpreted to accommodate modern needs. These alterations have drastically changed the whole meaning of Christian faith. They have affected the way we view God in relation to our selves, to life, and to history. They affect the way we think of his love, his goodness, his saving intentions, what his salvation means, how he reveals himself, how his revelation is received, why Christ was incarnate, and what significance this has for other religions. All of this and much more follows the moment that the formal categories of transcendence and immanence within the traditional doctrine of God are unsettled.

The contention that God is losing weight in the modern world may seem to fly in the face of some of the facts about church life that are now widely available. Over the past two decades in particular, religion has become a notable feature in the psychological landscape of America. In 1987, for example, Gallup found that 54 percent of adults said it was "very important" to them, and a further 31 percent said it was "fairly important." When the figures relating to Protestants are isolated, the story is even more dramatic. Among adults, 63 percent say religion is "very important" and 28 percent say it is "fairly important." Furthermore, among those who say it is "very important," a significant number, 31 percent, report having come to this position as adults, so this is not a matter of childhood belief that has lingered on into later years without careful examination.[3] This surge in reported belief seems to contradict entirely the argument that I am advancing here, that God has become weightless and is disappearing. How can a God who has become inconsequential be so important to so many people?

The answer, I believe, is that we are looking at two entirely different things. The net that Gallup casts out is designed to catch *subjective* belief. The pollsters are not asking whether this or that religion is true; they are not asking how people understand the nature and character of God; they are simply trying to find out how people feel about religion, what internal value it has for them. What they have found is that there is a sizable yearning for things religious in the American psyche. My comments on the weightlessness of God, on the other hand, focus on his *objective* significance — a matter of truth rather than psychology. I am talking about our relationship to God as the unchanging norm of what is true and right in all places, times, and cultures, a God whose reality is unaltered by the ebb and flow, the relativity, of life, unaffected by private perceptions or internal psychology. In the crude language of our commercial culture, if God is objectively true, then he has the same cash value for all people, in all times, in all cultures. And if he is objectively true, then he summons all people in all places, times, and cultures to know him in the same way (through Christ and by the written Word), to the same end (that they may love and faithfully serve him in the church and in all of their commerce with created reality), with the same results (that by the Holy Spirit and through the truth of his Word they will be transformed into his righteous character) such that his kingdom is extended and his name is made known throughout all the earth. All of this rests on the objective reality of God: when that begins to crumble, so does all that rests upon it. It is this crumbling of which I am speaking when I use the image of weightlessness.

I want to stress that there is no logical contradiction between a collapse of belief in the objective reality of God on the one hand and a surge of interest in things religious on the other. An interest in religion can be nothing more than a fascination with ourselves as

3. George Gallup and Jim Castelli, *The People's Religion* (New York: Macmillan, 1989), p. 37.

religious beings quite distinct from our standing before the true God. It is one thing to dwell on our hunger for God — or for mystery or something else that transcends the routines, trivialities, and pains of contemporary life; it is quite another to dwell on God as he is in himself. It is altogether possible for private, internal religion to flourish while belief in God as externally and objectively true fades.

The thesis I want to argue here, then, is that this anomaly of increased religious sensibility and decreased divine significance is perfectly comprehensible in light of the fact that religious interest is being stoked by a rearrangement (in some cases inadvertent) of what is immanent and what is transcendent in God's being.[4] More precisely, much of what should be understood as transcendent is either disappearing or is now being relocated to what is immanent, and what is immanent is then being filtered through the sieve of modern experience. The upshot of all this is that what was once objective in God's being, what once stood over against the sinner, is either being lost or transformed into something we discover first and foremost in ourselves in such a way that God's immanence is typically psychologized. These changes say a lot about our internal landscape and our worldliness,

---

4. Theology has often struggled to know what to make of the spatial image implied in transcendence. Is God's transcendence to be understood as something that is "above," "beyond," or "within"? Karl Barth, for example, argued for an infinite qualitative difference in the being of God as compared with our own and spoke of this under the language of hiddenness. He argued that "our knowledge of God begins in all seriousness with the knowledge of the hiddenness of God" (*Church Dogmatics*, 5 vols., ed. Thomas F. Torrance, trans. Geoffrey W. Bromiley [Edinburgh: T. & T. Clark, 1936-77], II/1:183). Jürgen Moltmann, by contrast, made divine transcendence a this-worldly matter and linked it to the Marxist vision of a coming age that would be qualitatively different fom the present (*Religion, Revolution, and the Future*, trans. M. Douglas Meeks [New York: Scribner's, 1969], p. 182; see further Gabriel Fackre, "The Issue of Transcendence in the New Theology, New Morality and the New Forms," in *New Theology No. 4*, ed. Martin E. Marty and Dean G. Peerman [New York: Macmillan, 1967], pp. 178-94). Existentialists have tended to think of transcendence not as above or as beyond but as within, as symbolic of the depths of experience in Being (see John Macquarrie, *Principles of Christian Theology* [New York: Scribner's, 1977], pp. 87-88, 120). Paul K. Jewett speaks simply of God in his transcendence as being "related to the world as prior to it, apart from it, and exalted above it" (*God, Creation, and Revelation: A Neo-Evangelical Theology* [Grand Rapids: William B. Eerdmans, 1991], p. 198). To this I would add the idea of God's holiness. That being the case, I consider it unwise to think, as Millard Erickson does, of God's "nearness" as his immanence and his "distance" as his transcendence (*Christian Theology* [Grand Rapids: Baker Book House, 1985], pp. 301-20). If God's holiness is distant — that is to say, not a present reality — the church loses its moral life.

for a God who has thus lost weight is no longer the God of biblical faith or classical Christianity. A God with whom we are on such easy terms and whose reality is little different from our own — a God who is merely there to satisfy our needs — has no real authority to compel and will soon begin to bore us. This is not the God of Abraham, Isaac, and Jacob. He is scarcely even the God of the philosophers, and certainly not the God of Jesus Christ.

Designer Religion

In the Western world, modernity has flowed along two quite different riverbeds — high culture on the one hand, and what has been characterized as low, popular, folk, or broad culture on the other. This is, to be sure, an artificial distinction, for in between these two types lie gradations that fill out the entire spectrum. I am simply referring, then, to two poles in culture that are further defined by class, educational, and economic differences. The distinction between "high" and "low" culture is not primarily moral or even aesthetic, with the one being invariably superior and the other invariably inferior. Richard Rorty's post-modern philosophical emptiness consists of essentially the same stuff as Madonna's post-modern philosophical emptiness, and Carl Rogers's psychological narcissism is essentially reduplicated in such magazines as *Self* and *Seventeen*.

What distinguishes these cultures is mainly the number who can participate in them. High culture is by its very nature an elitist matter. Only the few have the ability, training, and inclination to participate. Low, popular, or folk culture, by contrast, is where the masses play. If there is a difference beyond this, it is that high culture tends to be characterized by a greater degree of self-consciousness, a heightened awareness of its critical assumptions and habits of thought. Devotees of popular culture tend to be less aware of the internal mechanisms of their culture — and less interested in rectifying their ignorance about them. As the literacy rate declines in the West, the center of popular or folk culture is increasingly shifting away from print media (and the more exacting mental discipline associated with it) toward video.[5] Those who live by and within high culture typically want to think about their world and about themselves in that world; those who are borne

5. See Neil Postman, *Amusing Ourselves to Death: Public Discourse in the Age of Show Business* (New York: Penguin, 1985).

along by popular culture often wish to be spared such thought. But culture both high and low is driven by modernity; it simply comes to expression differently at the two poles. The connoisseurs of high culture and the enthusiasts of low may think that they have nothing in common with each other, but they are wrong.

Each cultural pole produces its own patterns of thought, its own ways of looking at the world, and in the past these have often been quite different. The profound influence of modernization has produced some important points of convergence between the two, however. Most significant in this regard is the way in which the self has been redefined by modern experience. This reordered self may come to expression differently in high culture and low, but in essence it is the same phenomenon that is coming to expression. We need to take a closer look at this convergence, because it is having a powerful effect on the way in which Christian faith is conceived and especially on how God is viewed.

In a nutshell, what appears to have happened in the larger culture is that the forces of modernization have increasingly robbed modern people of their external forms of connectedness. The yet more corrosive post-modern environment has eaten away every transcendent reference point and fatally weakened every attempt to find overarching meaning. Thus thwarted in their efforts to find meaning outside themselves, moderns have sought to relocate all reality internally, detached from any fixed moral norms. The self is altogether inadequate to bear the entire burden of creating this moral and spiritual meaning, however. It has succeeded only in blowing all its feelings and intuitions up to grandiose proportions to approximate the size of the external realities they have displaced — a size that only serves to reveal more clearly how inadequate these scraps of the self are to fill the role they have been assigned. At the same time, attempts to adapt to the chaotic patterns of modern life produce identities that are constantly changing and shifting, no longer integral portraits but mere collages of images. The fragile self adrift in the relentless tumult of modernity inevitably begins to experience the weariness and emptiness to which post-modern writers, composers, and artists have so uniformly pointed. This agonizing sense of weightlessness that we once thought only God would suffer in modern culture now turns out to be ours as well. That, in quick strokes, is the argument. I will now proceed to show how this development has, by an entirely different route, brought Western culture both high and low to the point of obsession with the autonomy of the self and to a corresponding rejection of all other authorities. We will begin by looking at popular culture and then look at the parallels in high culture.

Uprooted from the World

Long before the avalanche of literature on this theme began, Reinhold Niebuhr observed that the self draws its substance from three basic sources: family, community, and craft.[6] Connections to each of these sources are now either strained or lost to the modern self. It is worth recalling and expanding on Niebuhr's observations, although it should be noted that what he saw coming was but one part of the picture. It is true that the self has lost its capacity for connectedness in the world outside of itself, but it is also the case that it nevertheless seeks to adapt itself to the multiple shifting worlds of meaning through which it must pass each day and that this has a powerful effect on personal identity. Furthermore, with the collapse of the "metanarratives" of modernity after the 1960s — belief in such things as progress, rationality, and justice[7] — personal identity now is being shaped on the basis of a vision of freedom that amounts to little more than complete randomness.

First, the family is besieged not only by the plague of divorce and the huge increase in single-parent households generally but by the stresses and strains of life that exact their toll on the marriages that do manage to survive in the modernized world. Families that function together, and that do so with a set of common moral values, are becoming an endangered species. The significance of this change in the context of our discussion is that families have traditionally served as the chief conduit for the transmission of values from one generation to another, and now this conduit is breaking down. The new generation is inheriting a set of values and expectations that is so thin and pale as to be quite unsatisfying. Hungry for additional tutoring in the meaning of life, the young are turning first to the larger culture. Then, unsatisfied with the ambiguous and contradictory moral messages imparted by the popular media, they are turning inward in their search for signals about the meaning of life.

Second, modernization is progressively erasing geographical distinctions as a means of defining community. The modern individual

6. Niebuhr, *Reflections on the End of an Era* (New York: Scribner's, 1934), p. 104.

7. The fragile and sometimes tendentious nature of these concepts is revealed by Alasdair MacIntyre in *Whose Justice? Which Rationality?* (Notre Dame, Ind.: University of Notre Dame Press, 1988).

is almost wholly rootless, bereft of any psychological connections to place. To be sure, the new freedom from various parochialisms is in some sense exhilarating, but it does not come without a price. Those who belong everywhere can also be said to belong nowhere; they have been emancipated from the small town only to become anonymous, unconnected in our large world. Where the self wanders the earth as a vagrant, belonging nowhere, something that is profoundly intrinsic to being human has been lost.

Third, the self's connection to craft has also been seriously diminished by modernization, leaving many people perpetually dissatisfied with their work. In some case, machines have severed the link between the worker and the work. In other cases, layers of bureaucracy have severed personal links between ideas and products. In still other cases, the kind of work that is required by modernized societies is inherently undignified or boring, and the old virtue of taking pride in one's work becomes harder and harder to realize.

Were this all, the modern world would be easier to survive morally, spiritually, and psychologically than it has turned out to be. But in addition to this loss of connectedness to place, work, and family, there has been added the intrusion into the modern psyche of what Anthony Giddens calls our "large-scale social universe."[8] This is the world that we inhabit psychologically and cognitively through our technology, our cities, our saturating popular media. Modernity has produced a universal culture of commercialized life that has deeply and profoundly churned up the local cultures that were once tied to time and place and mediated by family and community. This universal culture is profoundly ambivalent. On the one hand, as Marshall Berman notes, it holds out the prospect of "adventure, power, joy, growth, transformation of ourselves and the world"; on the other hand, it threatens to destroy "everything we have, everything we know, everything we are."[9] And Giddens argues, as many others have, that there is an inescapable connection between our internal and external worlds, that in the midst of "massive waves of global transformation" that are threatening and overturning what were once settled values, stable hopes, and established beliefs, the individual is flooded with unrelenting anxiety.[10]

8. Giddens, *Modernity and Self-Identity: Self and Society in the Late Modern Age* (Stanford: Stanford University Press, 1991), p. 191.
9. Berman, *All That Is Solid Melts into Air: The Experience of Modernity* (New York: Simon & Schuster, 1982), p. 15.
10. Giddens, *Modernity and Self-Identity*, pp. 183-84.

Both Sartre and Freud distinguished between fear and anxiety. Fear is always specific: we fear falling bombs, burglars, muggers, unemployment. Anxiety is always nonspecific — indeed, its lack of specificity is a large part of what makes it so unsettling. A soldier may fear enemy bullets, but he will be anxious about his reactions to coming under enemy fire: Will he act with courage or with cowardice? Will he stand to resist the attack or run from the conflict?

There is much to fear in the modern world. Along with its innumerable benefits, modernization has also produced an increasing level of violence and a general devaluation and displacement of life as the forces of the marketplace move first in one direction and then in another. As communities have withered away, individuals have often been left to cope alone as well as they can in what may be bleak circumstances. But if fear has become commonplace, anxiety has become epidemic. It has become part of the fabric of modernity. It seems to be rooted most commonly in a sense of powerlessness, an inability to control the circumstances of personal life, a feeling that people are mere pawns in a game played by irresistible and unpredictable forces in society. Kierkegaard called it "dread," the sense of being utterly overwhelmed. It is a sense that does not simply settle upon the mind but sinks into the being, greatly destabilizing the self and seriously undermining one's capacity to cope in life.

Stripped of external connectedness and haunted within by anxiety, modern individuals drift in society like bits of cork on the ocean, moved about in ways beyond their understanding by deep and irresistible currents. Filled with dread, dis-ease, and foreboding and unable to secure a foothold in any external reality, they take refuge in the one certain thing remaining — the self. This turn to the self as the source of mystery, of meaning, and of hope is the key to understanding the shape that much religion in America is taking today. As Philip Rieff has pointed out, however, all this brave talk about the self and about its potential is actually evidence of a "disordering" of the self,[11] and it follows from this that any religion based on the self must itself be disordered.

Pastiche Personalities

Many of the modern individual's strategies for psychological survival are not working very well. Kenneth J. Gergen finds considerable evidence

---

11. See Rieff, *The Triumph of the Therapeutic: Uses of Faith after Freud* (New York: Harper & Row, 1968).

supporting this conclusion in our everyday language. We are constantly employing "the vocabulary of human deficit," he says.[12] Our lexicon of terms describing inward deficits has greatly expanded in this century, and most especially during the past three decades. Words and phrases such as "low self-esteem," "depressed," "stressed out," "obsessive-compulsive," "identity crisis," "mid-life crisis," "self-alienated," "authoritarian," "repressed," "burned out," "anxious," and "bulimic" have come to be used in connection with matters of self-identity only quite recently, and they all point to losses, to things that are inwardly awry or malfunctioning. In part, this profusion of new terminology could probably be attributed to growth in the field of psychology generally, but the fact that the terminology has left the category of specialized use to become commonplace in the larger culture suggests that the maladies to which it refers have become commonplace in the larger culture as well. It would seem that the experience of modernity is dismantling the self, and psychology is washing in to fill the hole. It is producing, in Christopher Lasch's words, the "minimal self."[13]

More than thirty years ago, David Reisman described a shift in modern culture from the "inner-directed" person to the "other-directed" person. People were becoming less inclined to define themselves in terms of an internal core of attributes and more inclined to define themselves in terms of attributes they perceived in respected contemporaries.[14] The years since have introduced a further refinement of this process. The mass media now churn out such a multitude of images, desirable personae, styles to be adopted and emulated that the young (and those who wish that they still were young) are left choking in confusion and sometimes despair. They have no internal gyroscope to help them settle on a direction amid the countless competing "products" in the market.

After the 1950s, personal identity became increasingly disengaged from beliefs about character and basic human nature and was associated instead with *consciousness* — that is to say, with something a good deal more shifting and elusive. This process evolved further during the 1970s, when personal identity became increasingly associated not with the narrative of one's inner life but with the projection

12. Gergen, *The Saturated Self: Dilemmas of Identity in Contemporary Life* (New York: Basic Books, 1991), p. 13.

13. See Lasch, *The Minimal Self: Psychic Survival in Troubled Times* (New York: W. W. Norton, 1984).

14. See Riesman et al., *The Lonely Crowd: A Study of Changing American Character*, rev. ed. (New Haven: Yale University Press, 1961).

of one's public *image*. Indeed, in the popular perception, image and inner life were disengaged from each other entirely. Great emphasis was placed on the skillful presentation of one's "image." Erving Goffman speaks of modern people as having become performers who stage their own characters and accomplishments, an art that often requires one to transcend the need to tell the truth in order to practice "the techniques of management impression."[15] A whole industry has now grown up to teach people how to market themselves by creating appealing and desirable images.

In this new world, the self is not something that *is;* it is something that is *constructed.* "As belief in essential selves erodes," says Gergen, "awareness expands of the ways in which personal identity can be created and recreated in relationships."[16] In the modern world, though, we are required to construct multiple selves because we live in so many different "worlds," play to so many different audiences, encounter so many different experiences, and juggle so many different values. Post-modern individuals are thus prone to develop "pastiche personalities" as a result of "constantly borrowing bits and pieces of identity from whatever sources are available and constructing them as useful or desirable in a given situation."[17]

The pastiche personality of the baby boomer, a personality suckled on rock music and television during the postwar years, is the major force behind the redrawing of the religious landscape in America today. Contemporary authors have made much of the return of the baby boomers to church, of their search for previously abandoned values, but they have not been so quick to see the similarities between the baby boomers who are in church (often megachurches) and those who have ventured out on self-directed religious quests that typically do not lead them to any sort of Christian church.

Among the boomers inside and outside the church, two traits are most evident. First, there is a hunger for religious experience but an aversion to theological definition of that experience. There is a hunger for God but a disenchantment with dogma or doctrine. And their characteristic abandonment of boundaries — boundaries between God and the self and between one religion and another — typically results in a smorgasbord of spirituality for which the only accepted criterion

15. Goffman, *The Presentation of the Self in Everyday Life* (Garden City, N.Y.: Doubleday, 1959), p. 208.

16. Gergen, *The Saturated Self,* p. 146.

17. Gergen, *The Saturated Self,* p. 150.

of truth is the pragmatic one of what seems to work personally. This is connected to the second trait, which is that baby boomers are inveterate shoppers. They are the children of a massively commercialized world who have learned the needed skills of commerce — principal among which is an ability to identify the products that will satisfy their inner needs. This generation is in the market for religious goods, and it is only to be expected that one person's purchase will be different from another person's, because every person is different, with special needs. In the fevered quest for individual fulfillment, commonality of belief is brushed aside as an irrelevance, if not an impossibility. The common *need* for religious experience of some sort is acknowledged, but no restrictions are placed on the sort of experience that will fill the bill for any given individual. Thus do we welcome the personalized, designer religion of the 1990s.

At the center of the new quest is the dichotomy that William James described between tradition and experience. Today it might more compellingly be characterized as a dichotomy between firsthand and secondhand experience. According to Wade Clark Roof, baby boomers want to "experience life directly, to have an encounter with God or the divine, or simply with nature and other people, without the intervention of inherited beliefs, ideas, and concepts."[18] It is the inwardness of experience, he says, that guarantees its authenticity in this expressive and narcissistic culture. He goes on to describe the very important implications of this approach with respect to both the character of the seeker and the nature of the search. For one thing, it renders the modern self "fluid, improvable, adaptable, manipulatable, and above all else something to be satisfied — the assumption being, of course, that the self's appetite is insatiable." Furthermore, it blurs the lines of demarcation defining religious identity, rendering it as fluid and malleable as the searching self. And it feeds naturally into pluralism by "demonopolizing any single version as *the* religious truth and by making a wide variety of religious options open to everyone."[19]

There is an irony in all of this that appears to be entirely lost on those at the heart of it. They labor under the illusion that the God they make in the image of the self becomes more real as he more nearly comes to resemble the self, to accommodate its needs and desires. The truth is quite the opposite. It is ridiculous to assert that God could

18. Roof, *A Generation of Seekers: The Spiritual Journeys of the Baby Boom Generation* (San Francisco: HarperCollins, 1993), p. 67.
19. Roof, *A Generation of Seekers*, p. 195.

become more real by abandoning his own character in an effort to identify more completely with ours. And yet the illusion has proved compelling to a whole generation.

Indeed, our generation is rapidly growing deaf to the summons of the external God. He has been so internalized, so tamed by the needs of religious commerce, so submerged beneath the traffic of modern psychological need that he has almost completely disappeared. All too often, he now leans weakly on the church, a passive bystander, a co-conspirator in the effort to dismantle two thousand years of Christian thought about God and what he has declared himself to be. That is to say, God has become weightless. The church continues its business of satisfying the needs of the self — needs defined by the individual — and God, who is himself viewed and marketed as a product, becomes powerless to change the definition of that need or to prescribe the means by which it might be satisfied. When the consumer is sovereign, the product (in this case God himself) must be subservient.

Intellectuals

The Breath of the Night Wind

This quick passage through the vagaries of the modern self has followed the path more of experience than of thought, but the same story can also be told of those who have conceptualized these changes. Nietzsche, the proponent of deep and unrelenting unbelief, was among the first to anticipate these changes. He noted the disappearance of God in the modern period. He declared that God had died, or, more precisely, that he had been murdered. He actually had in mind something a little different from what he is usually assumed to have meant, however. He was speaking of the passing of a world in which meaning and values had been rooted in the transcendent. He saw a world in which human beings were wresting sovereignty for themselves, and hence a world in which there were no longer ultimate values but only present possibilities — possibilities that were fluid, open, and unstructured by the divine or by an absolute moral order. This is the world that we describe under the rubric of secularization. Nietzsche never imagined that this brave new world would be idyllic. He understood that it would be filled with the clashing of egos and the thrashing of vice and decay. It would be a world without limits or constraints, a world in which power would provide the only path through the painful contortions of life. And this drifting, rudderless world has indeed been realized, producing the twin realities, in Jackson Lears's words, of "the diffusion of identity" and "the pervasive feeling of unreality" with which we are all too familiar today.[20]

Nietzsche understood both of these realities. The first had coalesced with the dreams of the Enlightenment, had seemed to give fresh evidence of the triumph of the ideas of its proponents, the philosophes, while the second had been persistently ignored, masked by liberal ideologies of progress and optimism.[21] Nietzsche maintained that these false hopes and dreams had died and that only the raw, dark forces of nature remained. In this regard, he was ahead of his time, but in the 1960s, as I have noted, many others came to argue that our bright new world is now devoid of meaning and ethical restraints because it makes no room for the transcendent realm in which that meaning and those restraints are properly anchored. As Jürgen Habermas has put it, modernity is now dominant but dead.

Martin Buber also noted the way in which psychological thinking has begun to fill in the holes in the modern psyche left after the sense of God faded in the modern period.[22] But this is only the first stage in the transformation. The second stage, which, in their quirky ways, the post-modern writers are now documenting, involves the disintegration of the self. It is not at all hard to find evidences of this process in both popular culture and the high culture ensconced in the universities, although we can look only briefly at the parallels between the two.

The Conquest of Reality

The question of knowledge, of how a subject comes to know an object, has produced an enormous range of philosophical speculation in every century since the writing of the New Testament and, indeed, before that as well. In this chapter, though, I am defining the difference between the subject and the object in terms of what distinguishes the

20. Lears, *No Place of Grace,* p. 41.

21. For the origin of these ideas in the Enlightenment, especially among its French thinkers, see Georges Sorel, *The Illusions of Progress,* trans. John and Charlotte Stanley (Berkeley and Los Angeles: University of California Press, 1969). For a critique of subsequent developments in this illusion, see Christopher Lasch, *The True and Only Heaven: Progress and Its Critics* (New York: W. W. Norton, 1990).

22. See Buber, *The Eclipse of God: Studies in the Relation between Religion and Philosophy* (New York: Harper & Row, 1965).

knower from what is known, the content of knowledge from the act by which that knowledge was acquired, the interior from the exterior.

Probably the simplest case in this regard involves our knowledge of objects in our physical world — trees, buildings, animals, food, machines — the things that we know through our senses of sight, touch, taste, hearing, and smell. Although this may be the simplest case compared to others, it is by no means simple in its own right. Philosophers have puzzled through the ages about whether the mind really is a mirror in which the external world is reflected and, if so, how this can be, and the matter has yielded no widely accepted solutions. But most people are content to resolve the question intuitively. They assume as a matter of course that there is a distance between what is being cognitively apprehended in the world and the person who is acquiring this knowledge. The self preserves its independence from trees, buildings, animals, food, and machines. It is precisely this over-againstness, this distance between the knower and the known, that allows us to know anything in the world at all.

When we shift our attention to God, however, the simplicity of this arrangement is immediately imperiled. God is not an object in space and time like a tree or a building, and the distance that otherwise distinguishes the knower from what is known now vanishes. God is not only exterior to the knower but interior as well. God and the self are known together in the context of religious experience.[23] Where is the over-againstness here? What is of God and what is of self? Can we tell?

In the twentieth century, these have not seemed like fruitful questions to ask, because the distance that once separated the creature from the Creator has steadily diminished. As traditional theism has fallen apart, God has increasingly been relocated within the human personality, and hence distinctions between the self and God have become harder and harder to make and the consequences of not doing so have come to seem less and less significant.

---

23. This is not an entirely modern discovery. John Calvin begins his theology with the assertion that wisdom in religious matters consists in perceiving the interconnectedness of self-knowledge and the knowledge of God. Calvin understood this knowledge of the self to be moral in nature rather than psychological, however, and held that its import was soteriological rather than therapeutic. To know one's self in truth was to know one's need for God's redemption. Furthermore, Calvin was arguing for the interconnectedness of the knowledge, not for some sort of infusion of the divine and redemptive into the human and psychological. See Calvin, *Institutes of the Christian Religion* 1.1.1.

From Kant to Rorty

This trend began with Kant, who altered the whole direction of thought in the West. Kant established the modern rules for discussing how it is that someone knows the external world, and in doing so he initiated the breakdown of the old distinction between subject and object. When this breakdown crossed over into theology, it resulted in an overemphasis on God's immanence and a diminished emphasis on his transcendence. This change had profound implications for the meaning of Christian faith.

Prior to Kant, the reigning epistemological paradigm held that the mind was simply a mirror in which the external world was reflected, that an objective world imprinted its reality on minds that were passive, inert, and uninvolved in this transaction. Kant rejected this model. Instead of beginning with the objective world, he began with the subjective conditions for knowledge, with the shape and functioning of the mind. He argued that the mind is active in and a constitutive part of what is known. It sorts into categories the stream of information contributed by the five senses and then synthesizes the data in ways that do not necessarily correspond to what is externally existent. He maintained that space and time, for example, are categories of the mind rather than realities in the world. Whatever can be said in favor of this, it should immediately be recognized that a fateful move had been made. Once the mind was seen as itself a source of knowledge, knowledge that was then superimposed on the data of the outside world, and once this knowledge was cut loose from control in the knowledge of God, a juggernaut was launched.

Indeed, the Kantian legacy has affected our understanding of all aspects of life. One might suppose that science would constitute some sort of stronghold against the new epistemology, that in this area at least hard data from the outside world would continue to exercise control over what was understood about that world, but Thomas Kuhn has showed that even in this realm, what is "seen" in the world is often dependent on what scientists expect to find.[24] It is only when these internal patterns of expectation shift, when a new paradigm slips into place, that the great leaps in understanding occur. Even before Kuhn's work had taken hold, Karl Popper compared the situation to how a searchlight works: "What the searchlight makes visible will depend

24. See Kuhn, *The Structure of Scientific Revolutions,* 2d ed. (Chicago: University of Chicago Press, 1970).

upon its position, upon our way of directing it, and upon its intensity, colour, etc.," although the scene that is illumined will also depend on what things lie in the path of the light.[25]

Outside the fields of science, the effects of the new epistemology have been yet more profound. Within the realm of science, the hard data supply continues to exercise at least some kind of restraint on human perception, but in the realm of the humanities, this boundary is a good deal fuzzier. Indeed, virtually the only remaining boundaries here are provided by aspects of personal culture — issues of race, gender, sexual orientation, and class. Meaning has largely been detached from what is objective and as a result has become radically subjective. In consequence, the perspectives that emerge, variously colored by personal and cultural biases, simply pour into the churning pluralistic pot. With no commonly recognized objective standard, there is no hope of resolving the differences among them.

In literature this inescapable pluralism has been pursued by the post-modernists with purposeful vengeance. In their different ways, such post-modern critics as Jacques Derrida, Harold Bloom, and Stanley Fish have each made the argument that texts have no stable, unchanging meaning, that they mean only what individual readers perceive them to mean. Fish asserts that this approach does not amount to imposing meaning on the text, that it is simply a recognition of the fact that words have no independent meaning apart from specific contexts.[26] Moreover, the contexts that are crucial for meaning reside not in the sentences and paragraphs of the texts but in the reader's internal psychology, in the ways the reader is inclined to understand life. Thus the subjective triumphs completely over the objective.

Take, for example, the sentence "The sergeant looked at her carefully and then smiled warmly." What does this mean? The deconstructionist's answer is that even in the context of a larger text, it all depends on which internal world of meaning fills out the words. A reader approaching the text as light entertainment might be inclined

---

25. Popper, *The Open Society and Its Enemies*, vol. 2: *The High Tide of Prophecy: Hegel, Marx, and the Aftermath* (London: Routledge & Kegan Paul, 1945), p. 247.

26. See Fish, *Is There a Text in This Class? The Authority of Interpretive Communities* (Cambridge: Harvard University Press, 1980), pp. 303-21. The contrary view is advocated by E. D. Hirsch in his books *Validity in Interpretation* (New Haven: Yale University Press, 1962) and *The Aims of Interpretation* (Chicago: University of Chicago Press, 1976). For a careful assessment of this literary terrain from a self-consciously Christian perspective, see Roger Lundin, *The Culture of Interpretation: Christian Faith and the Postmodern World* (Grand Rapids: William B. Eerdmans, 1993).

to view the sergeant's warm smile as simply the first small spark of a romantic interest. A feminist critic might be inclined to view the sergeant as making a deliberate calculation — "looked at her carefully" — in preparation for launching himself on a course of action that might end with seduction or harassment. A recent graduate of a military school might be inclined to find in the sentence a snapshot of the human face that the army is keener these days to show, in which control (the careful look) and humanity (the warm smile) are blended. The point is that it is the reader, not the author, who is providing the meaning here. And it should be noted that the significance of this shift in the source of the meaning is not simply that it unleashes pluralism in places where it has not been known so plentifully before but that it aims a blow at the entire Western academic tradition in which it has always been assumed that although all words have ranges of meaning, good authors also know how to limit for the reader what possibilities exist in any given passage. If the only meaning in a text is that which any particular community wants to provide, then what is normative in language, as well as in life, has been destroyed.

Richard Rorty has explored the limits of this position in the area of philosophy. He begins by rejecting Kant's model of knowledge as "inner representations" of the external world.[27] In fact Rorty engages in a thoroughgoing attack on the notion of such a mind, what Gilbert Ryle also ridiculed earlier in this century as the "ghost in the machine theory." There is no internal mirror, says Rorty. His philosophy therefore sharply breaks with psychology — he has no interest in what might be happening within a person at the moment of acquiring knowledge — and moves toward hermeneutics, an interest in the meanings that reside in words apart from any connection to any external reality. Rorty has no interest in epistemology because he has no interest in the notion of the self as knower.[28] In one sense, Rorty's philosophy pronounces the death (or at least the irrelevance) of the self, but in another sense it elevates the self to the position of an unchallengeable demagogue that can create meanings at will and that is wholly unconstrained by an external reality. In a world where there is no truth, what remain are possibilities that are always fluid and open, and life is simply a matter of pragmatically determining which work and which do not.

27. See Rorty, *Philosophy and the Mirror of Nature* (Princeton: Princeton University Press, 1979), p. 149.
28. On the disappearance of the self in Rorty's world, see especially *Philosophy and the Mirror of Nature*, pp. 357-94.

The Insurrection in Theology

We turn now to a consideration of comparable developments in the area of theology. Here, the initial conquest of the objective by the subjective is quickly followed by a fresh translation of the transcendence of God in terms that are wholly immanent. Though the terms are religious, the issue is the same: Is reality external to the knower allowed to exercise any sort of constraints on what is known? As we have already noted, this matter is complicated by the fact that, unlike physical objects in our world, God is not solely external to the observer but is also internal. In our experience, the line between flesh and spirit becomes blurry. But the distinction remains at the heart of knowing how to preserve a biblical understanding of God.

The bridge from Kant into modern theology was made easily. Kant initially argued that reason cannot establish the reality and nature of God, and then, in his *Critique of Practical Reason,* he went on to propose that it is only in *moral* experience that such knowledge can be grounded, for the knowledge we have of ourselves as moral beings is inexplicable if God does not exist. Friedrich Schleiermacher, the father of modern theology and the chief formulator of liberal Protestantism, agreed with Kant that the reality and nature of God are neither given by reason nor accessible to it, but he went on to propose that this knowledge is grounded in *religious* rather than moral experience. The general acceptance of this proposal has had profound implications for the doing of theology and has done much to give the popular culture of the modernized West the shape it now has. Our culture tends either to view experience as suffused with the divine or to confer divinity on the self.[29] The fact that popular culture has reached this conclusion with little knowledge of the learned discussions of the academy strongly suggests that both have been influenced by an overarching reality — namely, modernity.

First in his *Speeches on Religion* and then in his much more complex work *The Christian Faith,* Schleiermacher repudiated objective knowledge of God and then, like the romantics, reached down into his own being to find the grounding for his knowledge of God.[30] This being the case, a rehearsal of the divine attributes will tell us less about

29. Paul Vitz has argued that the practice of modern psychology has often produced a substitute religion; see *Psychology as Religion: The Cult of Self Worship* (Grand Rapids: William B. Eerdmans, 1977).

30. See Jack Forstmann, *A Romantic Triangle: Schleiermacher and Early German Romanticism* (Missoula, Mont.: Scholars Press, 1977).

God than about ourselves, for each of them is now simply an objectification of what we first find in our religious self. We experience sin in ourselves, and we project an understanding of God as holy; we find that we are able to resolve internal conflicts, and we attribute the resolution to God in terms of grace and love.[31] Schleiermacher dismissed entirely the vertical dimension of a God outside of experience summoning sinners through biblical revelation to pass beyond themselves into union with God through Christ. He maintained that the knowledge of God was restricted to the self, where the immanence of God was registered in feeling — specifically, awe deriving from radical dependence. Thus God became a kind of psychological deposit, a "something" deep in the self. Somewhere within, the divine signature could be read with enough clarity to secure some meaning in life. Thus it was that in the liberalism that followed Schleiermacher, in Europe as well as in America, poetry gradually edged out exposition, feeling replaced reason as the primary means of knowing God, the heart replaced the head, and intuition supplanted external, revelatory truth.

Barth says that Schleiermacher viewed God as the mirror image of the self.[32] If the result was, as Friedrich Schlegel charged, a God who was "a little skinny," the reason, of course, was that God could be no larger than the self of which he was a reflection. Barth later pointed out that we cannot call "God" by shouting "man" in a loud voice. For all his brilliance, Schleiermacher ended up knowing only himself, not God.[33] The reason so much attention has been paid to this aspect of Schleiermacher's thought, Barth said, is that modern theology suffers from a bad conscience. "Theology suffers from a chronic lack of objectivity" in our age; "we do not know what we are talking about when we talk about God but we still want to talk about him," so theologians have repeatedly returned to Schleiermacher to see if perhaps he might show us how to do it.[34]

Few at that time recognized the straw in the wind. But James

31. Schleiermacher's argument is that the divine attributes "are to be taken as denoting not something special in God, but only something special in the manner in which the feeling of absolute dependence is to be related to Him" (*The Christian Faith*, ed. H. R. Mackintosh and J. S. Stewart [New York: Harper, 1963], p. 194). That is to say, they speak primarily of our own inner experience of God rather than of God as he is in himself.

32. Barth, *The Theology of Schleiermacher: Lectures at Göttingen, Winter Semester, 1923-24*, ed. Dietrich Ritschl, trans. Geoffrey W. Bromiley (Grand Rapids: William B. Eerdmans, 1982), p. 217.

33. Barth, *Church Dogmatics*, II/1:339.

34. Barth, *Church Dogmatics*, II/1:193.

Turner is quite correct in observing that when these same ideas took root in America a little later, "many antebellum Protestants, without ever realizing it, teetered on the brink of secular morality."[35] Religious authority that was relocated from an external source such as the Bible or even the church to an internal source such as feeling or conscience unraveled easily because it was not in fact authoritative. Meaning that is gleaned from within is de facto independent of belief in God. There is nothing to keep the deep sense of dependence and awe before God that Schleiermacher associated with the religious experience from dissolving into a simple sense of mystery within the secular individual. The irreligious person will not find anything transcendent or supernatural in it.

Furthermore, granting the status of revelation to anything other than the Word of God inevitably has the effect of removing that status from the Word of God. What may start out as an additional authority alongside the Word of God will eventually supplant its authority altogether. At the beginning of the First World War, Adolf von Harnack earnestly defended the Kaiser's German nationalism as the expression of the will of God. When German nationalism once again became a potent force in the 1930s, the authors of the Barmen Declaration chose another course, condemning "the false doctrine that the Church could and should recognize as a source of its proclamation, beyond and besides this one Word of God, yet other events, powers, historic figures, and truths as God's revelation."[36] According to Barth, they were specifically responding to a demand that they "recognize in the political events of the year 1933, and especially in the form of the God-sent Adolf Hitler, a source of specific new revelation of God which, demanding obedience and trust, took its place beside the revelation attested in Holy Scripture."[37] Their declaration notwithstanding, the demand grew stronger over time. The additional revelation initially placed alongside the Word of God by some in the church eventually supplanted that Word. The Third Reich inaugurated a pagan millennium through a totalitarian state and set out to crush all Christian opposition. This dynamic has been repeated in every other case in which some other source of revelation has been placed on a par with God's truth.

35. See the helpful discussion in James Brown, *Subject and Object in Modern Theology* (London: SCM Press, 1953), pp. 140-67.

36. "The Barmen Declaration," in *Kairos: Three Prophetic Challenges to the Church,* ed. Robert McAfee Brown (Grand Rapids: William B. Eerdmans, 1990), p. 156.

37. Barth, *Church Dogmatics,* II/1:173.

Are we now to suppose that this will not happen when we place the ostensibly benign self alongside the Word of God as an authority?

By the 1960s, when it was clear that the neo-orthodox attempt to turn back the deeply subjective preoccupation of liberal theology had itself come apart, theology fell into disarray, but, interestingly enough, the old mechanism went back to work. Though the trend had been briefly arrested by Barth, in his wake the dominance of the knowing subject was linked up to fresh assertions that what has traditionally fallen into the category of the transcendence of God should now be transferred to the category of his immanence. Not all contemporary theologians have moved in this direction, however. As David Ray Griffin has noted, post-modern theologians "registered their conviction that that noble and flawed enterprise called *modern theology* had run its course."[38] They have abandoned their belief in the old Enlightenment project and its optimism, its expectation that reason would be able to pacify and comprehend the world. They have walked away from the old preoccupations with truth and meaning and the intellectual categories in which theology had been conceived, such as natural and supernatural, truth and error, transcendent and immanent. They repudiate the modern experience because it comprises not only abundance but also alienation, loneliness, rationalization, the abuse of nature, the abuse of minorities, and estrangement within the self. The result is that God is now under fresh construction, this time from the raw materials of disaffection and protest — but even here it is not uncommon to find some of the old Schleiermacherian themes, the same ousting of the truth of God by the preoccupations of the religious self.

Langdon Gilkey, for example, began by accepting the fundamental premise of modernity that there is nothing to which appeal can be made outside of modernity. There can be no address from a God who stands outside human experience, who holds human beings morally accountable, who provides meaning that is not itself the product of modernity and may well question much that is held dear by modernity. Gilkey rejects traditional notions of divine transcendence and winds up with a sense of the presence of God that is largely indistinguishable from modern experience. The foreign and even forbidding aspects of the otherness of God have thus been domesticated and rendered

---

38. Griffin, "Introduction: Varieties of Postmodern Theology," in *Varieties of Postmodern Theology*, ed. David Ray Griffin (New York: State University of New York Press, 1989), p. 1.

harmless. Gilkey equates the immanence of God with "the common, universal, and secular experiences of the reality, wonder and joy of life," and he equates God's transcendence with "our continual experience of the elusiveness of that security and meaning, in the experience of the radical relativity of our truth, and in our sense of alienation from the forgiveness and from the power of love."[39]

Alasdair MacIntyre has argued that modernity is by its very nature hostile to any expression of a traditional understanding of the transcendence of God.[40] In consequence, theism either retains its traditional character and becomes increasingly incomprehensible to moderns, or it adapts itself to the modern cultural context and becomes increasingly strained in its relation to historic orthodoxy. Schleiermacher and his many followers abandoned the traditional understanding of God's transcendence in favor of the knowledge of God as experienced immanentally within the experiencing subject. A God so understood can no longer stand outside sinners summoning them to the sort of knowledge of himself that might well violate everything they have experienced and presumed to be deep, profound, and therapeutic.

At the root of the remaking of the modern mind, in fact, is the refusal to allow external reality to impose constraints on the knower. For example, Rorty denies that reality has the power to impose itself on the mind, thereby emancipating the modern self from all external reality. The same mentality is evident in Fish, who maintains that the literary text is powerless to impose any limitations of meaning on the reader. And this mentality is also evident in much modern theology, which asserts that the will and reality of God are coextensive with religious experience and thereby deny that God has the power to contradict that experience. It is to this self that all external authorities such as the Bible and the church are now subjugated, thereby perpetuating the vision of the autonomous self with which the Enlightenment was launched.

The Therapy of Pride

It is important for us to see that modernization's reshaping of the world and (of the modern psyche as a part of that world) has promoted pride

39. Gilkey, *Naming the Whirlwind: The Renewal of God-Language* (Indianapolis: Bobbs-Merrill, 1969), p. 469.

40. See MacIntyre and Paul Ricoeur, *The Religious Significance of Atheism* (New York: Columbia University Press, 1969), pp. 3-29.

not only in the secular world but also in the religious world, not only among Protestant liberals in ecumenical structures but also among evangelicals outside these structures.[41] We usually associate pride with vanity, with a relentless striving for success, a need to lord it over others, an appetite for power and attention, being puffed up and stiff-necked, all of which came into being in the first sin. Moderns may be no more guilty of this vice than anyone else. However, it is important to see the shape that pride often assumes today. Pride is also self-centeredness that is pursued, protected, and given shape as an alternative to submission to God and to being God-centered. It is a preoccupation with the self as the goal of life. It is self-absorption and self-love. Thus it was that Dante pictured the proud man in hell bent over beneath the weight of an enormous stone: the gaze of the proud individual never leaves the earth.

Modernity stokes these fires of human pride by simultaneously marginalizing God and elevating the self as an alternative to God. It is in the self that meaning and morality are sought. And its authority is rendered absolute by that fact that it typically finds no substantial connectedness in the world and hence is simply left to itself. Defiance of God is quite unnecessary: he has been quietly replaced in a spiritual *coup d'etat*. The sun is now in eclipse, its bright light blocked by the impenetrable darkness of the self. The modern self has experienced the exhilaration of the complete freedom to choose a destiny without reference to God, without a thought to what is ultimately right or, for that matter, what anyone else may think or how they might be affected. In most quarters, however, this brief exhilaration has passed, and a weariness of soul has set in as the self creaks beneath the weight of all the functions it is now being called upon to serve. The tension, anxiety, and bewilderment that usually follow have become the calling cards of modernity.

On the religious side of the cultural divide, the new sovereignty of the self has vastly limited God's capacity to speak to us. Having identified God with the life of the self, we are no longer able to hear anything that would contradict our own intuition about what is true and right. We have ironically precluded the possibility of redemption in the area of our greatest need — tyranny of the self.

As the self comes to dominate the shape that truth can take, the universal reach of Christian faith collapses. It can no longer offer the

41. For a powerful exposition of pride, see Barth, *Church Dogmatics*, IV/1:413-78.

same word of grace to people in all times and places. The sovereignty of the self destroys the character of the church as the one people of God who are united by a common redemption in Christ, a common identity as children by adoption of the Father, and a common understanding in his written Word. It destroys as well worship of the God who stands outside all sinners and whose greatness and glory are the objects of their adoration. In place of God's unchanging glory, the sovereign self raises up the diversity of human need, the multiplicity of private meaning and personal expression. It is a fateful series of substitutions that we are now engineering, often with the very best of intentions, not understanding how modernity has toyed with our inner lives. The tragedy is that in the end we will find that both God and our own experience have lost all their reality, all of their weight.

The Saliency of God

So we can see a striking convergence in the way that God and self are being played out along the outer edges and along the broad avenues of our modernized culture. There has been far less self-conscious reflection on these matters in popular culture than in high culture, to be sure, but the results have been similar in each. How, then, is the saliency of God to be recovered? Certainly a biblical doctrine of God is indispensable for such a recovery, regardless of the difficulties that modernity now poses for the survival of such a doctrine. But the doctrine alone will not be adequate. I do not believe that modern evangelicals would ever knowingly deny biblical truth, and yet they have proved themselves regrettably liable to miscalculate the importance of that truth. So the question we now face is how we can recover the importance of truth, and specifically truth about God.

The answer, I believe, lies in the convergence of two separate but related lines of thought: we need to move away from Our Time's prevailing anthropology, and we need to move away from Our Time's prevailing theology. It is clear to me that we will not be able to recover the importance of truth unless we attend to both of these issues at the same time. That being the case, I regret that, given the limits of this book, I will be able to speak only very briefly to the issue of reordering our current anthropology. But I will devote the remaining chapters of this book to the issue of redirecting our current theology, in an effort to sketch the outlines of that half of my proposal for recovery.

The Caging of God

The first theme, then, is our need to move away from the prevailing modern anthropology, to convert our understanding of ourselves as consumers of inner experiences and things religious to an understanding of ourselves as moral knowers and actors.

We have turned to a God that we can use rather than to a God we must obey; we have turned to a God who will fulfill our needs rather than to a God before whom we must surrender our rights to ourselves. He is a God *for* us, for our satisfaction — not because we have learned to think of him in this way through Christ but because we have learned to think of him this way through the marketplace. In the marketplace, everything is for us, for our pleasure, for our satisfaction, and we have come to assume that it must be so in the church as well. And so we transform the God of mercy into a God who is at our mercy. We imagine that he is benign, that he will acquiesce as we toy with his reality and to co-opt him in the promotion of our ventures and careers. Thus do we presume to restrain him in a Weberian "iron cage" of this-worldly preoccupation. Thus do we tighten our grip upon him. And if the sunshine of his benign grace fails to warm us as we expect, if he fails to shower prosperity and success on us, we will find ourselves unable to believe in him anymore.

What has been lost in all of this, of course, is God's angularity, the sharp edges that truth so often has and that he has preeminently. It is our fallenness fleshed out in our modernity that makes God smooth, that imagines he will accommodate our instincts, shabby and self-centered as they so often are, because he is love.

In a psychologized culture such as ours, there is deep affinity for what is relational but a dis-ease with what is moral. This carries over into the church as an infatuation with the love of God and an embarrassment at his holiness. We who are modern find it infinitely easier to believe that God is like a Rogerian therapist who empathetically solicits our knowledge of ourselves and passes judgment on none of it than to think that he could have had any serious business to conduct with Moses.

This peculiarity of the modern disposition, this loss of substance and vigor, betrays our misunderstanding of God's immanence, his relatedness to creation. We imagine that the great purposes of life are psychological rather than moral. We imagine that the great purposes of life are realized in the improvement of our own private inner disposition. We imagine that for those who love God and are called according to his purpose, all things work together for their satisfaction and the inner tranquillity of their lives. Modernity has secured the triumph of the therapeutic over the moral even in the church.

The fact is, of course, that the New Testament never promises anyone a life of psychological wholeness or offers a guarantee of the consumer's satisfaction with Christ. To the contrary, it offers the prospect of indignities, loss, damage, disease, and pain. The faithful in Scripture were scorned, beaten, imprisoned, shipwrecked, and executed. The gospel offers no promises that contemporary believers will be spared these experiences, that they will be able to settle down to the sanitized comfort of an inner life freed of stresses, pains, and ambiguities; it simply promises that through Christ, God will walk with us in all the dark places of life, that he has the power and the will to invest his promises with reality, and that even the shadows are made to serve his glory and our best interests. A therapeutic culture will be inclined to view such promises as something of a disappointment; those who understand that reality is at heart moral because God is centrally holy will be satisfied that this is all they need to know.

We will not be able to recover the vision and understanding of God's grandeur until we recover an understanding of ourselves as creatures who have been made to know such grandeur. This must begin with the recovery of the idea that as beings made in God's image, we are fundamentally *moral* beings, not consumers, that the satisfaction of our psychological needs pales in significance when compared with the enduring value of doing what is right. Religious consumers want to have a spirituality for the same reason that they want to drive a stylish and expensive auto. Costly obedience is as foreign to them in matters spiritual as self-denial is in matters material. In a culture filled with such people, restoring weight to God is going to involve much more than simply getting some doctrine straight; it's going to entail a complete reconstruction of the modern self-absorbed pastiche personality. The cost of accomplishing this may well be deep, sustained repentance. It is our modernity that must be undone. Only then will the full weight of the revealed truth about God rest once more on the soul. Only then will we recover our saltiness in the world. Only then will God genuinely be known again in his church.

The Danger in God

The second and complementary change, which I will be discussing at greater length in the remaining chapters, has to do with God himself.

There are different ways in which we might speak of this. If it is the case that today we are suffocated by anthropocentric religion, then we need to recover that which is theocentric. If ours is an age much delighted by divine immanence and much given to perversions of that immanence, then we need to recover a sense of God's transcendence. These are the terms in which the problems are traditionally described and, indeed, the terms in which I have been describing the problems thus far. In what follows, however, I am going to change the language. I believe we can best get at the reasons why modernity eviscerates the reality of divine transcendence and our need for theocratic religion by speaking of the God who is *outside*.

Scripture indicates that there are two aspects of the outside God's transcendence. On the one hand, God is transcendent because he is self-sufficient, owing nothing to the creation for his own life, and so powerful that he can always act within that creation. He is dependent on nothing outside of himself for the realization of his will but, because the creation is always and at every moment dependent upon him, he is always over it. On the other hand, he is transcendent because his utter moral purity separates him from all of human life and defines him in his essential character.

It is because God is self-sufficient that he can both sustain the creation without being acted upon by what he made (contrary to the assertions of the process theologians), and he can also act within it. These acts are both "natural" (a matter of his upholding what he has made) and "supernatural" (a matter of his revelation of his character, will, and intentions). These acts occurred in the flesh and bone of our history, as God called out a people for himself, redeeming and leading them and providing institutions and rubrics to sustain them spiritually and morally. In these acts, he tied the objectivity of his truth to the flow of our history in such a way that the meaning of the acts, which he himself supernaturally provided, could never be any less objective than the events of which they were a part. This was important then, and it is important now. Then pagans listened intently to discern the meaning of the gods' and goddesses' intentions; now moderns listen just as intently to inner voices with the help of psychology. The modern self has simply replaced ancient divinities as the presumed source of mystery and meaning. Meaning then was subjective and variable even as it is now. By contrast, the meaning of God as given in history was not: events had either happened or they had not. This framework of objective historical fact secured the public relevance of God's revealed truth and disallowed all the pagan habits of privatizing truth, just as it now disallows all comparable modern proclivities. As Wolfhart Pannenberg points out, the resurrection of Christ, which completed this line of redemptive acts, sounded out God's public judgment on all religious mythologies, not to mention all private intuitions not in accord with the truth it declares. These historical acts, the prophetic words by which their meaning was given, and the inspired implications that were drawn from what God had said constitute truth for all time, all ages, all cultures.

I believe that the church has lost the transcendent truth and goodness of God, and I believe that if it fails to recover this truth and goodness, Christianity will buckle completely under the strains that are being exerted upon it by modernity. I do not mean to suggest that this recovery will be anything other than dangerous, however, for there is an unyielding flintiness to the purposes of God. His redemptive presence, in truth and holiness, is found only on his terms, and these are very different from what comes most immediately and most naturally to modern minds. He stands resolute and unmovable between the meaning he provides of himself and of life's purposes and the caprices of private intuition and consumer appetite by which these would be taken captive. If we grasp the reality of God, it will be on his terms and not on our own. But without this, we can have no binding address, no revelation given once and for all and to all, no Christianity that is universal in the sense that it calls all to the same knowledge of God through the same Christ. And unless God is understood to be transcendent in his holiness, the world can have no objective moral meaning, no accountability beyond itself, no assurance of salvation from guilt through Christ's death, and, in the end, no assurance that God will be the final line of resistance to all that is evil. And without this assurance, the hope dies that one day truth will be put forever on the throne and evil forever on the scaffold.

This is what I have in mind in speaking of the outside God. The brush strokes here, however, have been too quick and too broad. Let us now turn to a more careful exploration.

CHAPTER 6

The Outside God

There are few dangers threatening the religious future more serious than the slow shallowing of the religious mind. . . . Our safety is in the deep. The lazy cry for simplicity is a great danger. It indicates a frame of mind which is only appalled at the great things of God, and a senility of faith which fears that which is high. Men complain that they are jaded and cannot rise to such matters. That may mean that the matters of the world absorb all the energies of the great side of the soul, that Divine things are no more than a comfort. And, if so, it means much for the future of religion, and much which is ominous. And the poverty of our worship amid its very refinements, its lack of solemnity . . . is the fatal index of the peril.

P. T. Forsyth

No one should doubt the overwhelming power of modernization. In the West, in particular, its presence is crushing, intrusive, and inescapable. It is a machine that we have loosed on ourselves. As it reshapes our external world, gathering momentum as it goes along, it is also creating a universal cliche culture. The values of this shallow culture are now intruding on the innermost parts of our lives with insistence and with intensity. There is nothing on the horizon yet that could arrest the progress of modernization or even divert it. The question is whether there is anything that can arrest our taste for modernity, our sense of being completely at home in this new culture. Our thirst for the blessings of the modern world is not easily slaked. Can the church survive the modern world and the worldliness that it brings?

Modernity is unquestionably seductive, and, in the end, it will always triumph unless the church sees through its charms and seductions and determines that it wants something else. A hunger for the endless blessings of our world is not inevitable; we do not have to construct our lives around having them. Addiction to modernity can be resisted by a strong and passionate mind that has been shaped by God's Word of truth and infused with a due sense of what is right. In short, the one sure defense against modernity's conquest of the church is God. As mighty as modernity is, God is mightier yet, and though the embrace of the modern world is strong and extensive, it is still possible, by the grace of God, to evade it. The power and seductiveness of modernity do not impede God one bit in actualizing his truth in the church, introducing his character into the lives of ordinary men and women, realizing his saving purposes in the world, and exercising providential control over its direction and outcomes.

There are those who would argue that this view of the relationship between social structures and inward belief is simply naive, that it vastly underestimates the capacity of those structures to determine inward belief. Marx taught, and many continue to believe, that we are merely mirrors of our external world. Modern sociologists of knowledge scoff at the notion that the work of God's revelation and grace can survive with some integrity within the forms of modern life. They maintain that as society becomes more modern, it necessarily becomes less religious, because modernity inexorably relocates God to its periphery, rendering him first impotent, then irrelevant, and finally invisible.

Only those who minimize the enormity of the power and reach of modernity will dismiss this contention as just another academic conceit. I am not one of these; if fact, I am willing to grant that these sociologists are almost entirely correct. If modernity does not overturn all religion, it at least succeeds in rearranging it in a manner much more to its liking and in a way that greatly deprives that religion of its essence. But I include in my analysis something that sociology as a formal discipline excludes: the reality and character of God. This reality enables Christian believers to stand outside their culture cognitively, morally, and spiritually. More than that, the holy God, the Giver of truth, enables them to stand *against* worldly culture. And it is just this kind of distance, this kind of dissociation from modernity, this kind of opposition to modernity as an essentially ungodly worldview that is indispensable to the preservation of Christian identity.

This is to speak much too generally, however, for, if my analysis so far is correct, there are countless Christians, of all kinds and shapes, for whom a belief in God has proved to be no deterrent at all to a thorough immersion in and embrace of modernity. It is not simply a belief in God of which I am speaking, then, but a belief in the *biblical* God, the God who was there before the first foundations of the modern world were laid and who will be there long after it has self-destructed or been overwhelmed. But even that is not enough. It is unhappily the case throughout the church today that belief in God, in his eternity, in his power to act in life, and in the sovereignty of his purposes has been mixed together with ideas that modernity insinuates or requires — ideas about the centrality of the self, the inviolability of its demands, the easy conquest it can secure over all problems, regardless of whether they are moral or spiritual in nature, so long as it employs the proper concepts and techniques. All of these sorry capitulations to modernity are allowed to go hand in hand with a belief in the biblical God. But that is how modernity works: it dislocates the significance of God from life so that professions of Christian belief are emptied of their power to shape *praxis*. In the everyday matrix of doing, modernity becomes sovereign, dictating how, why, and when things will be done; in the world of believing, God can still hold his place, but his place must be emptied of its significance. He may still be king, but his kingdom has been taken from him by the modern world. So it is not just any doctrine of God of which I am speaking here.

I believe that our attempts to resist modernity at a cognitive, moral, and spiritual level will be successful only if we address two dimensions of the modern understanding of God. In this chapter, I want to focus on the aspects of this understanding that have incurred the greatest *loss* in the modern period. In Chapter 7, I will focus on the aspects of this understanding that have been subjected to the greatest *abuse* in the modern period. Unless we take action on both fronts, we stand little chance of preserving historic Christian faith. What I am doing, then, might best be called remedial theology or, were the term not so abused, contextual theology. It is not my intent here to assemble a complete doctrine of God, nor to review all that Scripture says in this regard. I will simply attempt to point out some central tenets that are on the point of being lost and to bring into better focus some that are now blurred.

What damage has modernity done to the church's appropriation of the doctrine of God? I believe the greatest loss we have suffered is not a matter of any particular aspect of God but rather of his *place* in the church and, beyond that, in society. If modernity is successful in diminishing the reality of God, in emptying him of his significance by pushing him to the periphery of interest, then it will manage to strip the church of the one thing that makes it the church. The church is nothing if it does not belong to God, and it ceases to belong to him when it loses a full-blooded understanding of him, when it ceases to be fully obedient to him, when it no longer worships in awe before him, when it gives up faithful service in his name. The New Testament speaks of the church as the people of God (1 Pet. 2:9-10), the household of God (Eph. 2:19), the body of Christ (1 Cor. 12:27), the bride of Christ (Rev. 21:2), a new creation in Christ (2 Cor. 5:17): it is made, owned, impelled, authorized, guided, and nourished by God in Christ. If the church loses this sense of ownership and intimate relationship — its sense of identity as *God's* people — then it ceases to be church.

Paul stressed this point emphatically. God was the center from which his thought arose and to which it was always returning, for it was in God that Paul found the ultimate meaning of life, the reality of grace, and the wonder of boundless glory.[1] "Oh, the depth of the riches and wisdom and knowledge of God," he cried (Rom. 11:33; cf. 1 Cor. 1:24). And since Paul was always God-centered in his thought, in the nature of the case he had to be Christ-centered as well, for it was in Christ that God had taken human flesh, revealed himself, and achieved his conquest over sin, death, and the powers of evil. It was in Christ, God's Son, that Paul saw "the light of the knowledge of the glory of God" (2 Cor. 4:6). To be Christ-centered is to be God-centered.[2] And Christ is the center, head, and groom of the church, without whom it has no existence, no salvation, no destiny. So, Paul's thought ran from God to Christ to the church to the world and then back to God. How does modernity imperil this kind of vision?

The church's awareness that it belongs to God at once mentally, morally, and spiritually, is dependent on an awareness that God stands outside the currents of modernity and, in important ways, over against them. The fact that he is holy means there is an otherness to him. In the context of modernity, this moral otherness has been converted into a relatedness that is wholly compatible with the morality of modernity. That is to say, the church's identity vanishes where

1. See Leon Morris, *New Testament Theology* (Grand Rapids: Academie Books, 1986), pp. 25-38.

2. On John's theocentrism, see Eugene M. Boring, "The Theology of Revelation: The Lord Our God the Almighty Reigns," *Interpretation* 40 (July 1986): 257-69.

transcendence melts into immanence. Or, we might also say that it disappears where theocentric faith (i.e., faith centered on God as an objective reality) becomes anthropocentric faith (i.e., faith centered on therapeutic interest in the self). Or, finally, we might say in the language I propose to use here that the church's identity as a body belonging exclusively to God always crumbles when his "inside" relationship to life is made coordinate with the experiences of modernity and his "outside" relationship to life (as the holy One who stands over against finite and corrupt human beings) is lost.[3] Where this happens, God becomes merely a convenient means by which to satisfy the self. He becomes too small to sustain a moral and spiritual enterprise as demanding and as large as the church. He becomes too small to sustain faith in a world where the normative beliefs are overwhelmingly erroneous, to sustain goodness in a world that overwhelmingly champions badness, to sustain life in a world where death is inescapable. Where this happens, the church no longer belongs to God in anything other than name.

God Who Is Above

Biblical Texts

We need to begin our consideration of God as outside by taking note of a large family of texts that speak of the plenitude of God's being, his bright excess, his overwhelming largeness, and the far reaches of his being that exceed all human understanding. These texts declare that God is exalted, that he is "high," that he is "above." They celebrate the fact that God in his being, character, and will is not subject to the ebb and flow of life, to its limitations and distortions, that such is the power God has that even in a fallen world he is able to effect his will, exercise his sovereign control, and act in the fabric of its life. When he does so, however, his ways may sometimes seem dark and mysterious to finite sinners.

In this family, we might first note those texts that speak of the greatness of God's being and character, of his being elevated or "above" this world. The Psalmist declares that God dwells "on high," for ex-

3. I have drawn on and adapted the language of the God who is inside and the God who is outside from John E. Smith, "The External and Internal Odyssey of God in the Twentieth Century," *Religious Studies* 20 (March 1984): 43-54.

ample (113:5; cf. 99:2-3), that his "greatness is unsearchable" and he is "greatly to be praised" (145:3). Isaiah, who had seen him in a vision sitting on a throne, "high and lifted up" (6:1), returned to the implications of this vision later when he saw God effortlessly exercising complete sovereignty over all creation (40:12-14), over all of human history (40:15-20), and in the lives of individual people (40:21-26). Similar references appear throughout the New Testament (e.g., in Rom. 1:10; Eph. 1:4-5; Col. 4:12). Stephen expressed his confidence in God's sovereignty when he gave his final speech, calling him the "Most High" (Acts 7:48).

It is this God, elevated over all of life, from whom Christ came. In John's Gospel, the contrast is drawn especially sharply in two forms. John distinguishes between two realms in life, sometimes contrasting "glory" with "flesh" and sometimes contrasting what is "above" with what is "below." It was from the realm of glory that Christ descended (3:13; 6:33, 38; 10:38) to take flesh (1:13-14). On forty-two occasions, John describes Christ as having been "sent" into this world, leaving God who is above and coming below (3:17; 9:39; 10:36; 12:46; 16:28; 18:37). Many have subsequently stumbled at this point, perplexed over the relation between the Father who was left and the Son who came. Did they share the same divine being? Could there be different grades of divinity? Did the separation require some kind of distinction between the divinity of the Father and the Son? The New Testament shows no such perplexity. Luke characterizes Christ as "the Son of the Most High" (1:32); Paul, citing Psalm 68:18, states that after completing his work on the cross, Christ "ascended on high" (Eph. 4:8); and all the New Testament authors affirm both implicitly and explicitly that the godness of the Son was not different from that of the Father.[4] And

4. In the Pauline writing, e.g., there is a complete linguistic identification of Christ with Yahweh. If Yahweh is omnipresent (Ps. 139:7-10), our sanctifier (Exod. 31:13), our victory (Exod. 17:8-16), and our healer (Exod. 15:26), then Christ is all of these things, too (1 Cor. 1:30; Col. 1:27; Eph. 2:14). The gospel of God (1 Thess. 2:2, 8-9; Gal. 3:8) is likewise the gospel of Christ (1 Thess. 3:2). The church of God (Gal. 1:13; 1 Cor. 15:9) is the church of Christ (Rom. 16:16). The kingdom of God (1 Thess. 2:12) is the kingdom of Christ (Eph. 5:5). God's Spirit (1 Thess. 4:8) is Christ's Spirit (Phil. 1:19); God's peace (Gal. 5:22) is Christ's peace (Col. 3:15); God's day of judgment (Isa. 13:6) is Christ's day of judgment (Phil. 1:6, 10; 2:16; 1 Cor. 1:8); God's grace (Eph. 2:8-9; Col. 1:6; Gal. 1:15) is Christ's grace (1 Thess. 5:28; Gal. 1:6; 6:18); God's salvation (Col. 1:13) is Christ's salvation (1 Thess. 1:10); and God's will (Eph. 1:11; 1 Thess. 4:3; Gal. 1:4) is Christ's will (Eph. 5:17). So, it is no surprise to hear Paul say that he is both God's slave (Rom. 1:9) and Christ's slave (Rom. 1:1; Gal. 1:10), that he lives for the glory that is both God's (Rom. 5:2; Gal. 1:24) and Christ's (2 Cor. 8:19, 23; cf. 2 Cor. 4:6), that his

by the fourth century, in the Nicene Creed, the early church had finally secured this position against the heretical alternatives.

Second, and related to these biblical texts, are texts that speak directly of the painful and sometimes terrifying reality of God's utter moral purity. This, too, is part of his elevation, the reason for saying that he is "high" and "above." This clearly was part of what Isaiah saw in the temple when he was led to cry out, "Woe is me! For I am lost; for I am a man of unclean lips, and I dwell in the midst of a people of unclean lips; for my eyes have seen the King, the LORD of Hosts!" (6:5). He was struck by the dreadful peril that he and the rest of God's people were placed by this holy God, for this kind of holiness, of necessity, asserts itself against what is dark, wrong, perverse, and dis-obedient. And yet, a little later, Isaiah says, "I will wait for the LORD, who is hiding his face from the house of Jacob" (8:17). Later yet he says, "Truly, thou art a God who hidest thyself" (45:15). Why would a God whose holiness so awed Isaiah now seem to disappear? Some-times the answer to this painful dilemma is that God's absence, his "hiding," his inaccessibility in the realm "above" is itself an expression of his judgment: he judges by withdrawing his presence. Though Christ's cry of dereliction — "My God, my God, why hast thou forsaken me?" (Mark 15:34) — may, in some ways, be different, the awful sense of abandonment he felt in the moment when he took our sin upon himself was in part an experience of God's absence as judgment. At other times, however, God's judgment is more overt; the Old Testa-ment gives a running commentary of those moments through the centuries when God's holiness asserted itself against those who were arrogant, unbelieving, or disobedient.

Finally, there are texts acknowledging that God's ways often elude human understanding. Paul, for example, says that God's judgments are "unsearchable" and his ways "inscrutable" (Rom. 11:33). God's apparent absence from our lives is not always a matter of judgment; sometimes, it is just a matter of the strange, unfathomable outworkings of his providence. Sometimes sufferers facing circumstances that seem to herald the defeat or flight of God simply have to trust that he is indeed good, that he is indeed present. God's government of the world

---

faith is in God (1 Thess. 1:8-9; Rom. 4:1-5) and in Christ Jesus (Gal. 3:22), that to know God, which is salvation (Gal. 4:8-9; 1 Thess. 4:5), is to know Christ (2 Cor. 4:6). See Walter Elwell, "The Deity of Christ in the Writings of Paul," *Current Issues in Biblical and Patristic Interpretation,* ed. Gerald F. Hawthorne (Grand Rapids: Wil-liam B. Eerdmans, 1975), pp. 297-308.

is often morally opaque from our perspective, and it will be so until the final day. "Why dost thou stand afar off, O LORD?" asks the baffled psalmist; "Why dost thou hide thyself in times of trouble?" (10:1). And Job, in his long anguish and confusion, knew "the dread of a silent and an absent God."[5]

In Deuteronomy we learn that what is unrevealed will remain unknown: "The secret things belong to the LORD our God; but the things that are revealed belong to us and to our children for ever, that we may do all the words of this law" (29:29). The God of the Bible is the God who reveals himself — which is to say that revelation is not a matter of human discovery but of divine self-disclosure. And the fact is that God could have remained completely inaccessible to our understanding had he chosen to do so, that he could have concealed all that he is from us, and that he could have done this because he does not need us for his own completion. The fact that he did choose to reveal himself to us is explicable only on the grounds of his grace.[6]

Having looked briefly at this family of texts, we now need to look into their implications. What are the consequences of saying that God is on high, that he is elevated over all of creation, and that Christ, who had been "above," came "below"?

Historical Developments

Perhaps it is the case that prior to the advent of modern science, the distinction between what is "above" and what is "below" was understood literally and spatially by some.[7] Certainly John A. T. Robinson sought to persuade the Christian public, long after the advent of modern science, that this was still what they were expected to think.[8] But this is clearly not what the Bible has in mind. In a literal sense, if God is everywhere, as Scripture affirms him to be, then there can be no place where God is not, neither "above" nor "below," "near" nor "distant," "inside" life or "outside" it, a point celebrated with joyful wonder in Psalm 139. No, images like this are not telling us about the

---

5. Samuel Terrien, *The Elusive Presence: The Heart of Biblical Theology* (San Francisco: Harper & Row, 1978), p. 363.

6. See Emil Brunner, *The Mediator: A Study of the Central Doctrine of Christian Faith*, trans. Olive Wyon (New York: Macmillan, 1934), pp. 548-60.

7. For a full examination of this theme, see Karl Heim, *God Transcendent: Foundation for a Christian Metaphysic*, trans. Edgar Primrose Dickie (New York: Scribner's, 1936).

8. See Robinson, *Honest to God* (London: SCM Press, 1963), p. 13.

internal architecture of God — what in his being might be geographi-
cally proximate and what might be remote — but rather truths about
his *relation* to the world.[9] And it is here, using the image of God "above"
in its figurative rather than its literal sense, that the early Church
Fathers began a line of thought that has not always proved felicitous.
In fact, their pattern of thinking, rearranged by the effects of modernity within modern evangelicalism, has produced a festering and
enfeebled spirituality.

In order to distinguish Christ from the Father, the early Church
Fathers set the Trinity within a spatial framework. Moreover, their
thought was increasingly colored by philosophical notions,[10] setting up
talking points along the way with Plato, Philo, and Aristotle.[11] The
solution that they increasingly settled on was that the Father above is
remote and distant — so remote and so distant that he has to dispatch
intermediaries to do his work. He could not break the spell of his own
transcendence to create, reveal, and redeem and had to send Christ
to do so. Thus they developed a bipolar vision of God — one pole
distant and the other pole near, one pole absolute, cut off from life in
this world, and the other pole related and connected with life. The
Father was associated with the distant pole, and the Son with the near
pole. The Father lived in eternity, but the Son came into the world;
the Father's power was boundless, but the Son's was circumscribed; in

9. Rudolf Bultmann categorized this language as mythological since it was
an attempt to describe an otherworldly reality in terms of this world, as this world
was understood in a premodern setting. Myth thus becomes a cipher of transcendence. For his straightforward defense of his position, see Karl Jaspers and Rudolf
Bultmann, *Myth and Christianity: An Inquiry into the Possibility of Religion without Myth*
(New York: Noonday Press, 1958), pp. 57-71. Once the foundations were thus
shaken, the next logical step was to ask whether there is any known divine reality
that is outside and beyond purely empirical human experience. That step was taken
by Gordon Kaufman, among others, in *God the Problem* (Cambridge: Harvard
University Press, 1972), pp. 41-81. Thomas Luckman has approached the matter
sociologically, arguing that modernity forces people to look for divine transcendence
within. As transcendence in any traditional meaning thus fades, the religion of
immanence flourishes. "Modern religious consciousness," says Luckman, "is characterized by a radically shrunken span of transcendence," and this demands a
redefinition of the sacred ("Shrinking Transcendence, Expanding Religion?" *Sociological Analysis* 51 [Summer 1990]: 135).

10. Cyril C. Richardson, *The Doctrine of the Trinity* (Nashville: Abingdon Press,
1958), pp. 19-27.

11. See W. R. Matthews, *God in Christian Thought and Experience* (London:
Nisbet, 1935), pp. 95-102. For a treatment of the theological meaning rather than
the philosophical content of the transcendence of God, see G. L. Prestige, *God in
Patristic Thought* (London: S.P.C.K., 1959), pp. 25-54.

the Son we see divine compassion and mercy, but in the Father we see only judgment.[12]

Once this polarity became settled in patristic minds, it was but a simple move to think of Christ as the one who was sacrificed and the Father as the one who sacrificed him. It took centuries more for this to blossom into a full-scale conflict between holiness and love. Still, this early distinction did introduce a clear gap within the Godhead, with the Father on the one side and the Son on the other.

This solution became severely strained during the Middle Ages, as traditional piety began to shift Christ himself in some small degree toward the pole of the Father's awesome distance, moving the whole of the godhead further away from human life. This produced an anguished spiritual emptiness and the perception of a need for a new intermediary or intercessor. Mary became the first candidate for this role of bridging the gap that now yawned not simply between the first and second persons in the godhead but also between the sinner and Christ. It was assumed that when Mary approached Christ, her Son, she could expect a far more gracious reception than common sinners, and Christ, in turn, could approach the yet more distant Father on their behalf.

This bureaucracy of intercession remained largely settled throughout the Middle Ages. A simple unquestioning acceptance of the doctrine, rather than any inherent conceptual connections, served to hold it together. But it exacted a fearsome toll on the church and its piety along the way. Martin Luther, who was raised in this piety, has given poignant and eloquent expression to the perplexities that he experienced prior to coming to a more biblical understanding of Christ and of justification.[13] In many places in his writings he speaks of his *Anfechtung,* the terrible burden of unrelieved anxiety that arose from his guilt and the seeming inaccessibility of God's grace:

---

12. The widespread acceptance of this arrangement explains why Arianism came so close to capturing the mind of the early church, for it posited an ontological chasm between Father and Son. This was rejected at Nicea in A.D. 325, but in 360 all previous credal symbols were disavowed and it was stated simply that the Son "was like the Father who begot him" — which was simply a different way of incorporating elements of dissimilarity into the godhead. It was not until A.D. 381, at the Council of Constantinople, that Nicea was reaffirmed and the ontological distinctions between Father and Son finally disavowed. But that did not prevent a fresh outbreak of Arian thinking with respect to the Holy Spirit.

13. See Gordon Rupp, *Luther's Progress to the Diet of Worms* (New York: Harper Torchbooks, 1964).

Hell is no more hell, if you can cry to God. . . . But nobody would ever believe how hard that is, to cry unto the Lord. Weeping and wailing, trembling and doubting, we know all about them. But to cry unto the Lord, that is beyond us. For our bad conscience and our sin press down on us, and lie so about our necks, so badly that we feel the Wrath of God: and the whole world could not be so heavy as that burden. In short, for our nature alone, or for the ungodly it is impossible to stand against such things and cry out to God himself, who is there in his anger and punishment and not go elsewhere.[14]

Nor did Luther find his approach to Christ to be any easier. "I knew Christ as none other than a stern judge, from whose face I wanted to flee, and yet could not," he wrote. "I used to turn pale, when I heard the name Christ." And again, "I have often been terrified by the name of Christ, and when I saw him on the Cross, it was a lightning stroke to me."[15] All of Luther's anxiety was finally resolved by his discovery of Paul's explication of the doctrine of justification and God's complete conquest over his own wrath in the person of his Son, through whom freedom from judgment is offered by grace through faith.

Nevertheless, this polarized understanding of the being of God that Luther inherited was not entirely set aside. It was simply translated into new terms — into the rhetoric of God "revealed" and God "hidden" — rhetoric still firmly planted in the medieval distinction between the Father remotely "above" and the Son "below." Luther characterized God's love as his "proper work" and his wrath as his "strange work." Because he associated the Father more closely with the latter, and the Son with the former,[16] Luther set up a conflict between the God who was revealed (the God of love) and the God who is hidden (the God of wrath). He never felt the need to resolve the contradictions inherent in this understanding; to the contrary, he seemed to revel in the paradox. Perhaps the explanation for this is that the stark and awesome conflict he perceived within the being of God — Father against Son, wrath against love — resonated deeply with his own psychological passage into faith. Outside of Christ, there was only darkness

---

14. Luther, quoted by Gordon Rupp in *The Righteousness of God: Luther Studies* (London: Hodder & Stoughton, 1953), p. 112.

15. Luther, quoted by Rupp in *The Righteousness of God*, p. 145.

16. See Philip Watson, *Let God Be God! An Interpretation of the Theology of Martin Luther* (Philadelphia: Fortress Press, 1947), pp. 132-37, 152-60.

and anguish; inside Christ, there was peace and light, a resolution of the horrifying and relentless guilt he had experienced.

On the Reformed side, matters were handled rather more cautiously. Nevertheless, when the Puritans later took their Calvinism to New England, they reintroduced the old polarity between God as absolute and God as related, between the Father and the Son. The scarce and tenuous ties between the two sides of God in this formulation rendered it inherently fragile, and when the Puritan experiment came to an end, it finally disintegrated, producing two entirely different kinds of belief. On the one side there emerged a Deism with a remote God, cool rationalism, and complete loss of christological interest. On the other side, there emerged modern evangelicalism, which looked to a God "invested with all the gospel's transformative passion" but with a greatly diminished aura of transcendence — the God "below," warmer, closer, more engaging, and more susceptible to be translated into a purely private deity.[17] In other words, evangelicals tended to dispense with God's otherness in the interests of promoting his relatedness through Christ and gospel faith. As we have already noted, this move was greatly accelerated during the nineteenth century by the increasing popularity of the democratic paradigm. A long series of powerful revivals sought to produce deep experience of the God within but all too often ignored the outside God, the knowledge of whom provides the only sure defense against the seductions of culture, to settle for false religious experience. God's otherness was increasingly lost, his immanence was cut loose from his transcendence, and today, under modernity's gathering momentum, these developments have been pressed yet further to produce a form of believing that is hollowing out the meaning of God.[18]

17. See Robert W. Jenson, *America's Theologian: A Recommendation of Jonathan Edwards* (New York: Oxford University Press, 1988), p. 11.

18. Peter Berger has proposed a twofold religious typology entailing "confrontation with the divine" (typified by Judaism, Christianity, and Islam) and "interiority of the divine" (typified by Hinduism and Buddhism). The former tends to offer divine transcendence without immanence, and the latter immanence without transcendence (see *The Heretical Imperative: Contemporary Possibilities of Religious Affirmation* [Garden City, N.Y.: Doubleday, 1979], pp. 168-81). Among the weaknesses in this typology is the fact that the line between the two types does not fall exclusively between East and West. There is much within Western Christian faith that, for entirely different reasons, also draws on the ostensibly Eastern "interiority." Emil Brunner has argued that the old Platonic and neo-Platonic thought that dominated medieval mysticism reappeared at the Enlightenment to produce ideas of universal "interior" religion and that this vision found new life again in Protestant liberalism. He expressed his own antipathy to this Western religion of

Boundaries

In order to redress this situation and think carefully about the biblical doctrine of God, it might be prudent to begin by establishing some boundaries. There are four points in particular that set out the parameters within which any biblical doctrine must be constructed.

First, while the Father and Son must be personally distinguished from one another, they cannot be disengaged, because they each fully share the same divine nature. Holiness, then, ought not to be associated exclusively or even predominantly with the Father, nor love with the Son. Jesus may address his Father as "Holy Father" (John 17:11) but the Father cannot be other than the God of love (1 John 4:16; 2 Cor. 13:11; 2 Thess. 3:5) whose love Jesus cites (Luke 11:42; John 5:42). And, while Jesus embodied God's love, he was not other than completely holy. Indeed, it may well be the case that the New Testament increasingly identified Christ's Spirit, who was sent to be "another Counselor" (John 14:16), as the *Holy* Spirit because it recognized in the Spirit the holiness it had seen in the Son. And it is by this *Holy* Spirit, Paul tells us, that "God's love has been poured into our hearts" (Rom. 5:5). We must not pit God's love against his holiness by identifying them exclusively with different members of the godhead. The Father, Son, and Holy Spirit are equally holy, equally loving.

Second, in a similar vein, Father and Son must not be set in opposition to one another with respect to their accomplishment of salvation. It is true that the Father "sent" the Son, "gave" his Son to

---

"interiority" as follows: "Religion without a Mediator . . . tries to incorporate the Christian faith into itself, by the assertion that what the Christian regards as essential, that is, relation to a unique historical event, is a non-essential psychological and educational aid to faith which can be discarded when we reach maturity. At this point the two views confront each other in opposite camps; here there can be no reconciliation. Only one of these views can be true" (*The Mediator: A Study in the Central Doctrine of the Christian Faith,* trans Olive Wyon [New York: Macmillan, 1934], p. 34). Berger is aware of this, too. He suggests that in America today one must choose either to be a "wimp" (following the religion of interiority, which makes concessions to modern culture) or a "thug" (following the religion of confrontation, which makes nonnegotiable religious demands). See *A Far Glory: The Quest for Faith in an Age of Credulity* (New York: Free Press, 1992), p. 149.

There is no doubt that the human heart, and not merely the *modern* heart, has persistently sought to sever the ties between what is transcendent and what is immanent. Still, modernity tends to do so a good deal more energetically. For an ancient illustration of this out of the book of Jeremiah, see Werner E. Lemke, "The Near and Distant God: A Study of Jer. 23:23-24 in Its Biblical Theological Setting," *Journal of Biblical Literature* 100 (December 1981): 541-55.

the world, but it is also true that the Son, by the Spirit, "offered himself without blemish to God" in his death (Heb. 9:14; cf. Matt. 26:36-46). While there was a penal dimension to Christ's death in that he bore in himself God's righteous judgment upon sin, it would be quite wrong to picture this in terms of the Son being led helpless to his death against his will. No, Father and Son were united in the common cause of saving those who were lost, and they had been so united from eternity (Acts 2:23).

Third, the New Testament does not allow for the possibility of pursuing the new pluralistic theological strategy of moving away from Christ-centered faith toward God-centered faith.[19] The reason, quite simply, is that the incarnation is fundamentally important: we know God only through Jesus. The permanent bonding of divine and human in Christ cannot be sundered. It is unacceptable to claim that Christ is anonymously manifested in other religions that specifically deny the particularity of that revelation in Christ. Jesus was not simply an exemplar of the truly religious person, an individual in whom God was specially coming to consciousness. On the contrary, he was the one who had come from God. The New Testament christology is a christology from above. How else would he have been able to reveal the nature and will of his Father? A Christ who was less than pre-existent, less than fully divine, or unaware of who he was would not have been able to reveal the Father or to redeem sinners.[20]

The only way in which we can be God-centered, then, is to be

19. Arnold Toynbee rightly predicted that the exclusive nature of Christianity's truth claim — what he calls a "family infirmity" — would become increasingly difficult to sustain as the twentieth century went along (*An Historian's Approach to Religion* [London: Oxford University Press, 1956], p. 11). Theologically, however, Protestantism's new infatuation with world religions is probably rooted in Barth, who, despite his animosity toward religion in general, nevertheless gave the impression of being more than a little interested in universalism. The logical consequence of his thought in this area, despite all protestation to the contrary, is that personal faith tied to the history of Jesus is not in the end necessary, a conclusion already intimated in his *Evangelical Theology: An Introduction*, trans. Grover Foley (London: Weidenfeld & Nicolson, 1963), pp. 15-62. Many of the early proponents of the new pluralistic theologies on the Protestant side were former Barthians. On subsequent developments, see Harold Netland, *Dissonant Voices: Religious Pluralism and the Question of Truth* (Grand Rapids: William B. Eerdmans, 1991); and Carl E. Braaten, *No Other Gospel: Christianity among the World's Religions* (Minneapolis: Fortress Press, 1992).

20. See James Denney, *Studies in Theology* (London: Hodder & Stoughton, 1908), pp. 61-62. This concept of Christ's pre-existence is frontally attacked by Karl-Joseph Kuschel in *Born Before All Time? The Dispute over Christ's Origin*, trans. John Bowden (New York: Crossroad, 1992).

Christ-centered, for God is salvifically known nowhere else (Acts 2:36-38; 4:12; 13:26-41; 17:29-31). It is popularly argued to the contrary that to be Christ-centered is to be other than God-centered because it excludes all religious options other than Christianity and hence excludes much of what God is doing in the world today. Whatever the attractions of this argument, it is simply unscriptural. It makes the reality of God diffuse, assails the uniqueness of his revelation in Christ, dispenses with Christ's saving death, and upends the premise of the entire biblical narrative, which is that God alone has reality, while the gods and goddesses of the pagans are nonentities. The New Testament unequivocally sounds the note of Christ's uniqueness, the clarion call of historical particularity, which vitiates every other religious claim.

Finally, we need to respect the relationship between what God has revealed to us and what he has kept hidden. It is, of course, true that God has not revealed everything to us — and even if he had, our finitude and sin would prevent us from fully comprehending it. But we can be assured that there is nothing in what remains hidden that will contradict what he has revealed to us. Moreover, as Wolfhart Pannenberg has noted, the tension between what is hidden and what is revealed is only temporary. "At the end of history," he writes, ". . . the God who is hidden in his overruling of history and in individual destinies [will] finally be universally known to be the same as the God who is revealed in Jesus Christ."[21] This has some fairly severe implications for mysticism. People who are attracted to mysticism usually assume that what is hidden in God is other than what is revealed, or that it is deeper or more interesting or spiritually nourishing. Such assumptions are as much in error in their way as the assumptions of the pluralists are in theirs.[22]

---

21. Pannenberg, *Systematic Theology*, vol. 1, trans. Geoffrey Bromiley (Grand Rapids: William B. Eerdmans, 1991), pp. 339-40. On his doctrine of God, see Herbert Burhenn, "Pannenberg's Doctrine of God," *Scottish Journal of Theology* 28 (1975): 535-49.

22. In the New Testament, "mystery" is typically associated with what is revealed and proclaimed (1 Tim. 3:9), never with what is obscure and unknown. The chief mystery is Christ (1 Cor. 2:2), promised long ago (1 Cor. 1:19), by whom the Gentiles now gain access to the Father (Eph. 3:14-15), and to whom Paul was bound in service (1 Cor. 9:16). To associate this mystery with the unknown rather than the known would be, as Eberhard Jüngel suggests, to render God unthinkable. "The strictest reference to God as mystery would then probably have to be a finger placed to the lips" (*God as the Mystery of the World: On the Foundation of the Theology of the Crucified One in the Dispute between Theism and Atheism*, trans. Darrell L. Guder [Grand Rapids: William B. Eerdmans, 1983], p. 251). See also A. E. Harvey, "The Use of Mystery Language in the Bible," *Journal of Theological Studies* 31 (October

Within these boundaries, then, I wish to look at two aspects of God's otherness that the church has lost, despite formal professions to the contrary — losses that I believe have provided modernity with easy access into the mind and heart of Christian people. I am referring to God's holiness and his knowledge, both of which are unlike anything that is to be found naturally in life.[23] Though they are both aspects of his transcendence, they must not be construed as belonging to what is remote or distant in God but must rather be understood as part of the means by which he confronts sinners directly and inescapably from without.[24] This is to say that they are profound and sometimes painful parts of the life of the church.

God the Holy

The Irrelevance of Holiness

Why does God's holiness weigh so lightly upon us? I see three main reasons.

First, it should be remembered that God in general, under the conditions of modernity, weighs lightly on everyone, that he has been so marginalized that his character and revealed will make few real intersections with the stuff of everyday life. Modernity makes him

---

1980): 320-36. Nevertheless, a fascination with mystery remains at the heart of interreligious dialogue. Heinrich Ott has argued, e.g., that there are numerous religions moved "by the same inexplicable mystery" ("Does the Notion of 'Mystery' — as Another Name for God — Provide a Basis for a Dialogical Encounter between Religions?" in *God: The Contemporary Discussion*, ed. Frederick Sontag and M. Darrol Bryant [New York: Rose of Sharon Press, 1982], p. 15). The role that mystery is accorded in Eastern religions makes such a proposal fairly encouraging, since much is unrevealed and hidden in Eastern concepts of the divine. But the proper Christian understanding of mystery as completely consistent with what is revealed clearly undercuts the proposal.

23. For a useful overview of the character of these two aspects of God's transcendent otherness, see Alan P. Sell, "Transcendence, Immanence and the Supernatural," *Journal of Theology for Southern Africa* 26 (March 1979): 56-66.

24. Protestants of all ages today tend not to dwell much on these aspects of God's transcendence. They are, on the whole, a good deal more interested in softer images of God associated with his immanence. Recent surveys indicate that, in order of preference, they think of God as creator, healer, friend, redeemer, father, master, king, judge, lover, liberator, mother, and spouse. See Wade Clark Roof, "Review of Polls: Images of God among Americans," *Journal of the Scientific Study of Religion* 23 (June 1984): 201-5.

irrelevant, and his holiness is rendered irrelevant along with the rest of his character. God's holiness often weighs lightly on us, for this reason, even when we can assemble all of the appropriate biblical passages and make the right confessions about their importance.

Second, the learning of virtue is so painful and haphazard an affair, attended by such a wild profusion of good intentions, grievous falls, unrequited hopes, gnawing regrets, shame, and embarrassment that we are often of two minds about the matter (cf. Rom. 7:13-25). Corrupted human nature does not take kindly to the venture and is likewise unenthusiastic about what drives the undertaking — namely, God's holiness. Paul declares that fallen human nature "is hostile to God; it does not submit to God's law, indeed it cannot" (Rom. 8:7). And our disinclination to seek virtue and form a godly character — a disinclination we know as a constant presence — clouds our perception of God and saps our interest in him and his holiness.

In fact, this moral disinclination can actually take on the appearance of a virtue in Our Time, making it that much more difficult to detect and hence to resist. I am referring to our unflagging preoccupation with psychological wholeness as a substitute for holiness. Faced with an epidemic of lying, theft, abuse, rape, and general depravity, we are more inclined to attribute the problems to the criminal's bad self-image than to bad character. Even in the church, the story is not much different. We have taken hold of the language of our therapeutic culture, from which moral responsibility has now more or less vanished, insisting that our preachers serve up psychological wisdom in place of biblical truth, and we have ended up with a form of Christian faith in which the holiness of God has little significance.

One of the surest signs of this deep cultural transition, though by no means the only one, is the ubiquitous language of victimhood that is heard both in society and in the church. There are, to be sure, genuine victims in our society — people who have actually been robbed, raped, beaten, and defrauded. But the number of those who *claim* to be victims, often on grounds as flimsy as gossamer wings, is rising exponentially and is attended by a vast new grievance literature. Our offices, factories, campuses, and homes are filled to capacity with pseudo-victims whose clamor obscures the troubling realities that real victims face. When everyone is a victim, the pain and grief of any individual becomes banal, unexceptional. Genuine victims are completely trivialized. What has brought this about? The explanation is no doubt complex, but at its heart is an unhappy union of hypersensitivity to individual rights and an associated refusal by individuals to take responsibility for their actions. The people of Our Time are strongly inclined to trace all internal confusion, pain, disappointment, or lost advantage back to someone else's door.

Charles Sykes introduces his study of this phenomenon in American culture with a string of anecdotes. An FBI agent who was fired for embezzling from the government, and who lost his ill-gotten gain at the gambling tables, was later reinstated because his love of money was judged to be the sort of "handicap" against which Federal law prohibited discrimination. A school district employee who was fired for being perpetually late mounted a legal defense based on the premise that he suffered from "chronic lateness syndrome." A professor in a Midwestern college wrote an essay detailing his experience of being treated as a minority and a social outcast. He is persecuted, he said, because he is a bicycle rider, and he concludes by putting disrespect for bicyclists on a par with cross burning, gay bashing, and anti-Semitic vandalism.[25]

This spiral into pervasive victimhood, now epidemic on college campuses and in other strongholds of the politically correct, marks a corresponding erosion of personal responsibility, and suggests that genuine moral discourse about what is right and wrong, irrespective of private interests, is increasingly less possible. Contemporary culture has so diminished our moral capacity, so robbed us of a concern to act responsibly, that we tend to resent moral demands from without or simply to dismiss them out of hand. To the extent that the church's garments have been soiled by this aspect of modernity, it will be that much less inclined to dwell on the holiness of God.

Third, Christians in Our Time sometimes act as though they were the first to recognize that God is a God of love. Of course the Bible tells us that God is love, but the Christians of modernity seem to think that this constitutes an adequate theology in itself, that God is fundamentally if not exclusively love — and hence that talk of divine holiness is distracting or intrusive. Protestant liberalism pioneered this displacement of God's holiness in the nineteenth century,[26] but in this century evangelicals have taken up with distressing

---

25. Sykes, *A Nation of Victims: The Decay of American Character* (New York: St. Martin's Press, 1992), p. 4.

26. See, e.g., Adolf Harnack, *What Is Christianity?* trans. Thomas Bailey Saunders (New York: Putnam, 1901), pp. 78ff. Cf. Anders Nygren, *Essence of Christianity*, trans. Philip Watson (Philadelphia: Muhlenberg Press, 1961), pp. 113-23.

carelessness the wholesale reordering of the Christian faith that it introduced, from the meaning of Christ's atonement to the meaning of Christian sanctification.

Today there is resistance to the tenet that has been most characteristic of Protestant thought since the earliest days of the Reformation — namely, that holiness fundamentally defines the character of God and that love is not an alternative to it but, rather, an expression of it. This must be so. If God's holiness is his utter purity, his incomparable goodness, the measure of all that is true and right, the final line of resistance to all that is wrong, dark, and malignant, then love must be a part of this. If love is virtuous and right, it must be an expression of divine holiness, the essence of which is truth and right. God's love is inescapably a manifestation of his holiness, as are his goodness, righteousness, mercy, and compassion. Holiness is what defines God's character most fundamentally, and a vision of this holiness should inspire his people and evoke their worship, sustain their character, fuel their passion for truth, and encourage persistence in efforts to do his will and call on his name in petitionary prayer.

We can be certain of the seriousness of this intrusion of modernity into the life of the church because the sort of religious talk associated with it constitutes a significant departure from the language of the Bible. Modernity's God is not nearly so morally angular as the God of the Bible. His sharp edges have all been ground down to make him less threatening, more comfortable, more tame. He is rarely perceived as the God of the outside who, in his awesome greatness, summons his people to worship, to hear that Word of truth that they cannot find within themselves or their world, to become agents of righteousness in a world that scorns this righteousness as alien and contrary. Robbed of such a God, worship loses its awe, the truth of his Word loses its ability to compel, obedience loses its virtue, and the church loses its moral authority. Why has this happened? Because it is the easiest route to take. The habits and appetites of modernity are more attractive than the sacrifice and discipline of orthodox faith. God's love seems less burdensome than his holiness. The church has succumbed to the seductions of our therapeutic culture, and in that context it seems quite natural to favor the relational dimension over the moral dimension, mysticism over cognitive conviction, self-fulfillment over personal surrender, self-image over character, pluralistic religious equality over the uniqueness of the Christian faith. When all is said and done, modernity dispatches the God who is outside, and all that remains is the God who is inside.

The Stranger in Our World

As Walter Eichrodt has suggested, a Christian faith "which has ceased to be aware of this ultimate fact of the opposition between God and his creatures, would have lost that note of absolute urgency without which the Gospel entrusted to it can never be other than unthinking and superficial."[27] The gospel of Our Time frequently is unthinking and superficial, frequently is believed and preached without urgency, and the reason is that it has yet to dawn on many in the church that God in his holiness is deeply and irrevocably set in opposition to the world because of its sin.

It is time to recover the biblical emphasis on the fact that God is in his very essence holy. The Bible "does not begin," Carl Henry notes, "like liberal theology, with an emphasis on divine love for the sinner to which divine wrath is and must be subordinated";[28] it begins with God's indignation at the fall into sin, which was an expression of his holiness. When James Moffatt wrote that "apart from the redeeming action of the Lord Jesus Christ, the early Church evidently saw no ground whatsoever for believing in a God of love,"[29] he exaggerated and identified himself with a view that the early church had in fact refused to accept. Nonetheless, his view is no more of a misunderstanding than its opposite, which in practice is widely assumed, that because of Christ's work there is no need to take God's holiness into account.

When God revealed himself as Israel's God, he spoke first from the burning bush to Moses: "Do not come near; put off your shoes from your feet, for the place on which you are standing is holy ground. . . . And Moses hid his face, for he was afraid to look at God" (Exod. 3:5-6). It was as holy that God had thus disclosed himself. In fact, this is God's characteristic revelation of himself in the Old Testament. As A. B. Davidson put it, holiness was "what he was in his being."[30] According to Louis Berkhof, holiness is "co-extensive with, and applicable to, everything that can be predicated of God."[31] J. Rodman Williams states that holiness

27. Eichrodt, *Theology of the Old Testament*, 2 vols., trans. J. A. Baker (Philadelphia: Westminster Press, 1961), 1:277.

28. Henry, *God, Revelation and Authority*, 6 vols. (Waco: Word Books, 1976-83), 6:325.

29. Moffatt, *Love in the New Testament* (London: Hodder & Stoughton, 1929), p. 5.

30. Davidson, *The Theology of the Old Testament* (Edinburgh: T. & T. Clark, 1911), p. 151.

31. Berkhof, *Systematic Theology* (London: Banner of Truth, 1959), p. 73.

"is the fundamental fact about God."[32] Anthony Hoekema writes that the holiness of God "is not so much a separate attribute as a qualification of all that God is and does."[33] And Barth says that the Holy One of Israel "is the most exact description of the name of Yahweh which determines the whole history of Israel."[34]

Perhaps the best place to start our consideration of God's holiness is with a review of those aspects of his character that most astounded the ancient Israelites, the things they considered to be most odd about Yahweh. Theodorus Vriezen has pointed out that the Old Testament frequently speaks of *knowing* God (e.g., in Hos. 6:6; 2:20, 22; 4:1; 5:4; Isa. 1:3). But what did this knowing entail? It involved more than just a philosophical comprehension of his existence. Certainly it included acknowledgment of God's existence, but it integrated into this awareness an acknowledgment of certain aspects of his character. For example, those who know God are inclined to walk humbly before him (Mic. 6:8), to be morally circumspect and reverent — that is to say, they will be inclined to demonstrate an appropriate "fear of the LORD" (Ps. 111:10; Prov. 1:7; Job 28:28). Why was this? And why did the Old Testament see this knowledge as properly penetrating the heart, shaping the life, and becoming part and parcel of thinking, being, and acting? It was because God is centrally holy.[35] Living in the midst of paganism (and not infrequently falling into it themselves), the Israelites could hardly have helped noticing that the holiness of Yahweh was different from that of the pagan gods and goddesses in at least three important ways.

First, God's holiness carries with it the demand of *exclusive* loyalty to him. This was formulated in the first of the Ten Commandments (Exod. 20:1-3), and it stood in striking contrast to what the Israelites saw around them. The surrounding pagan cults, says Gerhard von Rad, "were on easy terms with one another and left devotees a free hand to ensure a blessing for themselves from other gods as well."[36]

---

32. Williams, *Renewal Theology: God, the World and Redemption* (Grand Rapids: Academie Books, 1988), p. 59.

33. Hoekema, "The Attributes of God: The Communicable Attributes," in *Basic Christian Doctrines,* ed. Carl F. H. Henry (Grand Rapids: Baker Book House, 1971), p. 31.

34. Barth, *Church Dogmatics,* 5 vols., ed. Thomas F. Torrance, trans. Geoffrey Bromiley (Edinburgh: T. & T. Clark, 1936-77), II/1:363.

35. Theodorus Vriezen, *An Outline of Old Testament Theology,* trans. S. Neuijen (Newton, Mass.: G. Branford, 1961), pp. 153-57.

36. Von Rad, *Old Testament Theology,* 2 vols., trans. D. M. G. Stalker (New York: Harper & Row, 1965), 1:208.

The Israelites were allowed no such free hand because, as Hosea was to reveal, God in holiness loves with the deep, exclusive passion of a lover who will tolerate no rivals. This is why worldliness in the New Testament — the infatuation with what is fallen and fading in culture — is characterized as unfaithfulness (James 4:4). The love of the world and the love of God are mutually exclusive in an absolute sense: we must choose either one or the other, but we cannot have both (cf. 1 John 2:15-17).

Second, throughout the ancient Near East, holiness was more commonly ascribed to people, articles, and places than to gods and goddesses. The Old Testament presentation of God's holiness constituted a radical departure on this point, specifically reversing this arrangement. God alone is holy; whatever holiness is associated with persons, places, and articles derives not from what they are in themselves but only from the fact that they have been separated for use in the service of Yahweh.[37] This begins to get us to the heart of what holiness entails. It is not something that is first and foremost found in the depths of human experience. It is not our sense of mystery about life magnified many times over, nor our awe before the abyss of what is unknown, nor what is beyond reason, nor any of the other facets that Rudolf Otto suggested.[38] It is, rather, what originates only in God. Therefore, as von Rad observes, it is "the great stranger in the human world" that cannot be correlated with any aspect of human experience that is at home in this fallen world.[39] It comes as something alien, other, and outside the fabric of life. It comes with God. It is what he is in his essential being and character; it is what caused the psalmists and prophets to describe him as high and lofty.

Third, this loftiness in Yahweh, this burning purity, goes hand in hand with tenderness — another marked contrast between him and the pagan gods and goddesses. Through Isaiah, for example, Yahweh identifies himself as "the high and lofty One who inhabits eternity," the one "whose name is Holy," who dwells "in the high and holy place" — but who also dwells "with him who is of a contrite and humble spirit" (57:15; cf. Ps. 25:11; 79:9; Jer. 14:7, 9). The same prophet who describes God as exalted also declares that God is so near that no storm of trouble will overwhelm those who trust in him and that he will hold

---

37. Eichrodt, *Theology of the Old Testament,* 1:272.

38. See Otto, *The Idea of the Holy: An Inquiry into the Non-rational Factor in the Idea of the Divine and Its Relation to the Rational,* trans. John W. Harvey (New York: Oxford University Press, 1958).

39. Von Rad, *Old Testament Theology,* 1:205.

Israel's hand (Isa. 41:13; 42:6).[40] These two themes — the un-blemished purity of God for which he is so exalted and the consequence of this, his tenderness and compassion, increasingly appear together and are joined in the covenant. Indeed, as A. B. Davidson observed, while some might imagine tension between these two aspects, they are in fact integrally connected: "The Old Testament puts it differently — a righteous God, and *therefore* a Savior. It is His own righteousness that causes Him to bring in righteousness."[41] If it is God's holiness that reveals sin to be sin, says P. T. Forsyth, it is also God's holiness "that necessitates the work of Christ, that calls for it, and that provides it."[42] And John Piper argues that Christ's suffering "was the measure of his love for the Father's glory. It was the Father's righteous allegiance to his own name that made recompense for sin necessary." When the Son "took the suffering of that recompense upon himself," he declared that the glory of God was to be preserved and proclaimed against all that sin had sought to do in undermining it.[43]

These lessons about God's consuming and exclusive holiness were not easy to learn, and the Israelites frequently stumbled over what was unique in the God they served. There were two aspects of God's tutelage that they found particularly difficult to accept. These were important points then, and they are equally important for us today as we begin in our understanding at a place that is in many ways as remote from the actual reality of God as was that of these ancient Israelites.

First, we note that God's holiness and majesty belong together and interpret one another. In his majesty, God is separated and cut off from those who are finite and corrupted, and a sense of separation appropriately carries over into the language used to describe his holi-

40. See Norman Snaith, "God: Transcendent and Immanent," *Expository Times* 68 (December 1956): 68-71.

41. Davidson, *The Theology of the Old Testament*, p. 144.

42. Forsyth, *The Work of Christ* (London: Independent Press, 1938), p. 79. The requirements of God's holiness explain the way in which Christ's death is interpreted in the New Testament. In his death as our substitute, Christ reconciled us to the Father from whom we were alienated, bearing in himself God's righteous judgment, expiating our sin, propitiating God's wrath, and clothing us in righteousness that is alien to us and without which we could not stand in God's holy presence. These themes — reconciliation, propitiation, justification — are ably elaborated by Leon Morris in *The Apostolic Preaching of the Cross* (Grand Rapids: William B. Eerdmans, 1965) and *The Cross in the New Testament* (Grand Rapids: William B. Eerdmans, 1965); and by John R. Stott in *The Cross of Christ* (Downers Grove, Ill.: InterVarsity Press, 1986).

43. Piper, *The Pleasures of God: Meditations on God's Delight in Being God* (Portland: Multnomah Press, 1991), p. 176.

ness. Thus Moses was led to ask, "Who is like thee, O LORD, among the gods? Who is like thee, majestic in holiness, terrible in glorious deeds, doing wonders?" (Exod. 15:11). The holiness psalms (93, 96–99) convey the essence of God's reign by saying that he is "robed in majesty," that "honor and majesty, beauty and strength" go before him, that his name is "great and terrible," and that he is "a lover of justice." In passages such as these, God's holiness is more or less synonymous with his awesome majesty, his greatness, his power. However, there is also a profound moral aspect to this majesty. The reason that God is separate, high, and lifted up is his consuming, burning purity. This is what makes him dangerous, and this is what the Israelites had to learn by hard experience, because this holiness was foundational to God's entire working with them. This "transcendent holiness of God," said H. Wheeler Robinson, "was the majesty of a righteous and loving person. In that unity, all the deeper religious ideas of Israel find their source."[44]

The ark of the Lord, for example, was where God in his glory was symbolically localized. At one point, it fell into the hands of the Philistines, upon whom grave misfortune was visited, and so it was returned to Israel. When it was being retrieved, however, seventy men "looked into the ark of the LORD" (1 Sam. 6:19) and were immediately killed by God. Later, Uzzah put his hand on the ark to steady it as the cart on which it rested swayed, and "God smote him there because he put forth his hand to the ark" (2 Sam. 6:7). In his holiness, God is not to be trifled with; familiarity with God inherently borders on contempt and is subject to judgment. "God terrifies with his fearful punishment not only the Philistines and their gods," writes Eichrodt, "but also the Israelites . . . and by this means ensures that men will bow in awe before his majesty."[45]

In the church today, where such awe is conspicuously absent and where easy familiarity with God has become the accepted norm for providing worship that is comfortable and consumable, we would do well to remember that God is not mocked. It is true that the New Testament encourages a bold confidence in our access to God through Christ's holiness and by his work, but in our confidence we must never be careless of the purity of God or the requirements he has established for his people. The holiness of God begets and requires in those who

44. Robinson, *Religious Ideas of the Old Testament* (London: Duckworth, 1913), p. 70.

45. Eichrodt, *Theology of the Old Testament,* 1:272.

approach him the echo of his holiness. Ananias and Sapphira learned that the hard way (Acts 5:1-11), as did those who took the Lord's Supper so unworthily that Paul had to remind them that this was the reason that "many of you are weak and ill, and some have died" (1 Cor. 11:30). After considering the fact that God, in his holiness, asserts himself against the disobedient, the writer of the letter to the Hebrews concludes with the statement that it "is a fearful thing to fall into the hands of the living God" (Heb. 10:31). That God is dangerous in his holiness should not be dismissed as if it were a primitive idea, beyond which we have now evolved. It is, in fact, a reality toward which we are all moving, for in the end God's holiness will prove to be the final line of resistance to all that is wrong, all that is evil in the world. The day is coming when truth will be placed forever on the throne, and error forever on the scaffold.

Second, and growing out of this, is the fact that holiness is never a remote quality in the Old Testament: holiness is what God is in his essential character, what he is in his confrontation with sin and evil. This is why people, things, and places are referred to as holy only in a secondary sense, only in the sense that God sets them apart to serve his special moral or religious purposes.

There are numerous instances of this sort of special designation in the Old Testament, some of which are carried over into the New Testament and used to formulate the essential meaning of Christian life. For example, Israel's land is holy (Hos. 9:3; cf. Ezek. 37:28), as are Jerusalem (Isa. 52:1) and the site of an appearance of God (Exod. 3:5). The temple, too, is described as holy (1 Kings 9:3; cf. Lev. 8:10; Exod. 19:23) — not because of its elaborate design or because there was something magical about it but because it was where God was to be found and worshiped. That is to say, it was holy because of its distinctive purpose. Similarly, the animals offered in sacrifice had to be without defect (Lev. 1:3; 5:15), and yet their holiness lay not in the fact that they were different from other animals in this way but rather in the fact that they were put to a different use (Lev. 6:11). Indeed, each of these things was rendered holy by God's action in separating them out from common usage and dedicating them for his *exclusive* use.

This understanding of the nature of God's holiness is evident in the New Testament as well. For example, Christians are characterized as holy not because by nature they are less corrupt than others but because God has acted to separate them to himself through Christ. Thus all Christians are saints (Eph. 1:1, 18; Phil. 1:1; Col. 1:2) and priests (1 Pet. 2:9); their bodies are now temples (1 Cor. 6:19), sacrifices (Rom. 12:1-2). God's act of grace is not disjoined from the life of holiness; to the contrary, God demands true holiness of all the elect, and not merely in some remote apocalyptic sense but here and now in our daily lives.

God in his holiness is deeply intrusive, cutting to the very heart of our inner life. His truth is "sharper than any two-edged sword, piercing to the division of soul and spirit, of joints and marrow, and discerning the thoughts and intentions of the heart." He lays claim to the entirety of our inner life; all is open and "laid bare before the eyes of him with whom we have to do" (Heb. 4:12, 13). Specifically, he demands that the external expressions of our inner life be fully in accord with the fact that we belong to him through Christ, consistent with his truth, and obedient to his moral law. These are the demands not of a God who is far off, hidden behind intermediaries and a multitude of concerns, but of a God who in all his awesomeness is at hand.

So it is that when we succeed in cloaking the holiness of God, in focusing on his love to the exclusion of his wrath, we unsettle the whole moral universe. We create a God who may be patient, kindly, and compassionate but who is without the will to resist what is wrong, without the will to judge it, and without the power to destroy it. Such a God lacks the moral earnestness to attract our attention, let alone inspire our belief or warrant our worship. Such a God is not the God of the Bible, is not the God of Jesus Christ. We may place him at the center of our faith, but he cannot be the great protagonist in the moral drama of the world, the conflict between good and evil, for without holiness there is no drama and there is no hope. Hope dies when it can no longer see through this vale of tears to the triumph of God's sovereign goodness on the other side. Key to this triumph, of course, is the life, death, and resurrection of Christ, in whom the end is inaugurated and declared. When holiness slips from sight, so, too, does the centrality of Christ. A God who is not holy cannot deal with the great darkness of corrupted human life, the darker forces behind it, and the whole societal fabric in which this rebellion has become normative (cf. Eph. 2:1-10). He can scarcely comprehend the damnation that has already settled subliminally on the human psyche, and he is even less able to do anything about it. The best he can hope to do is offer counsel like a Rogerian therapist, listening carefully but non-judgmentally, necessarily detached in his kindness from the deepest pains, the most destructive realities of our lives. Such a God produces a Christianity that is attractively amiable and civil but utterly unable to come to terms with the suffering of this fallen world because it is simply not on the same moral scale as the transgressors to whom it presumes to speak a word of grace. It is a form of belief that is sympathetic but not searching, that confronts evil with attitude rather than action, that presents Christ as a pale Galilean who was overtaken by the combined opposition of his foes rather than as the eternal Son of God who took on flesh to triumph over sin, death, and the devil. It is a tame, nonthreatening form of belief with a toothless and accommodating God designed by consumers who are used to getting what they want the way they want it.

But the Holy, by its very nature, is in a realm we cannot enter as consumers but only as sinners, in sackcloth and ashes. Indeed, we cannot approach the Holy at all; we must wait for the Holy to approach and reconcile us to itself in Christ. The revelation of the Holy would be unbearable if we saw it in any way other than from within the redemption it grants us. The knowledge of God as holy, though taught throughout the Old Testament, must in the end be taught supremely by the Son, by his death in our place, before we can see all that God would have us see. The cross, writes P. T. Forsyth, "is the creative revelation of the holy, and the holy is what is above all revealed in the Cross, going out as love and going down as grace."[46]

Without this holiness of God, sin has no meaning and grace has no point, for it is God's holiness that gives to the one its definition and to the other its greatness. Without the holiness of God, sin is merely human failure but not failure before God, in relation to God. It is failure without the standard by which we know it to have fallen short. It is failure without the presumption of guilt, failure without retribution, failure without any serious moral meaning. And without the holiness of God, grace is no longer grace because it does not arise from the dark clouds of judgment that obscured the cross and exacted the damnation of the Son in our place. Furthermore, without holiness, grace loses its meaning as grace, a free gift of the God who, despite his holiness and because of his holiness, has reconciled sinners to himself in the death of his Son. And without holiness, faith is but a confidence in the benevolence of life, or perhaps merely confidence in ourselves. Sin, grace, and faith are emptied of any but a passing

46. Forsyth, *The Principle of Authority, in Relation to Certainty, Sanctity, and Society: An Essay in Philosophical and Experimental Religion* (London: Independent Press, 1952), pp. 4-7.

meaning if they are severed from their roots in the holiness of God. "Love," says Forsyth, "is but its outgoing; sin is but its defiance; grace is but its action on sin; the Cross is but its victory; faith is but its worship."[47]

Until we recognize afresh the centrality of God's holiness, until it once again enters into the innermost fibers of evangelical faith, our virtue will lack seriousness, our belief will lack poignancy, our practice will lack moral pungency, our worship will lack joyful seriousness, our preaching will lack the mordancy of grace, and the church will be just one more special interest pleading for a hearing in a world of competing enterprises. Until we acknowledge God's holiness, we will not be able to deny the authority of modernity. What has most been lost needs most to be recovered — namely, the unsettling, disconcerting fact that God is holy and we place ourselves in great peril if we seek to render him a plaything of our piety, an ornamental decoration on the religious life, a product to answer our inward dissatisfactions. God offers himself on his own terms or not at all. The deity who now appears to lie so limply upon the church is, in fact, the living and glorious God. His hand may be stayed by patience and grace, but it is certain that he will eventually pass judgment on the world. It is this holy God, glorious in his being, doing wonders, who beckons his people to a deeper working knowledge of himself, and it is he who breaks the power of modernity.

God the Knower

The Crisis of Authority

Why is it that today the implications of God's holiness often slide off the church like water off a duck's back? We have already noted how modernity lures us along an easier path, but there is also another fundamental factor at work: the general collapse of authority in the West.[48] This is another cultural trend that has seeped into the church with tragic results. For one thing, it has led the church to abandon the

---

47. Peter Taylor Forsyth, *The Cruciality of the Cross* (London: Independent Press, 1948), pp. 22-23.

48. Derek Phillips argues that modern therapeutic culture and the collapse of authority are the two major obstacles to the moral life today. See his essay "Authenticity or Morality?" in *The Virtues: Contemporary Essays on Moral Character,* ed. Robert B. Kruschwitz and Robert C. Roberts (Belmont, Cal.: Wadsworth, 1987), pp. 23-35.

transcendent Word, the means by which it understands God, and in so doing it has rendered itself unable to see through this world. And it has led the church to look to the self for a substitute Word. It has assigned the self all the tasks that biblical and, in a Catholic context, churchly authority once exercised. Today, we count the self as our only authority. "While the signs of the crisis in the churches proliferate," writes Paul T. Stallsworth, "the reason for the crisis remains constant: the sovereign self, understood apart from the Lordship of Jesus Christ, his Cross, his Church, and his Kingdom, is taken to be the maker and shaper of the self's nature and destiny."[49] But the problem here is that the self doesn't have the strength to take over the functions of God's Word; it doesn't have what it takes to provide vision in the modern world because it is cut off from the true source and foundation of that world. It is worth taking a closer look at the cultural context that has supplanted the true authority of God with the shallow authority of the self.

Western society has historically been held together by tradition, authority, and power. They long served it as essential garments, but of late they have been dropping away, leaving it exposed and indecent. Of the three, tradition was probably the first to go, although its demise was in many ways connected with that of authority. We have already noted how the institutions that once preserved tradition by passing on the accumulated wisdom, lore, beliefs, and values of one generation to the next have been overturned by modernity. Our families and our schools have become so enamored of the ostensible virtues of pluralism (or intimidated by the prospect of failing to be value-neutral) that they no longer even make a token effort to give the next generation moral instruction. The result is that rather than being introduced and connected to traditional values, the children of modernity are lifted away from them like so much flotsam on a rising tide.

The brave excursion into the future on which we are now embarked, unhitched from the past and stripped of many of the values that were once considered indispensable to the proper functioning of civilization and democracy, has until relatively recently been proceeding under the banner of progress. It is the conceit of modernity that the past is nothing more than a dead weight, that constant innovation is the only key to a better life and richer truth. We have, in other words, extrapolated from our experience in the areas of science and tech-

49. Stallsworth, "Time of Crisis, Time to Confess," *Lutheran Forum* 27 (August 1993): 51.

nology and concluded that what was judged true and wise yesterday must now be passé, that anything on the cutting edge must necessarily be superior. And we persist in this delusion despite the fact that the lives of us moderns, with our historically unprecedented wealth of knowledge, are everywhere characterized by emptiness, superficiality, banality, and destructiveness, whereas the lives of those who lived in previous ages and knew so much less than we do today were often comparatively more human, more serious, and more profound.

At the same time that our society is discounting the accumulated wisdom of the past, it is finding that it can no longer recognize appeals to any sort of authority, for any transcendent realm in which these appeals might be grounded has vanished from sight.[50] These changes are evident in a variety of ways in the areas of art, literature, philosophy, and politics, but they all follow a basic pattern. First, the Christian theism on which Western societies were built was replaced by idealism of one kind or another. This still had a transcendent interest, but it was no longer theistic. Then this idealism collapsed and was replaced by humanism. At first this humanism sustained elevated ethical and aesthetic interests, but this could not last, because it had no durable conceptual base.[51] In the political arena, for example, it gave way to various totalitarianisms — Lenin and Marx on the left, Hitler and Mussolini on the right. These individuals have now passed, but the moral vacuity on which they built remains, not only in politics but in many other aspects of life as well.

The forces that once bound Western culture together have thus been reduced to one. Tradition and authority have scarcely any remaining effect; only power remains. It is power alone that directs our corporate life, for instance — power severed from any moral order that might have contained and corrected it, severed from the values of the past that might have informed it. In the absence of any consensus about what is right, we have turned to law to settle our disputes. The

50. Stephen L. Carter has mounted a persuasive argument from his perspective as a constitutional lawyer that the disappearance of the transcendent in modern culture has been hastened by a widespread misappropriation of the doctrine of the separation of church and state. He asserts that the doctrine was devised to protect religion from the state, not to protect the state from the church. See *The Culture of Disbelief: How American Law and Politics Trivialize Religious Devotion* (New York: Basic Books, 1993).

51. On the older type of humanist, see the description and critique offered by Rosalind Murray in *The Good Pagan's Failure* (New York: Longman, Green, 1939); more generally, see Thomas Molnar, *The Pagan Temptation* (Grand Rapids: William B. Eerdmans, 1987).

duties that were once undertaken by family, school, and church have now fallen into the hands of lawyers and bureaucrats, who are preoccupied solely with the care and maintenance of networks of inviolable procedures. It is a terrible thing, Solzhenitsyn said, to live in a society where there is no law; it is also a terrible thing to live in a society where there are only lawyers.

Of course our current plight cannot be attributed solely to the outworkings of the impersonal forces of modernization. Our intellectuals have had a hand in it all as well, especially those who have carried along the revolution in thought that the Enlightenment unleashed. The Enlightenment introduced the notion that we have the power to remake all of life in our own image; modernization produced a world in which this illusion has taken on the feeling of reality. The resulting dissolution of religious belief has led many to reassign their source of "authority" to the private critical self-consciousness at either a popular or an academic level. Modern scientific method has provided a set of rules governing the outworkings of critical self-consciousness that has since developed into a substitute set of absolutes, a morality about what will be allowed to pass for legitimate knowledge and what will not. In almost every experience we have of the modern world — not only in the realm of science but in every area of life from the world of business to the world of television game shows — one thing is axiomatic: the only acknowledged authority is that of private preference.[52]

In the nineteenth century in particular, philosophers, novelists, and artists made numerous attempts to establish a system of morals based on something other than the existence of God or his revelation. These experiments were all the work of a small avant garde, however. What has changed is that now the whole of society has become avant garde. The whole of society is now engaged in this unprecedented attempt to rebuild itself deliberately and self-consciously without religious foundations. The bottom line of this endeavor is that truth in any absolute sense has been abandoned. Like life, truth is fractured. Like experience, it is disjointed. Like our perceptions of ourselves, it is uncertain. It takes on different appearances as we move among the small units of meaning that make up our social experience. Like our manners, it must be flexible and adapt to each new context. Truth is now simply a matter of etiquette: it has no authority, no sense of

52. This theme has been explored incisively by Van Harvey in *The Historian and the Believer: The Morality of Historical Knowledge and Christian Belief* (London: SCM Press, 1967).

rightness, because it is no longer anchored in anything absolute. If it persuades, it does so only because our experience has given it its persuasive power, but tomorrow our experience might be different.

The Centrality of Truth

If the concept of revelation presumes a prior act on the part of God — that is to say, if it is a matter of supernatural self-disclosure rather than something discovered as the result of a religious search by human beings — then it is a remarkable and a tragic thing that his Word should have become so silent in the church. God is the great knower of life, after all. Through his Word he brings to human life a knowledge that is not subject to the relativities of life even though he presented his revelation in the flesh and bone of relative cultural contexts. Because its content is transcultural, it can interpret life in all ages and places, spelling out its real meaning. The fact that this Word is now so silent, that it has so small a part to play in the church's worship, understanding, and spiritual nurture, goes a long way toward explaining why God, in his holiness, is also a stranger to the church.[53] We have to conclude that the collapse of authority in society is starting to infiltrate the church as well, along with the rest of the characteristics and habits of modernity. And so it is that God is disappearing from his church, being edged out by the self, naked and alone, as the source of all mystery and meaning.[54]

53. James Singleton has provided me with an unpublished study of two hundred sermons, half of which appeared in issues of *Pulpit Digest* between January-February 1981 and March-April 1991 and half of which appeared in issues of *Preaching* between July-August 1985 and January-February 1991. He placed each sermon in one of four categories. In 24.5 percent of the total, the content and organization of the sermon were determined by the biblical passage under consideration. In 22.5 percent of the sermons, the content was explicitly biblical, but the preacher took the liberty of imposing his or her organization on it. In 39 percent of the sermons, neither the content nor the organization arose from a biblical passage, but the substance was at least identifiably Christian. And in 14 percent of the sermons, neither the content nor the organization arose from a biblical passage, and the substance was not discernibly Christian at all. It says something about the status that the church in Our Time accords to the Word of God when, of two hundred ostensibly model evangelical sermons, fewer than half are explicitly biblical, and one in seven is not even discernibly Christian.

54. This is the key to understanding the growing fascination with Eastern spirituality, in and out of the church. Discussing the Hindu concept of God, e.g., T. R. V. Murti says that "if we are to look for God, we are to look for him in the composition or the structures of man, in the self (Atman). . . . The self-luminous and self-existent Self (Atman) is God *par excellence*" ("The Hindu Conception of

It is not possible here to develop a full doctrine of God's Word,[55] but it is worth pondering why so much of the effort in the evangelical world to do this, especially in the years after World War II, has apparently fallen on such barren soil. The debates, to be sure, have not always been elevated in tone or substance, but they have nevertheless been part of a serious effort to find formulations of the essential assertion that what Scripture says, God says. They have sought to underscore the point that God's revelation is coextensive with the written Scriptures, that his use of human authors in no way limited or distorted the nature of the intended revelation, and that the key to the interpretation of Scripture is included in Scripture. Much of the debate has taken place under the rubric of inerrancy, though the usefulness of this term has itself been much debated.

In retrospect, it looks like a case of Nero fiddling while Rome burned. The issue of inerrancy basically focuses on the *nature* of the Bible. It is entirely possible for those who have sworn to defend the concept of biblical inerrancy to function as if they had no such Word in their hands. Indeed, it happens all the time. And the sad fact is that while the nature of the Bible was being debated, the Bible itself was quietly falling into disuse in the church.

Without this transcendent Word in its life, the church has no rudder, no compass, no provisions. Without the Word, it has no capacity to stand outside its culture, to detect and wrench itself free from the seductions of modernity. Without the Word, the church has no meaning. It may seek substitutes for meaning in committee work, relief work, and various other church activities, but such things cannot fill the role for very long. Cut off from the meaning that God has given, faith cannot offer anything more by way of light in our dark world than what is offered by philosophy, psychology, or sociology. Cut off from God's meaning, the church is cut off from God; it loses its identity as the people of God in belief, in practice, in hope. Cut off from God's Word, the church is on its own, left to live for itself, by itself, upon itself. It is never lifted beyond itself, above its culture. It is never stretched or tried. It grows more comfortable, but it is the comfort of anaesthesia, of a refusal to pay attention to the disturbing realities of God's truth.

God," in *God: The Contemporary Discussion,* pp. 28-29). What in Hinduism is pursued as religious belief is, in the West, being pursued out of cultural habit.

55. For a detailed exposition of the doctrine that I am assuming here, see the first and third volumes of Henry's *God, Revelation and Authority.*

Some thirty years ago, A. W. Tozer observed that "the Christian conception of God current in these middle years of the twentieth century is so decadent as to be utterly beneath the dignity of the Most High God and actually to constitute for professed believers something amounting to a moral calamity."[56] We may be able to live on favorable terms with a God begotten in the shadows of the modern heart, but such a God will be completely unable to provide the intellectual vigor, the courage, and the moral fortitude that is so painfully lacking in modernity. Cognitive vigor, a conviction about God's truth, the courage to make it known in public and to live it in private, and the fortitude to do this day in and day out are born in the understanding of God's otherness. His transcendent holiness and knowledge enable us to stand outside the charms of modernity in order to act morally within it.

Only those who are countercultural by way of being other-worldly have what modern culture most needs to hear — a Word from God that can cut through the deceits of modernity to reach the hearts that lie within. These are the people for whom God has weight, and, because of this, they themselves have weight. In contrast, it is this-worldly Christianity, not merely in the old liberal forms but increasingly in the evangelical church today, that produces weightlessness in God and in its purveyors. It spreads something light and superficial, a mere gloss on modernity, under the illusion that it is actually offering the antidote to modernity.

So it is that evangelical faith and practice have unaccountably run aground in the shallow waters of modernity. If we are to survive, we must return to the deep waters of God's otherness — his holiness and truth — for that is where our safety lies.

---

56. Tozer, *The Knowledge of the Holy: The Attributes of God — Their Meaning in the Christian Life* (Harrisburg, Pa.: Christian Publications, 1961), p. 10. Cf. Deane W. Ferm, "Abuse of God," *The Christian Century*, 26 March 1975, pp. 307-10.

CHAPTER 7

God on the Inside

If the dangers and difficulties which now beset man are eliminated in postcivilized society and if he no longer has anything to fear but death itself, will not his creativity be diminished and may he not dissipate his energies in a vast ennui and boredom?

Kenneth E. Boulding

The pervasive experience of emptiness and meaninglessness in the modern world and an associated inhospitality to religion has in its way changed the shape of evangelical faith just as the abundance produced by our fecund economic system has changed it in its way.[1] As we have already noted, our culture of abundance has led the churches to refashion themselves into institutions better suited to satisfying consumers of things religious, and it has turned religious life into a field for entrepreneurs. Both the ethos of religious life and its structures have been overturned. And yet, despite all of the abundance into which evangelicalism has dipped, and despite a monumental proliferation of ministries to suit every need, churches organized to assuage every

1. The theme of meaninglessness, with its undercurrents of nihilism, was common among the earlier existentialists such as Albert Camus (as in *The Stranger, The Myth of Sisyphus, The Plague,* and *The Fall*). It is also evident in Balzac's *Comedie Humaine* and even in Tolstoy's *Death of Ivan Ilych.* For a brief review of this literature, see William Barrett, *Time of Need: Forms of Imagination in the Twentieth Century* (New York: Harper, 1972), pp. 3-42. The meaninglessness of which I am speaking here is cultural rather than literary, however; it is less reflective and more intuitive, less cogent and more inchoate.

demand, and magazines to fill every marketing niche, there is a hollowness within it all, an emptiness. It is my contention that the emptiness within is pulling in the walls of the evangelical church life quite as much as the pressures outside are pushing them in, and the two forces working together are having a devastating effect.

There is no way to prove this thesis empirically, but I believe that an oblique approach to the subject may in the end establish the point as convincingly as a cold assessment of the facts of the case. I want to ask whether the evangelical church has begun to try to fill the emptiness of modernity by means that are as much psychological as anything and at the price of things theological. Specifically, I want to ask whether two historically important doctrines have ceased to be influential in the evangelical worldview — the doctrine of providence, which asserts God's control over all of life's events, and the doctrine of the cross, which asserts that God has secured through the crucifixion of his Son a resolution of what has disordered the world and robbed it of its meaning. Have these doctrines lost their currency in the day-to-day commerce of life? Are we seeking substitutes for them in such things as political action, dramatic spiritual experience, strong charismatic leaders, and beguiling entertainments? Are the churches feeding their members sugary fluff and telling them pleasant stories simply to divert them from having to think too much about the painful realities of an empty existence — in a calculated attempt to hold on to their constituencies in a brutally competitive marketplace of ideas? Could it be that this is what Robert Schuller's "possibility thinking" is really all about?

If these things are indeed happening, then I believe we can explain them as a case of people seeking compensation for lost Christian substance both by deliberate appropriation from the culture and by an internal rearrangement of the faith. The end result is a culturally adapted faith that is driven by internal loss. It is as if human nature abhorred a vacuum of meaning, and so where something substantial in Christian understanding falls away or loses its efficacy, something else moves in to take its place. I believe that this dynamic best accounts for some of the massive changes in evangelical faith that have taken place since the 1970s.

The Sacred Canopy

Thirty years ago, Langdon Gilkey remarked on the fact that God's providence had virtually disappeared in learned discussion. Why, he asked, has this doctrine "been left a rootless, disembodied ghost, flitting from footnote to footnote, but rarely finding secure lodgment in sustained theological discourse"?[2] We might appropriately ask the same question today. It is no easy matter to straighten out doctrine when cultural and psychological pressures are weighing heavily against it. Today, at both an academic and churchly level, this doctrine is caught up in a process of internal bartering between what our experience of the modern world will allow us to believe about God's providence and what we think should be said about it theologically — and the gap between the two is wide and growing wider. We would do well, then, to take a closer look at the interplay between what we *can* believe and what we *ought* to believe in this area. What is it in the modern consciousness that so militates against the historic Christian understanding of God's sovereign, "inside" relationship to creation, history, and our own personal narratives? The answer is complex because our social world is complex, but I believe it involves three main factors.

A Peeling Canvass

First, there is little doubt that alongside the revelry that modern plenty and modern opportunity have provided, a deep foreboding has also been churned up, an apprehension that our world has gone dreadfully awry morally, socially, and spiritually. The point is not simply that the great strides that have been made in the twentieth century in improving diet, work conditions, living conditions, income, medical care, leisure time, opportunities of every kind have failed to satisfy the human spirit. That, of course, is true. But alongside this there is also apprehension. It flows like a dark and silent current beneath the surface of things, robbing much of what we do of ultimate meaning and, indeed, of any meaning at all. Our experience of the modern world produces the sense that there is no sure and steady purpose pervading life, that purpose, like life itself, has broken apart into small, unrelated fragments, that our daily routine is severed from the meaning that God once provided to it.

It may seem odd that those upon whom so much privilege and material good fortune has fallen should now look upon their world with such foreboding — what Robert Heilbroner has called our "civilizational malaise." But at least some of the reasons for it seem reasonably clear.

2. Gilkey, "The Concept of Providence in Contemporary Theology," *Journal of Religion* 43 (July 1963): 171.

First, there is the ominous realization that our world is becoming overcrowded, that its capacity to sustain those who inhabit it will, at some point, be exhausted unless the plague of AIDS or something comparably horrible substantially reduces the human population.[3] Second, we have despoiled the environment in our rough scramble to enrich ourselves, and no one seems to know what the final outcome will be.[4] Third, there is a deep unease that the technology we have used to manufacture the world we desire may in the future be put to truly catastrophic uses.[5]

Yet even realities such as these do not get to the heart of the matter. The deepest causes of our foreboding, I believe, lie in our intuitive sense that the fabric that holds our society together is in danger of unraveling. In 1993 the Heritage Foundation released a study of life in the United States produced by William J. Bennett. Among other things, he reported that since 1960 violent crime has increased 560 percent, the number of single-parent households has increased 300 percent, the number of births to unmarried women has increased 400 percent (68 percent of black children now fall in this category), and teenage suicide has increased 200 percent. These are the signs of a society that is disintegrating in fundamental ways.

And here we encounter one of the strange paradoxes of our time: despite the strong economic cords binding us together, despite the growing pervasiveness of government in society, despite the extensive legal protections we enjoy, our society seems more fragile than ever. It is now endangered *institutionally*. Law, commerce, government, and education have greatly expanded their reach, but, at the same time, their public credibility has plummeted. They are all in danger of losing their cultural legitimacy in America. In addition to this, society is now endangered *culturally* because there are fewer and fewer shared meanings and desires; the collective sense of what it means to be an American

3. See Heilbroner, *An Inquiry into the Human Prospect* (New York: W. W. Norton, 1974), pp. 32-40.

4. See Heilbroner, *An Inquiry into the Human Prospect,* pp. 47-52. The despoiling of our environment has provoked alarmed calls for curbs on our habits and appetites. See, e.g., Rufus E. Miles, *Awakening from the American Dream: The Social and Political Limits to Growth* (New York: Universe Books, 1976); and Al Gore, *Earth in the Balance: Ecology and the Human Spirit* (New York: E. P. Dutton, 1993).

5. Robert Lifton argues that the threat of global nuclear annihilation has broken the continuity, at a personal level, of the ways in which life moves into death, and this has resulted in a kind of nihilistic meaninglessness settling over society. See *The Broken Connection: On Death and the Continuity of Life* (New York: Simon & Schuster, 1979).

is shattering under the impact of relentless emphasis on distinctions of race, gender, sexual orientation, and class.[6] Finally, our society is endangered *morally* because binding and absolute norms now seem implausible to too many people. How, then, will we contain our life within channels that are beneficial and not harmful? We do, after all, have good reason to fear those who are toying with the secrets of life and death as they stumble along in our modern darkness.[7] We rightly fear them because our world champions brilliance without wisdom and power without conscience and because lawyers and bureaucrats have assumed the roles that moral leaders once held. In this precarious world, a world fragile beyond telling, it is no surprise that its turbulent, dangerous, unruly forces have come to look increasingly like a malevolent genie that has escaped the bottle of divine providence.

What I am describing here, of course, is the way in which Western culture in general has been secularized. This is a two-sided process. What is external and sociological I have called *secularization;* what is internal and ideological I have called *secularism*. From the one perspective, what I am describing is the outlook and the values that arise in a society that is no longer taking its bearings from a transcendent order; from the other perspective, what I am describing is the track that modernization has taken within the human spirit in producing and authenticating contemporary values. So what does the signature of this process look like?

We begin by noting again that this is a unique cultural moment. Historically, all major cultures have been based on religious assumptions.[8] But our culture, rooted in the Enlightenment and reshaped by modernization, has broken this connection. Our public life does not turn to a divine or supernatural order for justification or direction; as Bryan Wilson has suggested, it is in no way dependent on "the main-

6. See Arthur M. Schlesinger Jr., *The Disuniting of America: Reflections on a Multicultural Society* (New York: W. W. Norton, 1993).

7. See Hans Sachsse, "Modern Technology and the Contemporary Debate on It," *Universitas* 25 (1983): 85-92. What needs to be noted here is that technology does not simply enlarge our capacities for doing harm but also has the power to subtly reshape the way in which we view life. Jacques Ellul was among the first to explore this theme in *The Technological Society*, trans. John Wilkerson (New York: Alfred A. Knopf, 1965). More recently, Neil Postman addressed this theme in *Technopoly: The Surrender of Culture to Technology* (New York: Alfred A. Knopf, 1992).

8. Both Arnold Toynbee and Christopher Dawson considered the role of religion in culture to be axiomatic. With respect to Dawson's work, see *Religion and World History: A Selection from the Works of Christopher Dawson*, ed. James Oliver and Christina Scott (Garden City, N.Y.: Doubleday-Image, 1975).

tenance of religious thinking, practices or institutions."[9] It finds its justification, its life, and its direction solely within itself.

Our society no longer has a center of values that exerts a centripetal force on our collective life; similarly, our religion has lost the theological center that once held together thought and practice, private and public. The disappearance of the center in both society and religion has produced an emptiness, and for lack of anything better, this emptiness has been filled with various forms of pluralization. The once-whole worlds of society and religion have broken apart into a host of smaller independent worlds, each of which has taken off on its own trajectory.

In society, these subworlds consist of the small units of meaning within which we exist and through which we pass, perhaps even several times a day.[10] Each has its own values, its own cognitive horizons, its own reasons for and ways of doing things, its own class interests. Often, the only connections these worlds have with one another is the fact that the same people have to move amphibiously among them. Within short periods of time, people move from the family setting, with its unique relations and values, to an entirely different set of relationships and values in the workplace, from the company of professional colleagues to the company of personal friends, from service organizations to the larger business and bureaucratic structures in society, from engagement with the world's catastrophes and crises through the news media to the diversions of sitcoms, game shows, and, perhaps, the occasional blue movie.[11] Then we go to church. And lying across these worlds, sometimes identifying with them and sometimes disengaging from them, are the additional cultural distinctions of age, ethnicity, class, and occupation. To move among these multiple worlds smoothly, one has to master a variety of languages of survival and be fluid enough to accommodate a considerable variety of special interests, some of which may be mutually antagonistic. In fact, it is unlikely that such cultural diversity can be

9. Wilson, *Religion in Secular Society* (Baltimore: Penguin Books, 1966), p. 258.

10. For a discussion of the intersections of these subworlds of meaning, see Peter L. Berger, *The Precarious Vision: A Sociologist Looks at Social Fictions and Christian Faith* (Garden City, N.Y.: Doubleday, 1961), pp. 8-101.

11. With the advent of the videocassette recorder and the pervasive availability of pornographic material, ethical resistance is apparently crumbling among evangelicals. In a survey of clergy, 20 percent of those who rated themselves significantly above the laity in matters of sexual ethics admitted to viewing pornographic matter at least once a month. See the introduction to "The War within Continues," *Leadership* 9 (Winter 1988): 24.

surmounted without considerable cognitive dissonance. If society's emptiness produces what Durkheim called *anomie*, the cognitive dissonance generated by breakdown of social cohesion and the general collapse of meaning produces psychological confusion and anxiety. Our daily shuttling among the many small worlds of modernity is exacting a toll on us whether we recognize it or not.

While it seems to be the case that secularization is the cause of which cultural pluralization is the effect, there can be little doubt, as Peter Berger has noted, that each strengthens the other.[12] Our experience of cultural pluralization produces a greater emptiness in the center, and the emptiness in the center pulls in more pluralization by way of compensation. The resulting pressure away from any unifying focus gives powerful impetus to yet another form of pluralization — a breakdown in the unity of our knowledge and the emergence in its place of a mass of specialized fields and disciplines, each with their own assumptions, procedures, and criteria of judgment.

This development has been a boon to the publishers of popular magazines. Since 1950, magazines have proliferated at twice the rate of the population's growth. They have created nationwide congregations of individuals who don't known one another but who periodically share in a communion of appreciation for the glossy layouts of beautiful bodies, motorbikes, ski equipment, guns, or any of hundreds of other interests. As entertainment and diversion, this experiment in specialization may not be problematic, but it can perniciously undermine our attempts to make sense out of our world as a whole. We shop today in what Wilson has referred to as a "random supermarket of knowledge."[13] The randomness, the lack of connection, the independence of our private worlds of knowing is fracturing our perception of reality. If we understand what the physicists are talking about, the sociologists may make no sense to us; if we accept Carl Sagan's perspective on the world, we may not be able to enter into Solzhenitsyn's mind. The supermarket in which we shop for bits of knowledge is at once a testimony to our genius in mastering the world and our capacity for shattering reality.

The psychological fallout from this constant barrage of changing experiences, changing scenarios, changing worlds, changing world-

---

12. I concur with Berger's contention that, while secularization produces pluralization and pluralization increases the secularizing process, it is pluralization that produces the more serious threat to religion. See Berger, *The Heretical Imperative: Contemporary Possibilities of Religious Affirmation* (Garden City, N.Y.: Doubleday-Anchor, 1979), p. xi.

13. Wilson, *Religion in Secular Society,* p. 106.

views, and changing values — the multilingual commerce of our every-day experience — is dramatic. On the one hand, it greatly accentuates the importance of novelty and spontaneity, since each new situation, each new opportunity, each new alternative demands that we make a choice of some kind.[14] We are, in fact, caught up in a furious whirlwind of choices that is shaking the foundation of our sense of stability. If societies in central Europe under the dominance of Marxist regimes languished for lack of choice, we languish from having too many choices. Increasingly weary people long not for freedom of choice but the freedom to avoid having to make choices, the freedom simply to drop out.[15] On the other hand, the relativity and impermanence of everything from values to possessions creates a deep sense of "home-lessness," even of lostness, of not belonging, of not having roots in our world, of searching for but never finding a permanent niche into which we can fit.[16] Along with the lightning flashes of freedom we get thunderclaps of damnation — and the tumult of the storm is drowning out the melodies of divine providence.

The Tragic

Second, the suffering and brutality arising out of man's inhumanity to man have, as Wendy Farley says, "assaulted us in this century with terrible intensity. . . . War ravages every continent, while hunger murders countless millions with less fanfare but no less savagery. Bombs that could destroy life on the planet are suspended over our heads by the slimmest of threads."[17] In 1992 alone, human beings were engaged in ninety-three wars around the world and spent $600 billion dollars preparing for war. Does this not make the notion of God's control over world events seem a little precarious?

The problem of understanding the ways of God in the world is not new, of course, but it has taken on an intensity that is commensurate

14. The experience of pluralism creates a sense of *need* for spontaneity and unpredictability, an insatiable hunger for something novel, unusual, unpredictable. In a theological context, this hunger shows up as a desire for play. See, e.g., Jürgen Moltmann, *Theology of Play*, trans. Reinhard Ulrich (New York: Harper & Row, 1972).

15. See Erich Fromm, *Escape from Freedom* (New York: Avon Books, 1969).

16. Western individualism further accentuates the sense of loneliness that naturally arises within the context of modernity. See Peter L. Berger, "Western Individuality: Liberation and Loneliness," *Partisan Review* 52 (1985): 323-36.

17. Wendy Farley, *Tragic Vision and Divine Compassion: A Contemporary Theodicy* (Louisville: Westminster/John Knox Press, 1990), 11.

with the increased complexity of the modern world. From a philosophical standpoint, evil constitutes a problem if only one person is tortured on God's watch, but from a psychological standpoint, the matter of numbers magnifies the dilemma. We naturally find it more horrifying that six million Jews were slaughtered during the Holocaust than that one is murdered on the streets of New York during our lunch hour. Given the fact that the human race has doubled in size during the last fifty years, it is perhaps not surprising that we are beginning to see killings on an unprecedented scale. Moreover, the mass media make us more aware of the atrocities that do occur. The result, as Paul Hinlicky has noted, is that not since the wars of religion in Europe during the sixteenth and seventeenth centuries "has the perception of violence so dominated Western sensibilities as it does today."[18]

Television unquestionably introduces us to a larger, if filtered, reality. It takes us among the poor and desolate, among the starving and mutilated, among the homeless and abandoned of the world. It takes us to wherever the tragedy is — Africa, Asia, Europe, or our own streets. We gawk at more catastrophe than any previous generation has ever observed — perhaps more mayhem than the fragile human constitution can bear. Theodore H. Von Laue has suggested that this overload of tragedy and information has "engendered a mood of frustration, helplessness, and fatalistic escapism" among us, a mood that we often seek to dispel by turning to "the purveyors of hedonistic distraction and self-indulgence."[19] And is it not the case that the sheer weight of all of this calamity also extinguishes our hope that somehow there must be some meaning that can be retrieved from these ashes?

The Death of Progress

Finally, we need to note the special predicament in which our post-modern world has placed us. Divine providence was much easier to assert when Western culture still believed in progress, because this belief involved an acceptance of a kind of rationality and teleology, a sense that things were getting better, moving toward a goal. Langdon Gilkey maintains that this belief in progress was in turn grounded in three things: "The scientific consciousness represented the cognitive

18. Hinlicky, "The Human Predicament in Emergent Post-Modernity," *Dialog* 23 (Summer 1984): 170.

19. Von Laue, *The World Revolution of Westernization: The Twentieth Century in Global Perspective* (New York: Oxford University Press, 1987), p. 340.

heart of Enlightenment culture; scientific technology, the ground of
its deepest and most concrete hopes; and the economic, political, and
military power of the West, the foundation of its sense of continuing
security, reality, and power."[20] Each of these bases for confidence in
progress has either been shaken or has collapsed altogether, and the
dream of progress — what Christopher Lasch has called our "last
superstition"[21] — has now faded. Belief in progress was really a secularized version of belief in divine providence, complete with its own
"salvation history," but it is now clear that it was never more than the
opiate of Western intellectuals and had little basis in reality.

Sometime after the 1960s, dreams about progress began to die
in our culture, although it has certainly been a lingering death: the
dreams have proved remarkably impervious to the intrusions of reality.
Finally, though, belief in the essential rationality and benign intent of
life and in overarching structures of meaning are falling like loose
bricks from a condemned building. But while the death of an illusion
is itself hardly a cause for regret, the death of the idea of progress has
led many people to abandon *all* rationality, all purpose, all meaning
in life. In this new context of general bleakness, talk about divine
providence has a hollow ring to it for many people.

There is no denying the power of these three factors to alter our
belief in providence, although we are hardly the first generation to live
through a period of dramatic social change and decay. But in any
event, the point here is that the way in which we view our world should
be relativized by the truth of God's Word. Our view of the world should
arise not from our internal psychology, not from the sense that we
make of the world based on our experience, but from the God who is
outside, from what he has disclosed of his will for the world in his
Word. It is here that we find his meaning — meaning that comes not

20. Gilkey, "The New Watershed in Theology," *Soundings* 64 (Summer 1981):
123. In his subsequent development of this theme of providence, however, Gilkey
turned away from a traditional metaphysics and toward the thought that even as
our sense of what is ultimate fades, we secure meaning in daily life by assuming
that we are able to contribute to an "open future." Thus it would seem that we still
maintain a belief in progress, but it is a form of progress that has no substance.
See Gilkey, *Naming the Whirlwind: The Renewal of God-Language* (Indianapolis: Bobbs-
Merrill, 1969), pp. 342-48.

21. Lasch, "Progress: The Last Superstition," *Tikkun* 4 (May-June 1989):
27-30. He pursues this theme more fully in his large and complex book *The True
and Only Heaven: Progress and Its Critics* (New York: W. W. Norton, 1990). See also
Paul A. Carter, "The Idea of Progess in Most Recent American Thought," *Church
History* 32 (March 1963): 75-89.

from below but from above. Barth made this point in his address to the World Council of Churches assembled in Amsterdam in 1948.[22] There is no way, he said, that we can extrapolate from the world's pain and disorder, or even from what is good in the world, to what the designs of God might be. We cannot have any hope of success if we begin below. We cannot begin with "the good and bad manners of modern man, nor with the terrifying picture of a culture which is only technically oriented and only concerned with production, nor with the clash between a godless West and a godless East, nor with the threat of the atomic bomb."[23] Those who begin with the human perspective inevitably end with the human perspective. We must begin with *God*, for only in this way will we end with the divine perspective. Although Barth developed this point in a restrictive and unhappy way in his *Church Dogmatics*, the essential insight is correct. We must begin by reading the meaning of the world from the revelation of God's purposes in Scripture; we must not begin by attempting to read it from the text of the world's life. Beginning with divine revelation will not magically answer all our questions — we may still ask why evil appears to have such a free reign in the world, why God permits suffering, how personal responsibility and divine sovereignty play out with respect to one another, and how prayer works — but neither should our speculation on such matters be adequate to douse the fires of conviction that are fueled by the teaching of God's Word.

In saying this, I do not mean to speak lightly of the serious contemporary difficulties we face in this area. Modernity has gone a long way toward robbing us of our faith convictions. While we may believe in God's existence and his goodness, we find ourselves psychologically disabled in our attempts to bring this belief into incisive relation with the stuff of daily experience, unable to frame effectively our daily routines within the context of ultimacy. The result is that we find ourselves in the business of bargaining internally, daily negotiating between what we *ought* to believe about God's providence in life and what we *can* believe. I believe that such bartering accounts for some of the profound changes afoot in Christian believing today. So what is it that we should be believing?

22. On the assembly, see *A History of the Ecumenical Movement, 1517-1948*, ed. Ruth Rouse and Stephen Charles Neill (Philadelphia: Westminster Press, 1968), pp. 718-24.

23. Barth, "The World's Disorder and God's Design," *Congregational Quarterly* 27 (January 1949): 10-11.

The View from Outside

Christ the Interpreter

In the celebration of the greatness of Christ that opens the epistle to the Hebrews, the writer briskly sets out the two central affirmations in the doctrine of providence. First, Christ, by whom the universe was made, now upholds it "by his word of power" (Heb. 1:3). Second, this same Christ has been "appointed the heir of all things" (Heb. 1:2). The early Christians "taught that in Christ all creation was sustained; that in Him all creatures live, move and have their being; that in Him the universe is moving forward to its destined end; and that in Christ the believer has a share in the glory which is to be revealed in God's own time."[24] Here is the goal of the world, a matter not of empty hopes for life's progressive improvement but rather of eternal redemption in the midst of life's fiery conflicts and fearsome contradictions.

The prologue to the epistle to the Hebrews presents a third christological element as well, which, I shall argue, provides the aperture through which we should be looking at the first two. It is the fact that Christ, in his death and resurrection, has provided "purification for sins" (Heb. 1:3). Jürgen Moltmann is correct to argue that although the cross is not the sole theme of the Bible, it is nevertheless the center from which theological thought arises and to which it must always return. "All Christian statements about God," he says, "about creation, about sin and death, have their focal point in the crucified Christ. All Christian statements about history, about the church, about faith and sanctification, about the future and about hope stem from the crucified Christ."[25] And all thoughts about providence in the world must also be thoughts about Christ, for he is the architect of that providence, its origin, center, and goal.

The connection between Christ's atonement and the providential work of sustaining the world and guiding its life to the end for which it is appointed is to be found by steering a course midway between two dangerous shoals. On the one side is the older Protestant liberalism, which is now enjoying a quiet but considerable resuscitation; on the other is Barthian neo-orthodoxy. The older liberals equated Christ's

---

24. Thomas Hewitt, *Epistle to the Hebrews: An Introduction and Commentary* (London: Tyndale Press, 1960), 51.

25. Moltmann, *The Crucified God*, trans. R. A. Wilson and John Bowden (London: SCM Press, 1973), p. 204.

kingdom with the apex of high culture and hence spoke loosely and often of what God was doing in the world by pointing to what had been accomplished in culture. In reaction to this, Barth limited what could be known of what God was doing to what was revealed in Christ, thus contracting revelation into salvation.

Much of modern evangelicalism has joined Protestantism as a whole in drifting away from Barth and running aground on the shoal that brought Protestant liberalism to grief. To assert the essentially correct insight of Barth that God's providence needs to be read from the standpoint of Christ is to risk the appearance of embracing his christomonism and hence of reducing revelation to salvation, thus denying the proper roles of both Scripture and natural revelation. I believe it is possible, however, to build on this insight while also affirming the larger biblical framework that Barth, in his reaction to the liberals, disturbed. The question remains how we should think of God's providence.

There is some artificiality involved in slicing the work of God too finely, for his purposes were conceived in eternity and are worked out in history as an interconnected whole. What God did in bringing the world into being cannot be separated from his ongoing work of sustaining it, nor can his purposes in creating human life be separated from his purposes of redemption and judgment (John 17:24; 1 Pet. 1:17-20). The beginning must be read in the light of the end, because the end was present in the mind of God in the beginning and hence all that comes to pass has been in the mind of God from the beginning (Isa. 14:24, 27; 22:11; 40:10).

Nevertheless, we may distinguish, as B. B. Warfield did, between providence that is cosmic in nature and providence that is specifically soteriological. The former is what we usually have in mind when we speak of providence, whereas the latter is usually discussed using the language of election and predestination. It is indeed the cosmic providence that I chiefly have in view here, what Warfield describes as "the governing hand of God working out his preconceived plan — a plan broad enough to embrace the whole universe of things, minute enough to concern itself with the smallest details, and actualizing itself with inevitable certainty in every event which comes to pass."[26]

---

26. Warfield, *Biblical and Theological Studies*, ed. Samuel G. Craig (Philadelphia: Presbyterian & Reformed, 1952), p. 276. The issue of the relation between providence and predestination is thorny. In the 1536 and 1539 editions of *The Institutes of the Christian Religion*, John Calvin treated the latter as simply the par-

Under this general heading are two subthemes, what Barth calls God's work in "preserving" the world and his work in "ruling" it and bringing it to its appointed end — themes that are, of course, implied in one another. If God is preserving the world, it is because he has an end in view, and if he has an end in view, then he must preserve the world in order to realize this end.[27]

Over the years, however, there has been considerable debate, at least within Protestantism, about whether there is a third element — what Barth, in his own way, covers under the heading of the divine "accompanying" but that is more typically called "concurrence" or "cooperation."[28] This third element is actually an attempt to explore the *mechanics* of providence, to understand how God's work in the preservation of life and his nourishment of his covenant people relates to the so-called laws of nature, to human volition, to natural causes of all kinds in the world, and to evil. Does he use these, work around them, work despite them, or work through them?

While the metaphysics of God's purposes in the world are everywhere assumed in the Bible and everywhere acted upon, they are rarely the object of explicit examination. Even in the most troubling instances in which evil seems to be caught up at the fringes of God's actions, this remains the case. Evil is never treated, in these instances, as less than evil, and it is subject to God's judgment as such, but it is nevertheless seen as living out its life only by God's will, only within the boundaries that his providence prescribes, and, in the end, only as it serves his purposes. A consideration of the mechanism of God's providence might throw some light on how his preserving and governing roles are worked out, but such matters are really secondary to the issues at hand here. I want to take a closer look at such matters as the divine preservation of life, the fact that the universe is preserved by Christ's "word of power" (Heb. 1:3), and the fact that Christ governs

---

ticular application, in salvation, of God's generalized providence. In the definitive and final edition of 1559, however, he separated them and linked predestination more closely with the work of Christ, perhaps signaling a hope that the matter would be treated more pastorally and less speculatively. See Leigh Hunt, "Predestination in the *Institutes of the Christian Religion,* 1536-39," *Evangelical Quarterly* 9 (January 1937): 38-45; and Etienne de Peyer, "Calvin's Doctrine of Divine Providence," *Evangelical Quarterly* 10 (January 1938): 30-44.

27. See Barth, *Church Dogmatics,* 5 vols., ed. Thomas F. Torrance, trans. Geoffrey W. Bromiley (Edinburgh: T. & T. Clark, 1936-77), III/3:155.

28. For a discussion of these issues, see G. C. Berkouwer, *The Providence of God,* trans. Lewis Smedes (Grand Rapids: William B. Eerdmans, 1952), pp. 137-74.

the universe and is its destined end, for he is the "heir of all things" (Heb. 1:2).

The Big Picture

In the Bible, nature is never seen, as it is so commonly today, as a self-sustaining system with a self-contained meaning. It is never thus desacralized. On the contrary, nature is a veil behind which and because of which the Creator is seen. This is never expressed abstractly in the Bible but always as a vital part of understanding the meaning of life. This is especially evident in the Psalms. Because of the divine preservation, the heavens are "firm," as immovable as God's faithfulness (89:2); he is the one who has established "the moon and the stars" (8:3; cf. 33:6); in consequence, the heavens speak of his greatness (19:1-2). God is the one who has created the sun as a tent (19:4-6) and the winds as messengers (104:4), who makes "springs gush forth in the valleys" (104:10) and who gives to the animals "their food in due season" (104:27). And everywhere "he looks forth on all the inhabitants of the earth . . . and observes all their deeds" (33:14-15).

There is poetry in this, of course, yet it quite clear that here we have not the cool, detached God of the Deists, not an absentee landlord, much less the anomaly of a creation without a creator with which much modern thought is enamored. The Psalms paint the portrait of a God actively sustaining all that he has brought forth — including the lives of human beings. What changes in this conception as we come into the New Testament is simply the agent of this providence. While Paul says that it is in God that we all "live and move and have our being" (Acts 17:28) and that "from him and through him and to him are all things" (Rom. 11:36), this role can also be ascribed to Christ. It is through Christ that "all things were made" (John 1:3), "in him all things hold together" (Col. 1:17), and he is "upholding the universe by his word of power" (Heb. 1:3). The ease with which the writers move between God and Christ in this way is simply one more indication of the kind of high christology that informed their teaching.

No pious Israelite in the Old Testament or believer in the New ever doubted that God was everywhere present in the world and everywhere able to invest his will with reality.[29] Indeed, Psalm 139

---

29. Walter Eichrodt has argued that the corporate sense of providence was a real part of Israel's life long before any personal sense emerged. That there was early personal providence cannot be disputed (see, e.g., Gen. 24:1-67; Exod. 2:1-

joyfully celebrates God's omnipresence and his omnipotence together almost as if each were implicit in the other. And it would have been hard to miss the fact that if the world's Creator guarantees human existence, rather than the art of natural survival by itself, then life is sustained by his goodness.[30] And, in fact, God declared as much to Noah when he announced his gracious intention that so long as "earth remains, seedtime and harvest, cold and heat, summer and winter, day and night, shall not cease" (Gen. 8:22). Paul discerned a "witness" in the fact that God "did good and gave you from heaven rains and fruitful seasons, satisfying your hearts with food and gladness" (Acts 14:17). And Christ referred to this divine goodness, this forbearance with human wickedness across the ages and benevolence toward all in the provision of such gifts, in order to reinforce the ethic of love. He noted that the Father "makes his sun rise on the evil and on the good, and sends rain on the just and on the unjust" (Matt. 5:45), and he taught that this kindly benevolence should be emulated.

God's Hand in History

This general providence, extending to all of creation, has both continuities and discontinuities with the particular providence realized in God's calling, guiding, and sustaining of his people. On the general side, God's people experienced both the wisdom and goodness that the psalmists celebrate and the "wrath" and "eternal power" to which Paul refers (Rom. 1:18-20) in much the same measure as the rest of the created order. But there are also ways in which God relates specially to the history of his own people.

The understanding of God's superintendence of Gentile history came into focus quite late in the Old Testament. It is, nevertheless, unmistakable in the prophets. It is suggested in Jonah, for example, to the prophet's considerable displeasure, and it is overtly taught in Amos and Isaiah, where the sweep of God's judgment descends on the

---

10); the question is whether there was any consciousness of it. Eichrodt himself offers evidence that contradicts his doubt. He notes that when Joseph revealed himself to his brothers, he testified that through their act of betrayal, "God sent me before you to preserve life" (Gen. 45:5). Later Joseph makes the remarkable statement that "you meant evil against me; but God meant it for good, to bring it about that many people should be kept alive, as they are today" (Gen. 50:20). See Eichrodt, *Theology of the Old Testament*, 2 vols., trans. J. A. Baker (Philadelphia: Westminster Press, 1961), 2:176-85.

30. See Barth, *Church Dogmatics*, III/3:60.

surrounding nations for their injustices and naked ambition. When the power of God is unloosed, Isaiah tells us, these nations are of no more consequence to God than the fine dust on the scale which is blown off, or the drop running down the outside of the bucket (40:15). They are "as nothing before him" (40:17; cf. 31:1-2). In Daniel, the extraordinary visions recorded in chapters 7–12 reveal the destiny of God's people amid the rising and falling of civilizations, and we are informed that all of these rhythms across the ages are superintended by God. Many years later Paul returned to this theme, asserting that God has determined for all the nations "allotted periods and the boundaries of their habitation" (Acts 17:26).

It is important to note immediately that although the same sovereign will of God that dictates the rise and fall of worldly kingdoms also brings forth and directs his own people in their national life in the Old Testament, the consequences are nevertheless very different. There is never an inkling among the Gentile nations that the triumphs and misfortunes that attend their way are ultimately to be traced back to the will of God, but the way of God's people is, where needed, prophetically interpreted for them. They are told to look to the God whom they know, whose moral will has been revealed to them, whose hand is traced in what befalls them for an understanding of their situation. His providence is both the source of great comfort to them as they rehearse their history (Deut. 5:15; 7:18; 25:17-19; Ps. 9:11; 66:5; 74:12; 77:11-12; 86:10; 96:3; 103:6; 105:1; 106:2) and an alarm to warn them of their sins. To sound this alarm, to interpret what was happening, God sent a whole line of prophets. Yet even here, not everything is disclosed in the ways of God. Much remains hidden, for it "is the glory of God to conceal things" (Prov. 25:2). In looking back at how God had led his people across the ages, Paul marveled at "the depth of the riches and wisdom and knowledge of God," but then he immediately added, "How unsearchable are his judgments and how inscrutable his ways! For who has known the mind of the Lord, or who has been his counselor?" (Rom. 11:33-34).

Furthermore, God's providence effects no saving grace in the larger world, because God has not established a saving covenant with the nations. The providence he extends to his people, on the other hand, does rest on this grace, is explained by this grace, and is in fact an exercise of this grace which is given shape in the covenant. It is scarcely surprising, then, that the Bible rarely explains what God is doing at any given time by way of guiding the nations. Such matters belong to the divine counsels, which are entirely hidden from human scrutiny. Only in hindsight is it sometimes possible to surmise what was apparently occurring. Likewise, his sovereign circumstantial intentions for his own people are entirely hidden apart from the prophetic interpretation that God offers. Without such special revelation, it is quite impossible to read in the "text" of everyday events the narrative of what, in his providence, God has been doing. And yet, while those who belong to God may often be excluded from his secret counsels, they nevertheless enjoy the assurance of his grace, his unswerving faithfulness, and the fact that in Christ all of his promises find their divine Amen.

This takes us to the heart of many an experiential dilemma. The assurance of God's grace, vouchsafed in the death of Christ, may seem to be contradicted by the experience of pain, suffering, and affliction from which the children of God are not spared. The contradiction, however, arises only because of false expectations.

It should be enough to know that the God who provides for the fields will surely provide for those who are his own (Matt. 6:30), that even the most minute details of their lives are under his scrutiny (Matt. 10:29-31), and that "neither death, nor life, nor angels, nor principalities, nor things present, nor things to come, nor powers, nor height, nor depth, nor anything else in all creation, will be able to separate us from the love of God in Christ Jesus our Lord" (Rom. 8:38-39). Beyond this, God's people have no assurances that the dark experiences of life will be held at bay, much less that God will provide some sort of running commentary on the meaning of each day's allotment of confusion, boredom, pain, or achievement. Quite the contrary. The church is warned repeatedly that despite this providence, suffering and evil will befall all those who follow Christ. Those among us today who hold out promises of health and wealth as the essence of the Christian gospel are not only confusing conditions of middle-class American affluence with the message of Christ and sowing seeds that will eventually produce a harvest of bitter disappointment but are also propounding a palpably false doctrine of providence.[31] Genuine providence not only acknowledges the reality of suffering and deprivation but often grants them the status of seals of spiritual authenticity.[32] At the same time, this providence

31. For an excellent evaluation of the charismatic Faith movement, see Hank Hanegraaff, *Christianity in Crisis* (Ventura, Cal.: Harvest House, 1993).

32. For a careful elaboration of this theme, see Scott J. Hafemann, *Suffering and the Spirit: An Exegetical Study of II Cor. 2:14–3:3 within the Context of the Corinthian Correspondence* (Tübingen: J. C. B. Mohr, 1986).

which sometimes bears along with it harsh and disconcerting experiences is always the providence of a fatherly love (Heb. 12:3-11).

Moreover, we should note that neither Old Testament nor New Testament believers considered the doctrine of providence to be peripheral, something to be taken up and put down as circumstances required. Warfield was correct in saying that this belief in God's sovereign presence in the world "is fundamental to the whole religious consciousness of the Biblical writers, and is so involved in all of their religious conceptions that to eradicate it would transform the entire scriptural representation."[33]

Curing the World's Ills

This brings us to the heart of God's moral government of the world. While it is the case that God sustains nature and guides the destinies of nations, while he rules and overrules cultures that are heathen or secular, while his judgments are already experienced in the extent to which he gives men and women up to "the lusts of their hearts" to become the slaves of their own emptiness and folly (Rom. 1:21-24), yet he deals with evil decisively only at the cross. Evil may in some instances be restrained or used to serve God's purposes, but only in Christ's death is it dethroned. His conquest there has not yet run its full course, nor will it until his return. That is why evil is still in this world. But the cross does prefigure the day when all that is wrong, all that has defiled life, all that has mocked and defied God will be put forever on the scaffold and truth will be put forever on the throne. It is a bell tolling softly for the proud and arrogant, the defilers of life and the disobedient toward God, a reminder of God's certain judgment to come. God's abandonment of Christ foreshadowed the coming abandonment of those who have not found in his death their security. And God's judgment on his Son is the shadow of the executioner's ax that will surely drop on all that is morally dark, including the kingdom of dark powers from which it originates.

The cross, then, is the place where God's providence is most importantly interpreted, because that providence is centrally moral in its nature, and the world's offenses against God are decisively confronted in the cross. The cross is the revelation of God's love and his holiness, and as such it gives us important insights into those aspects of the doctrine of providence that otherwise seem so problematic. For

33. Warfield, *Biblical and Theological Studies*, p. 270.

example, it is abundantly clear that there is no balancing of the scales of justice in the world today. Many violate the law of God with impunity, and many who cherish moral integrity seem to be penalized for their goodness and honesty. We may be inclined to ask where the goodness and justice of God fit into this picture (cf. Ps. 73).

Liberal Protestants used to be offended by the notion that God's governance of the world might include judgment. How, they asked, can a loving God judge anyone? The biblical writers were most troubled by the fact that his justice is delayed. In the book of Revelation, for example, John is shown those martyred "for the word of God and the witness they had borne," and he hears them cry out with a loud voice, "O Sovereign Lord, holy and true, how long before thou wilt judge and avenge our blood on those who dwell upon the earth?" (Rev. 6:9-10). They are not giving vent to a desire for mere revenge but rather a desire to see the righteousness of God established and generally acknowledged. Everyone who knows the holy God experiences this desire. The church is specifically instructed to pray for it (Matt. 6:9-10). And it must be acknowledged that the delay of this reign of righteousness does create dilemmas for believers.

The church knows that God's reign or kingdom was inaugurated in the ministry and death of Christ; it now anxiously awaits the consummation of this reign at his return. The church lives in the time between the two comings of Christ, the first in grace and the second in glory, one in lowliness and one in majesty, one that ended in shame on the cross and the other that will be bright with glory on the clouds of heaven (Tit. 2:11-14). And it is here, in these comings, that God's own theodicy is laid out for us.

The early church confessed with confidence that Christ's death had broken the back of evil. Christ "delivered us from the dominion of darkness and transferred us to the kingdom of his beloved Son" (Col. 1:13); "he disarmed the principalities and powers and made a public example of them, triumphing over them" (Col. 2:15); he "gave himself for our sins to deliver us from the present evil age" (Gal. 1:4); he took on our humanity "that through death he might destroy him who has the power of death, that is, the devil" (Heb. 2:14); and it is through him that "death is swallowed up in victory" (1 Cor. 15:54).

Gustav Aulén has argued that our whole understanding of Christ's death should be framed in terms of this conquest over evil.[34]

---

34. See Aulén, *Christus Victor: An Historical Study of the Three Main Types of the Idea of the Atonement,* trans. A. G. Hebert (London: S.P.C.K., 1968).

But in making this proposal, he failed to take proper account of the fact that this conquest will not become cosmic until Christ's return in glory; until that time, the people of God experience a more narrowly focused conquest through the gospel. The New Testament message is not that we are innocents who have been taken captive by the powers of evil but rather that we have willingly participated in our own captivity. Paul speaks of three sources of our bondage: (1) the powers of darkness, (2) our own fallenness, and (3) the cultural norms in which that fallenness is made public and normative. He told the Ephesians that once they had been "dead through the trespasses and sins in which you once walked, following the course of this world, following the prince of the power of the air," but through Christ they had been made alive (2:1-2). The gospel, in other words, had liberated them from the world, the flesh, and the devil.

The deliverance that the gospel declares, then, is deliverance from our complicity in this rebellion against God, our love of darkness, our devotion to all of the worldly ideologies that authenticate our rebellion. When the New Testament authors speak of the conquest of evil, they do so firstly and foundationally in the context of our relation to God, and hence they use the conceptual terms of *justification* (Rom. 3:24; Gal. 3:13; Eph. 1:7; 1 Pet. 2:24), *reconciliation* (Rom. 5:10; 2 Cor. 5:18-21; Eph. 2:16), *propitiation* (Rom. 3:25; Heb. 2:17; 1 John 2:2; 4:10), *sacrifice* (Matt. 26:28; 1 Cor. 5:7; Eph. 5:2; 1 Pet. 1:18-19; Heb. 9:14), and *redemption* (Eph. 1:7; Tit. 2:14; 1 Pet. 1:18-19).

The New Testament vision, then, is not about winning a victory but about entering into the victory that Christ has won, not of gaining the world but of saving the soul. Its message is not about making this worldly age more secure but about entering the "age to come" through Christ, not about manufacturing happiness but about finding holiness, not about purchase but about faith, not about amusement but about repentance, not about distraction but about knowing God. That is to say, the message is grounded not in ourselves but in Christ. It presents a teleology of redemption, not of progress. The purpose of the world, under the hand of God, is redemption from sin, death, and the devil, from what is fading and passing to what is eternal and enduring. "That," remarks P. T. Forsyth, is "the only teleology of the world which is as sure as sorrow, death, the soul, or its God."[35] It assures the world that, despite the ravages of poverty and sorrow, the presence in every

---

35. Forsyth, *The Justification of God: Lectures for Wartime on a Christian Theodicy* (London: Latimer House, 1948), p. 54.

society of the "wretched of the earth," the fearful prospects of nuclear warfare — despite these and many other awful realities, there is a future. It is not a future managed by human beings, a future constructed for their ends, but the future opened by the cross of Christ, the future of God's ends.

That is the aperture through which God's larger providence in the world must be seen, for all of these purposes have as their intent the establishment of his kingdom and the ultimate glorification of his Son. His government is not bureaucratic but moral and spiritual. It has sharp edges. It does not so much control evil as destroy it. God refuses to patch together the best that human life can offer; instead, he creates in human beings, by the Word and by the Spirit, more than they could find within themselves with even the most effective psychological and sociological techniques. God allows the worldly kingdoms to strut for a while before running themselves out, but for all of their "boasted pomp and show" none contributes an iota to the makings of his kingdom. Instead, he chooses the weak and foolish, the low and despised, and those who have no standing as a judgment on the worldly who do (1 Cor. 1:26-29).

It is essential that the church grasp the implications of the fact that it lives in an interim time, between the first and second comings of Christ, in the murky twilight between the inauguration and the consummation of the kingdom, between the moment when the world heard unmistakable rumblings of God's justice at the cross and the moment when the storm of his judgment will arrive.[36] Divine judgment is, in fact, the foundation of God's moral order and the fundamental premise of the gospel. As such, it is proclaimed in both the Lord's Supper and baptism, for common to both is the thought that life outside of Christ is life under God's wrath.

Although God's ordering of life is as extensive as life itself, it does have a center. The center is Christ, in the establishing of his kingdom, in the redeeming of his people, and in his own ultimate glorification, when every knee will bow "and every tongue confess that Jesus Christ is Lord, to the glory of God the Father" (Phil. 2:11). This is the key to what God is doing, the focus of his providence. But how much of this doctrine is actually believed in the church today?

36. See Leon Morris, *The Biblical Doctrine of Judgment* (London: Tyndale Press, 1960).

The View from Inside

Bartering for the Real

It is unfortunately the case that we sometimes have trouble matching up what we *ought* to believe about God's providence with what our experience of life seems to tell us is actually happening. The problem lies in the invisibility of God's providence. Daily experience has an urgency and intensity to it that often drowns out other considerations. Certainly spiritual reality is often made to appear foreign and unwelcome in the modern world, and belief in providence in particular is often relegated to the periphery of our attention. Modernity renders the reality of God's presence implausible, and the cut-and-thrust of daily existence empties it of its meaning. As God becomes increasingly weightless, the doctrine of providence is one of the first things to go.

What we call the "real world" is the world that confronts us most intensely, and this is typically not the world providentially ordered and sustained by God but the disconcertingly contingent and accidental world of modernity, not the moral world in which God's character is central, in which his holiness required the death of Christ, but the world in which values shift and slide like fads and fashions, in which we find no evidence of a canopy of meaning stretching over the whole noisy human enterprise. Perhaps it is the painful and dangerous emptiness of this world that makes it seem real to us, the cacophony of competing truth claims, the jostling for power, the relentless breakdown of family, the growing inconsequentiality of people in the giant money-making machinery of modern commerce, the callous disregard for life, the strain, fear, anxiety, and unhappiness that attend the whole process. Even the church seems inclined to view this sea of horrors as the "real world." Rather than standing apart from it, the church has entered into negotiations with this world, has made extraordinary efforts to accommodate it, and to a significant extent has absorbed its values, apparently oblivious to the fact that this world has no ultimate reality — and to the fact that that eternal world which seems so faded and threadbare by comparison is nonetheless the genuinely real world, the domain over which God is sovereign. This capitulation to worldliness seems to have taken two quite different forms, one more liberal and the other more evangelical.

The more liberal form involves an outright surrender of the Christian faith to the modern mindset. This is what Leonardo Boff enthusiastically describes as Christianity "in a maturity of consciousness, in frank and open dialogue with the realities of the world, with a view to a new incorporation of Christianity in a new society."[37] There are a host of variations on this theme. One example of a broadly accepted approach can be found in David Pailin's embrace of radical relativism. Operating on the assumption that we are always captive to our culture, he asserts that when theologians "consider the divine ultimacy, it can never be known for certain that they are describing God's own nature and not simply reflecting their entertainment, probably largely unconscious, of the prejudices of their own culture."[38] It can never be known? Or one thinks of Daniel Liechty, who has revived an old contention of some of the death-of-God proponents of the 1960s and employed the trendy tools of the deconstructionists to argue that God is simply the projection of our desires, that there is no God above who corresponds with the God we have constructed below.[39] No God above? Or one thinks of Norman Pittinger, who has relocated future realities such as heaven and hell into the present and characterized the unfolding of everyday events as an unfolding of God's own narrative.[40] God is prisoner to our history? Or one thinks of James McClendon, who, like many narrative theologians, is of the opinion that human experience provides us with the script of our theology and that the more this leads us to erase distinctions between religions, the better.[41] Psychology is theology? Or we might think of Jürgen Moltmann, who maintains that the meaning of life is not provided by God above but by the way in which human societies below are being recast such that what now breaks them apart — class and gender differences, greed, violence, and economic abuse — will one day all be put behind us when the "cosmos opens itself to the apocalyptic process."[42] Marxism is Christian eschatology?

37. Boff, "Images of Jesus in Brazilian Liberal Christianity," in *Faces of Jesus: Latin American Christologies*, ed. José Míguez Bonino (Maryknoll, N.Y.: Orbis Books, 1977), p. 9.

38. Pailin, *The Anthropological Character of Theology: Conditioning Theological Understanding* (Cambridge: Cambridge University Press, 1990), p. 75.

39. Liechty, *Theology in Postliberal Perspective* (London: SCM Press, 1990).

40. See Pittinger, *Unbounded: God and Man in Process* (New York: Seabury Press, 1976), p. 89; and *God's Way with Men: A Study of the Relationship between God and Man in Providence, Miracle, and Prayer* (London: Hodder & Stoughton, 1969), pp. 101-22.

41. See McClendon, *Biography as Theology: How Life's Stories Can Remake Today's Theology* (Nashville: Abingdon Press, 1974), pp. 87-111.

42. Moltmann, *Theology of Hope: On the Ground and the Implications of a Christian Theology* (New York: Harper & Row, 1967), p. 137.

The Evangelical Version

Evangelicals typically go in for something a little different from these daring excursions across the mud flats of modernity. Broadly speaking, they capitulate to modernity's bifurcation of life into public and private spheres, but rather than take the liberal Christians' route of losing themselves in the public sphere, evangelicals seek their meaning in the private sphere.

The private sphere of the modern world, as we have already noted, consists principally of a small circle of friends and family, perhaps of a neighborhood, in which personal relations are important. The public sphere is everything else in the larger world, the "real world," in which personal relations are often viewed as an impediment to efficiency and productivity. Dominated by bureaucracy and large structures, the public sphere runs on anonymity and subordinates values to productivity and profit. With its rude combat, inhumanity, and endless competition, the public sphere is pointedly inhospitable to genuine Christian faith. Evangelicals have substantially agreed to accept this distinction between public and private spheres and have relegated their faith to the private sphere, reinterpreting it in therapeutic terms. They assume that what they find to be meaningful internally will probably not be meaningful in the public square, and as a consequence they have tended to ignore or abandon those elements of the Christian faith that have historically been related to the public square — among which, significantly, is the doctrine of divine providence.

The need for meaning persists, however, and so evangelicals have followed their inclination to seek meaning within and have squeezed the doctrine of divine providence down to a sense of God's presence within themselves. When this treatment is further modified by their consumer mentality, the doctrine is further diminished into little more than a matter of God satisfying the needs of the self. What God is doing in the world is thus contracted into what he is doing for us personally and privately. The whole process turns God into a product and believers into customers.

In this regard, I want briefly to consider two extraordinarily successful novels by Frank Peretti, *This Present Darkness* (1986) and *Piercing the Darkness* (1989). Some might argue that they constitute an attempt to restate the doctrine of providence in such a way as to recover ground lost in evangelical capitulations to modernity. I would argue to the contrary that they constitute evidence of how difficult it has become for evangelicals to sustain a belief in God's providential presence in the world and that they demonstrate in stark fashion how completely the private elements of Christian faith have been sundered from the public elements.

The astonishing success of Peretti's books (both of the titles I mentioned have sold over a million copies) clearly suggests that he has struck some special chord among Christians. What is the secret? It's not a matter of any exceptional literary merit. His characters are two-dimensional and undeveloped, his plots are contrived, and his writing style is flat. I believe the secret lies in the fact that Peretti is offering an explanation for what has gone wrong in the world that is perfectly tailored to match the tastes, assumptions, and expectations of the evangelicals of Our Time.

The books are described as novels, but they are actually spiritual thrillers, literary docudramas that purport to reveal that much that passes as quite ordinary and unexceptional in our modern world is, in fact, the work of unseen spiritual forces, both angelic and demonic, with exotic-sounding names like Tal and Rahal. In other words, the places and people in the books are fictitious, but the *worldview* is intended to be taken literally and, in fact, to serve as a key to understanding what is going on in the world today and specifically why Christians have become so marginalized in modern society.

Peretti portrays a hidden drama going on behind the backdrop of small town life — a drama of which no secular person has any knowledge — in which angels "corkscrew" through the air, leaving behind them bright vapor trails, flashing their swords, descending upon and blasting off from the earth, and sometimes transforming themselves into mere, garden-variety, white males as they "unglory." All of these startling pyrotechnics are carried out in pursuit of the larger strategy of unhinging the aims of yellow-eyed demons with sulphurous breath, a number of whom go up in puffs of red smoke when caught in the crossfire of angelic war maneuvers. The premise is that everything that takes place in the world is the outcome of invisible conflicts being waged by supernatural beings for whom human life is both the battleground and the prize. What is there about this cosmology that is attractive to so many Christians?

First, I think Peretti is successfully capitalizing on a deep Christian dis-ease with the state of the modern world, with the diminished role Christians play in the public square. This dis-ease may register only as a troublesome apprehension, a sense that things seem to be so terribly awry in the modern world, but it also seems to be connected to an awareness that Christians have been dislodged from a place they once occupied in the world, that they have been banished from the centers of cultural power, and that no one seems to be able to provide a satisfactory explanation for why it has happened. Peretti has an explanation.

Behind the scenes of life, behind the local newspaper and the local university, behind the chief of police and the town's liberal pastor is a legion of dark, satanic forces intent on routing all Christian influence from the world. This is why Christians have been dislodged from the public square. It has nothing to do with the restructuring of the world on the basis of Enlightenment ideals or the corrosive effects of modernization. It seems to have little to do with the worldliness that has accompanied these changes and that is hostile to the will and truth of God. It doesn't even seem to have much to do with human corruption. It is all a matter of the triumph of supernatural forces over benighted Christians. I would contend that these books are statements of cultural grievance.[43]

In *This Present Darkness* and *Piercing the Darkness* we have virtual duplicates. The chief difference between these books lies neither in the plots nor in the characters but in the evils being exposed. In the one, we have a New Age conspiracy under the guise of the Universal Consciousness Society, attempting to take over Ashton, a small town, and in particular its college; in the other, we have the American Citizens Freedom Association (ACFA) and the Child Protection Department, both of which are simply fronts for satanic forces attacking the Good Shepherd Community Church for permitting both prayer and corporal punishment in its school. Here, then, are the opening shots at the list of Christian enemies: public education, modern intellectual life, public life itself, the A.C.L.U., liberal Christianity, and Eastern spirituality. Each of these is pilloried as a tool of the demonic.

Of course, these books are not really meant to be read as serious cultural criticism. Peretti offers no overt cultural criticism at all, doesn't engage in any sort of formal discourse about what, humanly speaking, motivates life. He simply speaks in terms of a basic conflict between Christians and all that is non-Christian, and the enemies of the Christian are — literally — demonized. This approach may be attractive to some Christians displaced from their culture in that it offers a specifically supernatural explanation for their malaise, but in the end it is

---

43. See John Seel, *The Evangelical Forfeit: Can We Recover?* (Grand Rapids: Baker Book House, 1993), pp. 43-46.

filled with mischief because, as Robert A. Guelich argues, whatever comfort it may offer comes through a cosmology that is more Gnostic, or early Jewish apocalyptic, than Christian.[44]

It is true, of course, that in an ultimate sense the Bible also views all of life in terms of the difference between Light and Darkness, but life is presently being lived out on a plane that is altogether more ambiguous. No one in Christ is presently all Light and, excepting the case of the unforgivable sin, no one outside of Christ is all Darkness. Christians are not yet perfect, for sin is always a residual presence, and Paul says that unbelievers, "who have not the law," are nevertheless able to "do by nature what the law requires" (Rom. 2:14) in a formal way because they are still in God's image. There is ample evidence in the letters of the New Testament that Christians are still capable of telling lies, indulging in gossip, committing sexual sins, and finding it difficult to believe God's Word. And we know that unbelievers can be kind, care for their children, and act with honesty and compassion. Although believers proceed along the path of sanctification, and unbelievers along the path of spiritual disintegration, this kind of categorical ambiguity persists through all of life.

In Peretti's cosmology, however, this ambiguity is resolved by the simple expedient of attributing all of life's activity to either the angelic or the demonic. This is Zoroastrianism in modern garb. The result of resolving the moral murkiness of life into either pure Light or pure Darkness is perfectionism on the one side and demonization on the other, and this radical bifurcation has serious ramifications for the nature of Christian faith and its function in the contemporary world. It amounts to a major reordering of the faith on the basis of a relatively minor theme in the New Testament. Peretti turns the conflict at the cross with the powers of darkness into the sole issue of faith, and in the process he subverts the true significance of the "world" and the "flesh."

I believe a second principal source for the the appeal of these books lies in Peretti's capitalization on a recognition, however inchoate, among evangelicals that secularization has taken its toll on their world as well. Religious though they may be, evangelicals have found it difficult to think that God is working out his sovereign purposes in modern society. Secularism has flattened what is spiritual in society and, often, what is spiritual in the church. It has drained the human

44. Guelich, "Spiritual Warfare: Jesus, Paul and Peretti," *Pneuma* 13 (Spring 1991): 58.

spirit, Christian and otherwise, of its capacity, as well as its need, to understand itself against the backdrop of what is eternal. Even among Christians these secular habits of thought have become so ingrained as categories for evaluating the meaning of modern life, and distinctions between Good and Evil have become so remote, that Peretti's exuberant plunges into the supernatural have had the effect of sounding a call to arms, awakening slumbering belief, and reviving a perception of the world that should never have perished. It is in this sense that it might be possible to argue that his books constitute an attempt to retrieve the lost understanding of God's providential presence in our world.

And yet as replete with supernatural presences as these books are, they are empty of the presence of God. That is what I find most striking about them. Human beings are more or less incidental to the warfare that rages between the opposing forces of demons and angels — but so, too, is God. The outcome of the battles appears to be in doubt because God is a far-off presence who has delegated the fight against evil to the angels. So what we really have here is the introduction of the angelic hosts as a surrogate for God and his providence. Like the evangelical world in which they have attained great popularity, these books are conspicuously supernatural on the surface but, ironically, quite secular underneath. Peretti has made his concessions to modernity, too — not the public capitulation of the liberals but the private capitulation of the evangelicals. This helps to explain why the outcome of his fictional battles is so indeterminate: the engagement with the demons arises not so much from a conquest already won by Christ but from a desire to win a conquest *for* Christ. While I am sure it is not his intent to empty the cross of its accomplishment, that is the result of his strategy.

Oscar Cullmann has noted the uncommonly large number of New Testament passages in which Christ is spoken of as being at God's "right hand" (e.g., Acts 2:34; 5:31; 7:55; Rom. 8:34; Col. 3:1; Eph. 1:20; Heb. 1:3; 8:1; 10:12; 1 Pet. 3:22).[45] These passages testify to the powerful rule that he is now exercising in heaven and on earth. Paul admonishes his readers about Satan's strategies in Ephesians 6:10-20 only after he has told them that by virtue of the cross and resurrection, Christ is already "far above all rule and authority and power and dominion, and above every name that is named, not only in this age

45. Oscar Cullmann, *Christ and Time: The Primitive Christian Conception of Time and History*, trans. Floyd V. Filson (Philadelphia: Westminster Press, 1964), p. 151.

but also in that which is to come" (Eph. 1:21). That is to say that the warfare with demonic powers is not still awaiting some ultimate resolution: it has been won already, and Christians have entered into the victory through their union with Christ. When Paul comes to deal with spiritual warfare in Ephesians 6:10-20, he counsels believers simply to "withstand" and "stand," drawing on the weapons of Christian character, the Word, and prayer.

Peretti's cosmic dualism, ironically, bears some resemblance to Eastern thinking, and it ends up emptying the world of God's effective presence because, although it confesses the cross, it significantly mutes what has actually been accomplished on the cross. I cannot help but think that the enormous popularity of books that are flawed in these ways constitutes a rather bleak testimony to the profound ways in which belief in God's providence and Christ's cross has been eroded even among those who are most insistent about spiritual reality.

What God Is Doing

It is a truism that the Puritans who came to New England were intent on establishing a theocracy. But, as H. Richard Niebuhr has suggested, their intentions in this regard were hardly unique.[46] Common to so many of the religious who came — the followers of Roger Williams in Rhode Island, the Germans in Pennsylvania, the Quakers in the middle colonies, the Dutch Reformed in New York, and the Presbyterians of Scottish and Irish descent who came later — was the belief that their existence as religious people could be explained only in terms of the sovereign actions of God in establishing his kingdom, that this kingdom was at odds with much of the world in which they found themselves, and that its principles had to be made supreme in society. It is true that these different groups worked out the contradictions between Christ and culture in different ways, but at least they shared the belief that, under God, life should be something other than what it is. The ideals of Christ's kingdom are realized too little in the world, his name acknowledged too infrequently, and his truth believed and obeyed too inadequately.

But if we profess that God is sovereign in his providence, are we unreasonable to think that he is presently resolving this contradiction between what is and what should be? Might it not be possible to identify

46. See Niebuhr, *The Kingdom of God in America* (New York: Harper & Row, 1937), pp. 45-87.

the places and the ways in which this is happening? If so, we would have in our hands a means by which to reduce the power of this contradiction and to find meaning in the wasteland of modernity. And hence we stumble onto one of the great religious nostrums of the day: what is meaningful, religiously speaking, is what God is currently "doing."

Reasoning along these lines would seem to account for the widespread habit, not only among charismatics but broadly throughout the evangelical world, and not only on the conservative end of Protestantism but at its theologically liberal end, too, of announcing what God is "doing" in the world today, as if the script of human life yielded plain descriptions of the details of divine providence. The older, culturally elitist liberalism was given to declaring that Christ's kingdom was breaking through wherever the latest evolutionary development happened to be taking place. Liberationists of all kinds today catch sight of God wherever social injustice (as defined by leftist standards) is being overthrown. South American liberationists see God's hand in the defeat of entrenched political power and North American capitalism. North American black liberationists see God's hand in the rattling of the white establishment. Feminist liberationists see God's hand in the erosion of male power. The World Council of Churches, with its strong commitment to pluralism, sees God doing all kinds of things in other religions. And too many televangelists have heard God whispering in their ears that he wants them to find their way into the wallets of their viewers. Everybody sees God "doing" something different.

We are all anxious to have a line on what God is providentially doing in the world to direct its outcomes. And since American culture is therapeutic and deeply psychologized, we tend to focus on what he is doing within the self. There we can get an intuitive take on what God is up to. We sense what he is "doing" in the world from our place in it.

In our rush to identify where God has shown his presence actively, we frequently overlook the biblical assertions that the providential work of God is hidden in the world and that we are called to walk not by sight but by faith, because sin is so pervasively present in human nature that human beings will always be inclined to find ways of dominating and controlling the reality of God unless God's grace redeems them from this proclivity. Unless God specifically grants an individual the power to declare what he is "doing" in the world (as in the case of the biblical prophets), the attempt to name such things is nothing more or less than an attempt at such control. More than that, it actually detracts from Christ's cross, which is the one thing that the church today is called to declare with assurance and conviction that God has done.

It is not insignificant that it is thus that the work of the Holy Spirit is narrowed in the New Testament. The Old Testament indicates that the Spirit's work was manifold. In addition to instilling obedience and faithfulness in God's people (Neh. 9:20; Num. 11:16-29; Deut. 34:9) to the will of God that he revealed (Num. 24:2; 2 Sam. 23:2), the Spirit also gave skills for work (Exod. 31:1-11), controlled nature and history (Ps. 104:29-30; Isa. 34:8-16), and was involved in the creation itself (Gen. 1:2, 7; cf. Ps. 33:6). The New Testament never denies this wider work of the Holy Spirit in the world, but neither does it dwell on such activity. The focus shifts wholly to Christ. The work of Christ and that of the Spirit are now correlated with one another. It is now the Spirit's work to apply to men and women what Christ accomplished on the cross, to produce in them faith, love, and hope of which Christ is the source and object.

It is true that the authenticity of the links between Jesus and the Spirit described in the synoptic Gospels (e.g., Luke 1:35; 2:25-27; 4:1, 14; 10:21) are disputed by some on the grounds that they are too advanced theologically. But we need to remember that the synoptic Gospels were being composed at a time when Paul's teaching had circulated widely, and, given his extensive teaching on the Spirit and his correlation of Spirit and Son in the work of salvation, it is surprising that the synoptic authors say so little about it, not that they say as much as they do. Their reticence has the mark of authenticity about it. As sparse as the development in the synoptics is, in John and in Paul the connections are strong and clear. Paul's identification of Christ with the Spirit is both developed theologically and signaled linguistically in expressions such as "the Spirit of Christ" (Rom. 8:9; 1 Pet. 1:11), the "Spirit of his Son" (Gal. 4:6); the "Spirit of life in Christ Jesus" (Rom. 8:2), and the "Spirit of grace" (Heb. 10:29). In New Testament theology, this correlation is inescapable and it is filled with importance.[47]

The point of all this for our discussion here is that Christ's work on the cross and the glory of his person are the sole criteria that we have for reading what God is doing in the world today. Anything that does not arise from Christ's saving death as interpreted by Scripture,

---

47. For a brief overview of the presentation of the Holy Spirit in the New Testament, see my book *God the Evangelist: How the Holy Spirit Works to Bring Men and Women to Christ* (Grand Rapids: William B. Eerdmans, 1987), pp. 4-10.

that does not promote Christ's glory as understood by the apostles' teaching, that does not bear the stamp of his grace as seen in obedience to his Word, love of his gospel, commitment to his church, and service of others cannot rightly be characterized as the work of God.

The earnest insistence on finding this work elsewhere — in other religions, for example, or in political or cultural developments — not only constitutes what is probably the gravest abuse of the doctrine of God today but is also, I suspect, a poignant testimony to our failure of nerve. The presumption is that if we cannot identify God's presence in the world, if we cannot with boldness and certainty say what God is "doing," and unless what God is doing meets with the approval of modernity, then it must be the case that he has been doing nothing, that he is absent. And this, in turn, speaks powerfully to the way in which our world has, in fact, been emptied of the presence of God, leaving us stripped of meaning — a condition that we now feel driven to remedy with bold pronouncements.

The recovery of an appropriate vision of God in our world is much needed today not only because the wholeness of Christian faith requires it but also because the alternatives that we have been feverishly supplying (viz., the insertion of our own agendas or our own selves as prima facie evidence of the presence of God) are so destructive. It is a tragedy that we should attempt to rest our tired and empty spirits on these broken reeds, forgetting that God's greatness and sufficiency are accessible to faith and not to sight. This is the story told by the gallery of heroes that the writer to the Hebrews parades before us, the ones who received "divine approval" (11:2). What is preeminently clear from these sketches is that belief in God's presence and in the individual nurture he provided was very often sustained against the most contrary of evidence, including martyrdom, and was not read off the self or off the nations at all. Obedience to his Word was often maintained with little or no sense of what God was elsewhere "doing" in the world.

This is the courage, faith, and conviction that the church will have to find again if it is to rise above its failure of nerve in the modern world, a world that is now so fragile, so haunted, and so filled with tragedy. For the cross is not only the place where salvation is found: it is also the place where evil has been judged and where God's triumphant holiness has been revealed. It is because of this judgment and this holiness that the church is called to be bold in its declaration, confident in its witness, and joyful in its service as it acknowledges the fact that it has been pardoned from sin and freed from the powers of darkness. The church is called to declare the message of the cross, not to uncover God's hidden purposes in the world or the secrets of his inner therapy. It is called to tell the world what God has said about its sin, not to guess at what he might be saying through daily circumstances or whispering to private intuition. And it is called to make known the coming judgment. God's glory requires this judgment, and the church awaits in hope the moment when truth will be put forever on the throne and error forever on the scaffold. And so the church looks to that time when "night shall be no more" and God's servants will "need no light of lamp or sun, for the Lord God will be their light, and they shall reign for ever and ever" (Rev. 22:5). This, then, will be the final word of God's own theodicy to which all of his providence has led.

CHAPTER 8

The Coming Generation

It would be superficial simply to say that Evangelical theology as practiced by the coming generation is becoming more liberal. Yet the evidence is suggestive of a common trend, one in which the theological tradition is conforming in its own unique way to the cognitive and normative assumptions of modern culture.

James Davison Hunter

The title of this chapter exaggerates its scope. Its scope is not the coming generation as a whole but the coming generation in leadership, and not leadership in every sphere but just in the church, and not the church in general but just those churches in which the graduates of evangelical seminaries will worship, serve, and exercise leadership.

It is of course impossible to predict with any accuracy exactly what this leadership will eventually look like. We can take a look at what these potential leaders are like today, what is important to them, how they see themselves and their world, but it is not possible to know how these predispositions will play out in the churches in the years to come. Will these leaders change? Will the churches change to accommodate them when differences in agenda and outlook arise? We cannot know. Yet it is clear that this new generation has been shaped by its passage through a deeply modernized culture as well as by its experiences in home and church. It has developed its own new agenda, been attuned to a new set of issues, and worked out its own ways of addressing those issues. Its new inclinations and strategies have a large potential to reshape the meaning as well as the direction of evangelical faith in the future.

186

In order to understand this better, I worked with Rodger Rice, director of the Social Research Center at Calvin College, and Assistant Director Ann W. Annis to survey the beliefs of students in seven representative seminaries during 1993. The students were asked a wide range of questions that help to give us a picture of how they view themselves and their world and how important their theological beliefs are in that view of the world. We were fortunate to be able to obtain the raw data from a study that James Davison Hunter conducted on seminarians in 1982, which made it possible for us to develop some illuminating comparisons. Despite some differences between the studies, there were numerous close correlations, which strengthens our belief that these are very accurate studies.[1]

In the material that follows, I will at times venture beyond the data to propose some possible explanations of their significance. Although these suggestions may be slightly speculative, three main findings are beyond dispute:

1. Seminarians say that theology is very important to them.
2. Seminarians believe that the church has lost its vision and that its theological character is crumbling.
3. The theology that seminarians say is so important to them does not, in fact, intersect very cogently with the world they inhabit mentally and practically.

1. The seven seminaries that participated in the 1993 survey were Asbury Theological Seminary, Bethel Theological Seminary, Calvin Theological Seminary, Denver Conservative Baptist Seminary, Fuller Theological Seminary, Gordon-Conwell Theological Seminary, and Talbot School of Theology. The seven seminaries that participated in Hunter's 1982 survey were Asbury Theological Seminary, Conservative Baptist Theological Seminary, Fuller Theological Seminary, Gordon-Conwell Theological Seminary, Talbot Theological Seminary, Westminster Theological Seminary, and Wheaton Graduate School. Hunter has published an analysis of the results of his survey in *Evangelicalism: The Coming Generation* (Chicago: University of Chicago Press, 1987).

Of the 3,255 seminarians on the seven campuses who were eligible to participate in the 1993 survey, 1,591, or 48.9%, were given the questionnaire. A total of 730 seminarians completed and returned questionnaires — a response rate of 45.9%, constituting 22.4% of all those eligible in the sampling pool. Hunter's 1982-83 survey of seven evangelical seminaries had an overall response rate of 64%, ranging from 50% (Talbot) to 79% (Asbury). Response rates on our survey were lower, ranging from 22.4% (Talbot) to 70.0% (Asbury). For fuller details on the study and a profile of the students surveyed, see Tables 41 to 52 in the Appendix.

The estimated sampling error in the 1993 survey (based on 730 respondents from a finite population of 3,255), when comparing percentages based on the entire sample that are in the neighborhood of 50%, is ±3.2% at the 95% confidence level.

Several different worldviews are evident in these students, and they apparently move, somewhat amphibiously, among them. It is certainly the case that their theology exercises a lax discipline over their internal world. They are at least as self-focused, self-absorbed, and therapeutically driven as their secular counterparts. All of this has potential consequences for the directions and ways in which they might seek to lead the church in the future.

There was some tantalizing evidence, which we were unable to confirm, suggesting that seminaries have succeeded in modifying at least some of the values and habits with which students entered, for we did detect differences between students who had just started and those who had been in the seminary for some time. To establish the conclusion that it was principally the seminaries that were responsible for these changes, however, it would be necessary to test the *same* students upon entry and then again four years later. It is possible that our findings can simply be attributed to differences between the students who entered at these two points. Still, there is a *possibility* that the seminaries were responsible for these changes.

An Extended Family

All of the seminaries participating in the 1993 survey are typically considered to be evangelical; in describing themselves, their students overwhelmingly chose this term. Nevertheless, there is a sense in which this conceals as much as it reveals. For example, the term does not tell us what is really important to those who identify themselves as evangelicals, nor does it tell us which broad theological traditions they belong to or what their denominational affiliation might be.

In any event, this term was clearly the most favored by the students. In the 1982 survey, 73.9% designated themselves evangelicals; in 1993, 68.3% did. A 1993 pretest survey indicated that some students found it difficult to choose only one of the possible designations, so in the main survey that followed, we allowed for a primary and a secondary choice (absent from the 1982 survey), and this introduced some nuances that proved helpful. However, although some changes have occurred in the decade that lies between the two studies, the term *evangelical* is still favored by seven to one over any alternative. The order of preference following *evangelical* in the 1993 survey was Traditional-Confessional (10.0%), Charismatic (8.4%), Fundamentalist

(4.8%), Pentecostal (3.7%), Neo-orthodox (1.5%), Liberal (1.4%), and other (5.3%; see Table 1 in the Appendix).

The students predictably gave evidence of different understandings of what constitutes evangelicalism. Some define it chiefly in theological terms, some more in terms of the practice of piety, and some in ways that might be characterized as sociological. Typical of the first group was the student who defined it as "a catch-all for orthodox belief." Another filled out this sentiment a little by saying, "I am evangelical in the sense that I believe that the Bible is God's authoritative Word and that we can only be saved through faith in Jesus Christ." These two Reformation principles, the formal having to do with authority and the material having to do with salvation, were sometimes also mentioned in their connections with other matters — for example, as going hand in hand with the "ecumenical creeds" or as entailing obedience to Christ in "all dimensions of life (business, political, environmental, social, etc.)."

The theme of practicing what is believed was frequently mentioned, especially in terms of evangelism. One student reported being "very much concerned with evangelism and missions" and stressed that this is important to what it means to be an evangelical. I was a little surprised to find that some students looked on the term from a political or sociological angle. "I find evangelical to be a middle position between liberal and fundamentalist," said one. Another appreciated the fact that "evangelicalism is a *balanced* tradition." Yet another said, "It's broad enough to include my mainstream conviction." Despite the many nuances of the term, despite its varying connotations, and despite the fact that to some it has become definitionally anemic, *evangelical* remains the chief label that these students used to describe themselves.

The students can be further classified in terms of the major religious strands in contemporary evangelicalism. Hunter identifies four such categories: the Baptist tradition (which includes more than just those churches or denominations that specifically call themselves Baptist),[2] the Holiness-Pentecostal tradition, the Reformed-Confessional

2. In Hunter's reworking of Weber's typology of ascetic Protestantism, it might be said that the Baptist tradition is that religious tradition which is not contained within the Holiness-Pentecostal, the Reformed-Confessional, or Anabaptist traditions, provided that it emphasizes congregational church polity and personal conversion arising from belief in Christ's work on the cross. The other three traditions are easier to define because they are less diffuse than the Baptistic tradition and more easily identifiable denominationally. Hunter views the Holiness-Pentecostal tradition as intensifying the pietistic undercurrents in the Baptistic

tradition, and the Anabaptist tradition (which was only lightly represented in the two studies). Of those who identified themselves denominationally in the 1982 survey, most identified with the Baptist tradition
(56.5%); in the 1993 survey, 55.5% placed themselves in this category.
The number identifying themselves as Reformed-Confessional declined
from 1982 to 1993 from 28.9% to 22.9%, and the Holiness-Pentecostal
increased from 11.5% to 16.6% (see Table 2). In the two surveys, about
a hundred denominations were named by students, and only 3.0% of the
participants did not fall under one of these classifications or were un-
affiliated with any denomination.

Yet another form of classification is that of the broad family
groups outlined by J. Gordon Melton.[3] This method initially appears
to give a picture different from Hunter's, but in fact they are not all
that different. What Hunter calls the Baptist tradition is differentiated
by Melton into Pietist-Methodist, Baptist, Independent Fundamentalist, and Adventist family groups. Hunter's Reformed-Confessional
category combines what Melton differentiates into the Reformed-
Presbyterian, Lutheran, and Liturgical families. Hunter's Holiness-
Pentecostal group comprises what Melton breaks down into distinct
Holiness and Pentecostal families. And Hunter's Anabaptist tradition
is equivalent to what Melton calls the European Free Church group.
In the 1993 survey, the largest family group of denominations represented among the responding seminarians was the Pietist-Methodist
family (29.2%); the Reformed-Presbyterian was the second largest
(18.6%), followed by the Baptist (16.4%), Independent Fundamentalist
(10.3%), and Holiness (9.9%; see Table 3).

A classification scheme used by Wade Clark Roof and William
McKinney makes distinctions in terms of the liberal-conservative denominational continuum.[4] On this basis only 8.5% of the seminarians in the

---

tradition, on the Holiness side leading to spiritual and moral perfectionism and on
the Pentecostal side leading to the intensification of spiritual experience evidenced
by tongue-speaking. He views the Reformed-Confessional tradition as rational and
objective in its temper, oligarchical in its governance, and more spiritually ascetic
in its outworking. Finally, he views the Anabaptist tradition as distinguished by a
more objective attitude toward matters of salvation, an emphasis on the interde-
pendence of the church community and the priority of the community over the
interests of the individual, and a concern for social activism and pacifism. See
Hunter, "Operationalizing Evangelicalism: A Review, Critique and Proposal," *Sociological Analysis* 42 (1981): 363-72.

    3. See Melton, *Encyclopedia of American Religion* (Detroit: Gale Research, 1993).
    4. See Roof and McKinney, *American Mainline Religion: Its Changing Shape and
Future* (New Brunswick, N.J.: Rutgers University Press, 1987).

1993 survey were classed as liberal, and the remainder were classed as either moderate (45.5%) or conservative (41.9%; see Table 4).

The picture that emerges from all this is one of very considerable diversity beneath the simple designation *evangelical*. The denominational diversity is itself sometimes an expression of other kinds of diversity that have both historical and theological components and involve issues of both worldview and religious practice. The result is that it is now impossible to predict exactly what people who refer to themselves as evangelicals will think, how they will view the world, or how they will act. However, I would argue that in the case of the evangelical students who participated in our survey this unpredictability is tied less closely to their formal theological professions or specific profile in the midst of the sort of diversity I have just described and that it is tied more closely to the sort of weight those theological professions have in the students' lives. The key issue here is not so much what their theological professions are as what efficacy those beliefs have in shaping the way they view and experience the world.

Even if this is the case, though, we would still do well to begin by taking a look at matters of formal belief. What do these students think about theology in general? What do they understand it to be, and what are their basic beliefs on some matters of doctrine?

The Vision of Theology

For the 1993 survey, we used an uncomplicated definition of theology, characterizing it as "reflection on the truth of God's Word and application of that truth to ourselves and our world." More than 90% of the respondents agreed that this was an acceptable working definition; 47.3% strongly agreed, and 43.9% simply agreed (see Table 5). The definition understandably elicited numerous proposed additions, but only rarely were these comments of disagreement; for the most part they simply proposed additions to alter a given emphasis. If there was a somewhat mildly voiced dissent on the part of some students, it had to do with their insistence that any theology that is not God-focused is for that reason quite inadequate. "So long as theology remains *theocentric*," said one student, "it is theology. If this focus shifts, then the study becomes anthropology within the context of religion." Likewise, another suggested that theology is "more a study of God and how He works with people."

A significant number of the elaborations on the basic definition had to do with the understanding of "application." These typically went in one of two directions. Some focused on the application of God's Word to the self. At its most basic level, one student wrote, "I see theology as being done by people who are seeking who God is. If a person has no faith to start with, it is impossible to understand him." But others added sentiments such as "We need application for holiness"; "If theology is not practical in some way, it does little good to those less cognitive"; and "Reflection on truth demands application in life." Other participants focused on the importance of application to society. Theology, wrote one student, "must also analyze the world, the assumptions and beliefs of the surrounding cultures. It is not enough simply to apply culture, we must critique and creatively interact with culture without compromising the gospel." And another said that theology "is essentially about communication of the Word (and its own worldview) to our contemporary world. Thus Word and world become the twin foci of our theological reflection."

Granted that the group of respondents gave evidence of different emphases and interests with respect to their perception of theology, it is nevertheless clear that they consider theology to be important. Two thirds (66.4%) indicated that without theology the rest of their lives would not have much meaning, and only 15.6% indicated that this was not the case for them (see Table 6). Furthermore, 74.9% indicated that most of their important decisions are consciously based on their theological beliefs (see Table 7).

Since a majority of the students indicated that a biblically founded and shaped theology constitutes the foundation for their life, it is important that we take a closer look at their views on the Bible. What views do they hold on the nature and function of Scripture? How do they expect to derive truth from the Bible in order to function theologically in the world?

Both the 1982 and 1993 surveys solicited the students' views on the nature of the Bible, although the 1993 survey modified Hunter's language slightly. In both years, the students very largely settled on one of two possible affirmations about its nature. In 1982, a majority of 53.8% held a view that did not entail a commitment to biblical inerrancy: "The Bible is the inspired Word of God, not mistaken in its teachings, but it is not to be taken literally in its statements concerning matters of science, historical reporting, etc." A position that *does* entail a commitment to inerrancy was held by 43.3%: "The Bible is the inspired Word of God, not mistaken in its statements and teachings and is to be taken literally, word for word" (see Table 8).

Because the phrase "is to be taken literally" is problematic inasmuch as it might be understood to mean that poetry, for example, should not be read as poetry or that figures of speech should be read as something else, we chose to omit it. With that change, the majority of respondents to the 1993 survey (54.9%) affirmed the inerrancy position, agreeing with the statement "The Bible is the inspired Word of God, not mistaken in its statements, and therefore what it teaches is authoritative and is to be followed without question" (see Table 9). The second largest group (41.8%) agreed with the statement "The Bible is the inspired Word of God, not mistaken in its teachings, but it is not to be taken as speaking factually in matters of science, details of history, etc." The changes in the figures — the decline from 53.8% to 41.8% in the number endorsing the second statement and the increase from 43.3% to 54.9% in the number endorsing the inerrancy position — could be attributable to a growing conservatism among the students, to the change in the wording of the question, or to some combination of both. Since there is considerable evidence that such changes in wording do affect the results, sometimes substantially, it would probably be safest to assume that the students' outlook on this point has not changed much since Hunter's survey. Those who were most inclined toward the inerrancy position were in the Baptist tradition; those least likely to endorse it were in the Holiness-Pentecostal tradition (see Table 10), though the differences between the groups were not great.

On this matter at least, the tilt within academic culture toward a more liberalized perception of the world, in which the constituents of the new knowledge class have numerous vested interests, has apparently not triumphed over these students. Their views have on the whole remained consistently conservative during the past decade.

On average, students reported that they study the Bible at least five days a week. The largest group (39.3%) said they studied it for 15 to 29 minutes each day; the second largest (30.9%) said they studied it for 30 to 59 minutes a day. An interesting split showed up in their responses to a question about the benefits resulting from such study. The majority (58.0%) said that the Bible "instructs me about God and His will for His people," but the next largest group (32.1%) said that it helps them discern "God's speaking to me within" (see Table 11).

There is no question that under modernity's aegis, listening to the self, finding the source of morality and meaning in the self, and leaning on intuition in making life's decisions have become routine and acceptable for many. Still, the overwhelming majority of respondents stopped short of endorsing anything like the kind of bare therapeutic absorption in the self characteristic of secular culture: only 1.0% said that the most significant gain they received from Bible study was help in getting "in touch with myself or my feelings." This is not to say that they are untouched by the therapeutic impulse, however. There is evidence that the streams of pietism and of charismatic experience now pervasive in the evangelical world have brought into it the broader cultural self orientation in a variety of ways. For example, in their response to other questions, the students showed a dramatically greater interest in aspects of divine immanence as compared with divine transcendence. So, while the students may repudiate the rhetoric of the self movement, it is quite possible that they have inadvertently baptized some of its habits for divine service, thereby blurring the distinction between how God works and how culture works.

We will examine these matters at greater length later. At this point it is enough simply to underscore the point that on the whole the survey respondents view as central to their calling and their work efforts to reflect on God's truth, relate it to themselves, and work out its implications and its relevance in the contemporary world. It is upon this truth, derived from God through his Word, that they are building their lives and typically basing their decisions about life.

Ships in the Night

A rather striking indication of the surveys is that the responding students did not find the church particularly helpful in developing their spiritual lives. The data suggest that this is not because these students began with disaffection toward the church. Quite the opposite is true. As measured by attendance, at least, their commitment to it is rather solid. The majority of participants (55%) reported attending worship services more than once a week; 42.5% reported attending once a week, and only 2.5% reported attending less than once a week.

Nevertheless, a strong majority, 71.6%, agreed or strongly agreed with the statement "Most churches today have lost a clear sense of the spiritual nature of religion" (see Table 12). This was not simply a judgment about churches and denominations other than their own; they prove to be no more sanguine about their own. And while some might have expressed this judgment out of a desire to see more charismatic activity in the churches, that was not the majority position.[5] What is it, then, that lies behind this loss of confidence in the church?

Although denominations appear to be losing their strength at present in the United States, this is not at the core of the students' discontent either. They are somewhat inclined to want the denominations to reduce their differences (see Table 13), and they believe that the churches are insufficiently concerned with matters of social justice — indeed, 59.6% asserted this (see Table 14) — but the fullest answer to their discontent seems to lie elsewhere.

We asked the students how much of their life was influenced by their church's theology, and the answer was not altogether reassuring. The largest concentration (56.8%) said that it was a "strong influence," but 36.3% reported that it was a "small influence" (see Table 15). They have little confidence that the church's "long-standing" doctrines are "the surest guide for knowing ultimate religious truth." That proposition was affirmed by only 26.6% (see Table 16). And they expressed minimal confidence that their own denomination had managed to get matters of Christian belief straight (see Table 17).

Theology as it was defined for this study really has three components. First and foundationally, theology builds from the truth of God's Word and hence must centrally be about the God of that Word, the God to whom people have access through the Word by the Holy Spirit. Second, it involves the internal culture of the believer, the process of becoming a spiritual and moral person. And third, it is about the way in which biblical truth (its teaching about the nature, character,

---

5. One third (33.3%) of the respondents to the 1993 survey reported having spoken in tongues; the corresponding figure in the 1982 survey is 34.2% (see Table 53). Where are they to be found *denominationally?* It is not surprising that 38.7% come from conservative Protestant denominations and 27.9% from moderate Protestant denominations. Somewhat more surprising is that fact that 35.0% come from liberal Protestant denominations (see Table 56). Using Hunter's grouping of denominational affiliations, 53% of those in the Holiness-Pentecostal tradition had spoken in tongues, 31.7% of those in the Baptist, 30.8% in the Anabaptist, and 22.0% of those in the Reformed-Confessional traditions (see Table 54). By denominational family, 84.2% of Pentecostals had spoken in tongues, 47.3% of Independent Fundamentalists, 30.1% of those in the Pietist-Methodist family, 25.4% of those in the Holiness family, 23.7 of those in the Baptist family, and 20.3% of those in the Reformed-Presbyterian family (see Table 55). And where are tongues-speakers located *theologically,* using as the base the students' own self-classifications? They are to be found across the entire spectrum. Using their first-choice labels, we find the following breakdown: Charismatic, 86.9%; Pentecostal, 81.5%; Neo-Orthodox, 36.4%; Evangelical 28.8%; Fundamentalist, 29.4%; Traditional/Confessional, 12.5%; and Liberal, 11.1% (see Table 57).

and acts of God) should be worked out in the daily commerce with the created order and in the surrounding culture. Where, then, has the church lost its vision?

We can only surmise from the data we have. Perhaps the disaffection is grounded in the virtual collapse of biblical preaching in the contemporary church that some have noted or in the perception that even where biblical preaching is done, it is not always sufficiently nourishing. Perhaps the disaffection can be attributed to the profound influence of modernized culture on these students. They may be dissatisfied with the church for failing to intersect substantially enough with the habits and appetites native to this modernized culture or, alternatively, they may be fully invested in the culture and feel that it is not able to make large enough connections with what goes on in the church. In that sense, they may feel that the church is no longer "relevant." Whatever the answer may be, it seems clear that the church's failure to confront internal confusion (a point we will presently explore further) is a significant part of the students' charge that the church has lost sight of its spiritual mission.

The effects of this breakdown in the church's function has shown up in the seminaries. Students now enter seminary with less biblical literacy than they used to have, often with less moral literacy, and with a considerable indebtedness to modernity for their self-understanding and for the values by which they live. Somehow, the high commitment to the inspiration of Scripture has failed to work itself out in lives centered on and disciplined by the truth of Scripture, not only in matters of doctrinal belief but also in matters of internal culture. The seminaries are being asked to remedy these serious deficits in a few short years, so that the church can have as its ministers people whose calling to serve is clear, whose Christian character is solid, whose spirituality is deep, whose biblical knowledge is excellent, and whose pastoral skills are impeccable. Without years of effective teaching and nurturing by the church, that may be asking altogether too much.

The Enchanted World

What shapes the inner world of the seminary student? We've already noted two key factors: the theology they profess and the nurture and training the church has provided. We turn now to a third ingredient — the external world. What images do they have of that world? How does it cross the line into their inner lives? What images do they have of themselves?

In order to explore these issues in the 1993 survey, we used a series of seven-point scales patterned after those used during the 1980s in the General Social Survey conducted by the National Opinion Research Center at the University of Chicago. This enabled us to contrast the responses of the 1993 seminarians with those of nationwide samples. An important pattern began to emerge. The students do endorse theological affirmations, but they also tend to separate these beliefs from the way in which they view the rest of their world — even when the theological affirmations directly impinge on that world. We can see an example of this in the way they correlate their belief in human corruption with the way in which they view culture and with the way they view the self.

First of all, the seminarians gave evidence of a belief in the corruption of human nature that stands in sharp contrast to the views of those in the national sample. Respondents were asked to judge basic human nature using a seven-point scale in which 1 = "Human nature is basically good" and 7 = "Human nature is fundamentally perverse and corrupt." In the national survey of a general population, 16.6% of respondents adopted positions on the continuum leaning toward the assertion that human nature is basically perverse and corrupt (i.e., points 5-7 on the scale). Among the seminarians responding to the 1993 survey, 79.4% adopted positions in this range, and only 9.0% asserted that human nature is basically good (i.e., selected points 1-3 on the scale; see Table 18). Furthermore, 79.5% of the seminarians characterized the world as basically "a place of strife and disorder" rather than of "harmony and cooperation," compared with 33.8% of the national sample (see Table 20).

However, in responding to other questions designed to gauge their perception of the outside world, the seminarians' belief in its perversity and corruption was substantially muted. When presented with a scale that ranged from "The world is basically filled with evil and sin" to "There is much goodness in the world which hints at God's goodness," 28.0% of the seminarians selected positions characterizing the world as basically good (compared to 53.3% of the national sample), and only 38.4% selected positions characterizing the world as basically evil (compared to 18.5% of the national sample; see Table 19). How do we account for the fact that a large majority (nearly 80%) of the seminarians endorses the theological assertion that that human nature is fundamentally perverse, but only a minority (38.4%) views the outside world as filled with sin. They seem to be applying different standards to human nature on the one hand and human culture on the other. It may be that the students have adopted the secular presupposition that culture is essentially neutral, immune to the sort of corruption that infects individual human nature.

Selecting positions on a scale that ranged from the assertion that "Human achievement helps to reveal God in the world" to "Most human activity is vain and foolish," the seminarians were quite divided, though as a group they adopted positions somewhat different from those adopted by the general sample. Among respondents, 37.5% of seminarians took positions weighted toward the assertion that human achievement reveals God (compared to 89.3% in the national survey). On the other hand, 37.1% adopted positions weighted toward the assertion that human activity is essentially vain and foolish (compared to 12.7% in the national survey; see Table 21). A clearer majority, 51.9%, nonetheless chose positions weighted toward the assertion that "Good persons must be deeply involved in problems and activities of the world," compared with 20.5% who chose positions weighted toward the assertion that "Good persons must avoid contamination by the corruption of the world" (see Table 22).

This same pattern is evident in responses to other questions. For example, 90.1% of the students participating in the 1993 survey affirmed the belief that Jesus Christ is "the only absolute Truth for humankind" (see Table 23), but 49.4% of them maintained that "other religions contain some truth and should not be seen as completely wrong" or positions yet more inclusive (see Table 24). In the area of evangelism, they were asked whether it is "in poor taste when sharing the gospel to emphasize damnation and repentance," and 41.9% indicated that they thought it was, either always or under most circumstances (see Table 25).

The reasons offered for this diffidence appear to be cultural in nature. Of course it is true, as one respondent put it, that "every situation is different and needs to be handled differently." However, the concerns of our pluralistic culture were also evident. To the question of whether an unbeliever should be told of his or her fate, one student said, "It always depends"; a second wrote, "Eventually, but not initially"; and a third maintained that an unbeliever should not be told "unless you have had repeated discussions and earned the right to be heard." This is a rather different sentiment from that recorded in the book of Acts. The essential relativism of our culture demands a considerable civility of all of us and often forces views that are distinctive into a completely privatized, inner realm.

This gap between the beliefs that the students profess to hold and the beliefs that actually shape their behavior and worldview is even more significant in matters of the self. Again, despite the strong affirmation they make of the essential corruption of human nature, their responses to a number of questions seem to indicate their conviction that the self is essentially innocent. They seem to be as uncertain about how sin works within the self as they are about how it works in culture. They also give evidence of being much taken with the pursuit of self-fulfillment.

For the most part, the seminarians affirm something like the biblical doctrine of sin, which locates the source of rebellion against God in the self. This rebellion is characterized by pride, by a refusal to submit to God and to his law, and it issues in all the human vices that break apart human relations, creating a world in which greed, corruption, violence, and inhumanity are pervasive and sometimes even become institutionalized. As we noted earlier, this is what the Bible pejoratively describes as the "world," a public context that makes righteousness appear strange and that makes many expressions of human fallenness appear normal and even normative.

This is not to say that the Bible views the self exclusively from the perspective of its fallenness, for while the fall remains a present reality in human life, the *imago Dei* remains as well, preserving the human capacity for moral experience, for meaning, and for God. Thus we experience the strange ambiguities of human life, informed by an inner sense of the difference between right and wrong through the conscience, while all too often filled with a painful sense of how that moral sense has been violated, a sense of obligations refused, duties abandoned, people trampled, families betrayed, and unethical actions perpetrated. On balance, however, the 1993 survey seems to suggest that at the center of the lives of the participants, a vision of the self as individually discovered or created is more powerful than a vision of the self as fallen, perverse, and corrupt. This vision quite clearly has less to do with their professed theology than with their debt to their culture.

Beginning in the 1960s, a sea change occurred in American culture as secularization took hold. While self-mastery remained a virtue in the marketplace, self-mastery in personal life, expressed in such things as attempts to prevent or rectify moral failure, increasingly diminished. It certainly disappeared in our public discourse as a *religious* obligation. In fact, in its place there arose an ideology of the self that moved in an entirely different direction. The moral work of self-discipline was replaced, according to Hunter, by "the virtual veneration of the self, exhibited in deliberate attempts to achieve self-understanding, self-improvement, and self-fulfillment."[6] Nor was any significant resistance to this change offered by those who professed belief in the traditional Christian doctrine of sin.

Daniel Yankelovich conducted research in an attempt to plot this sea change and turned up some disquieting evidence.[7] On the basis of his findings, he argued that America had, for some time, been searching for new meanings by which to live. This search began on college campuses during the 1960s but soon spread into mainstream society and older age groups; by 1980, many people well into middle age had involved themselves in the search. Yankelovich defined culture as I have in this book, as the set of shared values that are held to prescribe what is normal in a society. These values encompass the small and great things of life — what it means for a man to wear an earring, say, or a woman to use the title *Ms.*, what it means to drive a Cadillac, to be a Republican, to be a Black Muslim, to support abortion, to carry a handgun, or to be a Christian believer. Each of these means something to us — to ourselves and to other people. Each has its own significance in the cultural shorthand in which we all communicate. The accumulation of all of these values provides the texture of contemporary culture, its biases, its distinctive point of view. Yankelovich argued that the set of values that prevailed in the 1960s had been stood on its head by 1980. Traditional mores were routed. And at the heart of the change was a new emphasis on finding "the full, rich life, ripe with leisure, new experience, and enjoyment, as a replacement for the orderly, work-centered attitude of earlier decades."[8] It was a change so pregnant with significance that Yankelovich likened it to the shifting of tectonic plates beneath the earth's surface.

These new cultural impulses, now experienced by a substantial majority in the nation, are rooted in a fresh insistence that life consists of more than the daily routines of work, that it is more important to enjoy its pleasures than to deny them out of a moral concern, that the chores of living need to be transcended in the search for a fuller and deeper life in which there are richly experienced moments of self-expression and self-discovery. The new search is, in fact, being driven

6. Hunter, *Evangelicalism: The Coming Generation*, p. 65.

7. See Yankelovich, *New Rules: Searching for Self-Fulfillment in a World Turned Upside Down* (New York: Random House, 1981).

8. Yankelovich, "New Rules in American Life: Searching for Self-Fulfillment in a World Turned Upside Down," *Psychology Today* 15 (1981): 310.

by an intuition that we can find meaning only to the extent that we get in touch with the self (understood here as a hierarchy of inner needs) through a process of inner discovery involving self-help, self-satisfaction, and self-expression. And, having grown up in generally affluent conditions, this new generation of self-seekers largely assumes that the wealth that our strapping economic system produces in such rich abundance is essential to this process. They assumed that to have is to be, and so they have anointed economic well-being as both a right and a necessity.

Both Hunter in his 1982 survey and we in our 1993 survey employed some of Yankelovich's questions, so we have a basis for some interesting extended analysis. Our findings bear out in some detail the conclusions that Hunter arrived at about a decade ago — principally that these students, who represented a distinct group within society (what he called "strong formers"), are oriented toward self-fulfillment, self-expression, and personal freedom to a degree that often exceeds that of the more general sample of citizens surveyed in Yankelovich's study.

The gap between a biblical view of the self and what these "strong formers" affirm is quite evident. In our 1993 survey, 40.2% of the respondents affirmed that "realizing my full potential as a human being is just as important as putting others before myself" (see Table 26). Had Christ held this belief, for example, it would have ended all prospects of the incarnation. He did not consider his own potential in glory as something to be weighed alongside considerations of service to sinners, to those who were under God's judgment. He forsook his own place in glory for those sinners (cf. Phil. 2:5-12; 2 Cor. 8:9). Furthermore, 86.7% of the respondents to the 1993 survey indicated that they believe self-improvement is important and they work hard at it, 74.5% want to be well rounded, 64.6% reported feeling a strong need for new experiences, and 52.3% acknowledge spending a great deal of time thinking about themselves (see Table 26). Similar sentiments show up in their responses to questions about their attitudes toward work (see Table 27) — responses that Hunter characterizes as very similar to those of a sample from the general population.

There is a further difficulty involving the relationship between ends and means in this search for personal satisfaction. The process of seeking self-fulfillment is itself both end and means for the modern individual, and it inevitably conflicts with the efforts of others who are similarly engaged. Consensus is impossible where everyone blindly pursues self-interest. Stable societies depend on some level of self-restraint, some degree of willingness to set aside self-interest in the name of cooperation and harmony. But our therapeutic age condemns such restraint as repressive and pernicious. Rules are typically anathema. It is clear now that this elevation of the self is based on patently humanistic premises, including the naive assumption that the world is benign, neutral. It is inevitable, then, that the journey of discovery into the wonderful, sanitized world of the inner self is consistently interrupted by the disillusionments of reality.[9]

The orientation toward self is also evident in the seminarians' views concerning salvation. While 41.6% indicated an orthodox belief that the most important benefit of salvation was that they had been spared God's judgment because of Christ, 45.5% listed as the most important benefit such things as an experience of inner peace, divine power, an ability to love others, and a sense of community within the church (see Table 28) — all benefits that are consistent with the values of a therapeutic culture.

This fascination with the self is not a uniquely Christian or uniquely American phenomenon; it is the calling card modernity leaves behind wherever it goes. Edward R. Norman, Dean of Chapel at Christ Church College in England, has noted the same patterns among students there — "the idea that life owes us personal fulfillment; that it is all about the internal development of our sensibilities and material satisfaction; that we have a wide range of 'rights' so sacred that we are justified in developing or enjoying them without regard to their effect on others; that self-expression is more important than self-control." He goes on to say that of all of the shifts he has seen in the past two decades, especially in the world of education, he believes this will prove to be "the most far-reaching and, for man, the most devastating."[10]

Is it not at least a little strange, though, that these patterns should have shown up with such intensity among evangelical seminarians? L. Guy Mehl, a psychologist at Lancaster Career Development Center who has counseled more than a thousand ministerial candidates over the past twenty years, has also noticed this deeply ingrained therapeutic interest in the self. He believes it is rooted in the fact that many of these candidates are coming out of dysfunctional homes in which there

9. For a development of this theme, see David G. Myers, *The Inflated Self: Human Illusions and the Biblical Call to Hope* (New York: Seabury Press, 1981), pp. 47-81.

10. Norman, "Freedom in an Age of Selfishness," *Intercollegiate Review,* Spring 1993, p. 3.

has been trauma and pain, sexual abuse and divorce.[11] He argues that in these troubled family settings the seminarians learned how to become "rescuers" (i.e., to intervene in problem situations in an effort to set things right) and in doing so typically developed traits of co-dependency. In evangelical faith they find deliverance from life's darkness and ugliness, but they carry with them the insecurities and uncertainties of their past. They continue to serve as co-dependent rescuers in their professional capacity in the church, typically fashioning their ministry in terms of counseling. Mehl argues that this sort of pastor tends not to become a leader. Rescuers are inclined to identify with the wounded, with the church's failures, and while they typically do a good job of conveying compassion and empathy in that regard, their co-dependent mentality tends to keep the church in its weaknesses rather than leading it out of those failings.

Mehl's observations do seem to accord with a common situation in evangelical seminaries today: their counseling services are often overloaded, unable to provide enough help to all of those who have brought into the seminaries unresolved problems from the past. His observation may also help to explain the considerable popularity of seminary degrees in counseling.

The extremely strong evidence of the therapeutic mind-set among respondents to the 1993 survey suggests that this mind-set may well soon be spreading yet further among the evangelical laity to which they will be ministering. They will likely offer leadership that is more consensual, that takes large account of the feelings of those being led, and that will place as much emphasis on preserving relationships as it does on acting on principle. Although this form of leadership has its virtues, I have to wonder whether it will be strong enough to face the profound challenges that modernity will pose to the church in the years ahead.

The World in a Lens

The complexity of the modern world with its growing diversity and pluralism, the daily jousting between competing belief systems, and

---

11. Mehl has detailed his findings in an unpublished paper entitled "The Quality of Ministerial Candidates from a Counselor's Perspective" (1991). With regard to his thesis concerning the source the therapeutic impulse among seminarians in troubled childhood, it is interesting to note that 79.9% of the respondents to the 1993 survey indicated a belief that forgotten childhood experiences could have an effect on them (see Table 60).

the vast range of our knowledge are making it more and more difficult for any worldview to function consistently or, perhaps, even survive. Worldviews are interpretive grids that enable us to understand our experience, to read its meaning, to see it in its wider perspective. They enable us to see the world as a whole and, in that light, to find meaning in the many parts of the whole that we encounter. Worldviews are thus rooted in our understanding of what the world is, and in this sense they push our thought to the edges of ultimacy. Worldviews reveal and are the outgrowth of what is religious (or what takes the place of religion) in our lives. It is therefore a matter of some importance to discover what sorts of worldviews the seminarians we surveyed were holding.

In an earlier work, Robert Wuthnow delineated the essential characteristics of four basic worldviews: theistic, individualistic, social-scientific, and mystical. He was seeking to find those beliefs that would be *likely* to place a person in one worldview or another. In assembling the 1993 survey, we used the same questions Wuthnow had developed for this attempt at locating students in one meaning system or another.[12]

Of Wuthnow's four basic worldviews, most of our respondents placed themselves in the theistic, individualistic, and mystical categories; only small number showed any attraction toward the social-scientific worldview (see Table 29). The theistic worldview entails belief that life is derived from God, sustained by God, and given meaning by God. The individualistic worldview is somewhat more difficult to describe, but it entails a belief that individuals are in the center of their world and in charge of their own destinies. This goes beyond a simple belief in free will, however, to a conviction that individuals transcend all social forces and are personally responsible for all of their own achievements and failures. In this sense, the individualistic worldview stands in marked contrast to the social-scientific worldview, which entails a belief in the force of social and cultural factors external to the individual. Finally, the mystical view is less cognitive in nature than the others. It entails a belief that the meaning of life resides in intuitively comprehended peak experiences — typically experiences in which a person feels at one with the universe or a close proximity to something unusually holy or sacred. These experiences make lasting impressions but also feed a mind-set that favors symbols, myths, and fantasies.

12. See Wuthnow, *The Consciousness Reformation* (Berkeley and Los Angeles: University of California Press, 1976), pp. 136-42.

Responses to the 1993 survey indicated that most of the participants held the theistic worldview: 61.2% of those placing in this category had the highest possible score, 29.1% the next highest, and no one scored beneath the midpoint of the scale (see Table 30). The second most popular worldview proved to be the individualistic, with 17.3% in the highest classification: 48.8% of those placing in this category fell into the two highest scoring groups, and 51.2% fell into the two lowest scoring groups — indicating that about half the seminarians exhibited a high likelihood of functioning with this worldview and half exhibited a lower likelihood (see Table 31). Finally, with regard to the likelihood of holding a mystical worldview, 51.6% of our respondents placed in the two highest scoring groups, and 48.4% placed in the two lowest scoring groups (see Table 32). We can draw three clear conclusions from this material:

1. There is no single, exclusive way in which these students are likely to view their world. They apparently operate with more than one worldview, depending on the circumstances.

2. The apparent popularity of the individualistic and mystical worldviews and the comparatively unpopularity of the social-scientific worldview suggest that these students see their lives as being somewhat impervious to the forces that shape society and hence to the values that arise from those forces today — namely, modernity. This confirms a conclusion we drew earlier on the basis of other evidence from the survey: while the students affirm the corruption of human nature, they were inclined to view culture as neutral and resisted the notion that it has the power to corrupt individuals. Those who subscribe to the mystical worldview are likewise inclined to view cultural forces either as essentially benign or as positively beneficent, the locus within which the sacred is to be found.

3. The strong showing of the individualistic and mystical worldviews appears to be providing soil in which the therapeutic interests can take root and grow.

The Maze of Modernity

It has become hard to escape the conclusion that the reality of God now rests somewhat inconsequentially upon the church, and yet it is not always easy to identify the mechanisms, the psychological devices that have made this the case. However, some pieces in this puzzle now seem to be coming together.

The seminarians in the 1993 survey would likely contest the assertion that theology is not a central, defining reality in their lives. Of the respondents, 66.4% said that life would not have much meaning without theology (see Table 6), and 74.9% said that their most important decisions are consciously based upon theology (see Table 7). A further 23.2% said they thought these decisions rest on their theology in a general or unconscious way. Thus fully 98.1% affirmed that their important decisions about life are in one way or another intimately connected to their theology. Obviously they do not consider their theology to be an inconsequential factor in their lives.

This is not to say that the seminarians are sanguine about the role of theology in other people's lives, however. When asked to assess the statement "While evangelical theology is still professed, it is losing its power to define what being an evangelical means and how evangelicalism is practiced," 61.2% agreed and only 14.2% disagreed (see Table 33). In additional comments, the great majority of students went on to lament the state of theology in the church. Their explanations of the loss of the church's theological soul generally took one of two directions: they either asserted that people are losing their faith in the truth quotient of theology or they maintained that the culture is becoming so intrusive that theology can no longer function as it ought.

Following the first line of argument, one student lamented that evangelical theology "is losing its power because evangelicals have lost their pursuit of truth" — a variation of another's respondent's observation that "evangelicals are discouragingly uninformed about their theology." Evangelicalism has become too "inclusive," they said, or it is "becoming wishy-washy in doctrine," or it has allowed its theological interests to focus on petty concerns while allowing the "big concerns" to fade from view. Doctrinal lines, said one student, "seem more fluid" now.

The preponderance of the student analysis, however, followed the second line of argument. They maintained that theology has lost its power to define what evangelicalism ought to be because of a "growing worldliness" in the church. They characterized this worldliness in a variety of ways, but they generally shared a perception that modernity is intruding on the inner life of the church. One student characterized this influence as "devastating." Another stated that pluralism "has led to minds that will accept *anything!*" One student explained the loss of the church's theological vision as "the result of the fragmentation, specialization, individualism, secularization, relativization of life in the modern Western world. The evangelicals have not grasped the depth of the problem nor have they any useful correctives." Both the academic world and "liberal church bureaucracies" were charged with having "harmed evangelicalism" along these lines. As the churches correspondingly come to embrace "many of the postmodern ideas," the church itself has lost its meaning and sense of purpose.

So the seminarians expressed considerable unanimity in affirming the importance of theology in the life of the church and the very serious consequences that follow once it is dislodged. Still, these obviously deeply held sentiments were difficult to correlate with our findings about the role of theology in the students' own lives.

I believe that we can account for the disjunction between seminarians' high regard for theology in the life of the church on the one hand and their more ambiguous regard for theology in the context of their own day-to-day lives on the other hand by looking to their ambiguous use of the term *theology*. They appear to be using the term to refer (1) to a certain group of biblically derived core beliefs linked to a sense of the transcendence of God and (2) to a more nebulous group of beliefs that are perhaps more accurately described as *religious* rather than theological and are linked to a sense of the immanence of God. The use of the term in the first sense is grounded in revelation rather than personal experience and includes belief in such things as the divinity and perfection of Christ, the corruptness of humanity after the fall, and the atoning power of Christ's sacrifice on the cross. The use of the term in the second sense is connected more to personal experience of God's presence in one's life than to a self-conscious interaction with Scripture. The students tended to link both of these senses to the term *theology*, and it is this amalgam that 98.1% of the respondents reported as undergirding their important life decisions in one way or another.

Where questions more closely distinguish between theological and religious beliefs, there are more dramatic differences in their responses. For example, while 94.8% said "Without *my religious faith,* the rest of my life would not have much meaning to it" (see Table 36), only 66.4% said "Without theology, the rest of my life would not have much meaning to it" (see Table 6). Religious belief apparently makes life meaningful for a fair number of students in ways that theology does not.

The distinction between specifically theological and religious beliefs does seem to speak to the issue of the disjunction between the seminarians' affirmation of the importance of theology and the lower level of efficaciousness that they accord it in their day-to-day lives. We sought to gauge this disjunction by employing a theological saliency scale.[13] The results of this test indicated that the seminarians do grant theology some practical importance in their lives, but not to the degree that their profession would lead one to expect. On the four-part scale, 17.0% scored in the highest bracket and 38.3% in the next highest, while 43.8% placed in the lower two categories of the index (see Table 34). While only 13.0% scored below the midpoint of the index, the *perception,* or perhaps profession, of the importance of theology in these students' lives is still at odds with the reality. Why is this so? There may be many reasons for this that our study was not able to identify, but some important findings relative to how the participants understand God may well hold part of the answer.

God is clearly not just important but central in the lives of the respondents to the 1993 survey. When asked to identify which of six items have influenced their lives (e.g., genetic makeup, socio-political powers), God ranked high. In response to another question, 69.0% of the respondents indicated their belief that God "determines my life almost entirely," and a further 30.6% indicated their belief that God exerts a "strong influence on my life" (see Table 35). As we have already noted, fully 94.8% indicated that without their religious faith, the rest of their life would not have much meaning, and, among these, 69.4% asserted this *strongly* (see Table 36). However, it seems rather clear that the seminarians were making an implicit distinction between experiential religious faith on the one hand and theology on the other. The key to this distinction seems to lie in their understanding of God.

The students were asked to locate their views on a seven-point scale that ranged between the contrasting statements "God is almost totally removed from the sinfulness of the world" and "God reveals Himself in and through the world." Since this test had also been used nationally, it was possible to compare the views of our respondents to those of a general sample. Nearly eight out of ten seminarians (79.0%) placed somewhere between the midpoint and the pole affirming that God reveals himself through the world; they clearly rejected the view that he separates himself from the world's sinfulness (see Table 37). This affirmation of divine immanence on the part of the seminarians

13. The test we used in our survey was modeled after a test used by Wade Clark Roof and Richard Perkins; see their article "On Conceptualizing Salience in Religious Commitment," *Journal for the Scientific Study of Religion* 14 (1975): 111-28.

was even stronger than that of the national sample, in which only 70.9% chose this view.

This strong attraction to divine immanence rather than divine transcendence appears also to have been a factor in another answer. Given a bare choice between two statements about God, rather than being able to place themselves on a scale, 80.3% of the seminarians preferred the statement "God's love includes all people; His desire is that all should know him" to the statement "God is holy; evil will not triumph." Only 18.5% indicated a preference for the second statement, and only 1.1% indicated that they affirmed both statements equally (see Table 38). Some students wrote that they did not like having to choose between the two statements, since they believed both were true. The question was designed to investigate their *foundational* understanding of God, however, and by a ratio of more than four to one they chose the God of love over the God of holiness.

How are we to explain the ascendancy of the religious dimension in these students' lives over the theological dimension? The answer seems to be that they are attracted to the immanence of God, a sense of divine presence that does not require mediation or interpretation by the Word of God. This certainly jibes with our survey's indication that the students' religious consciousness ranked higher than the saliency of their theology: 84.4% *strongly* declared that God "constructs reality and makes life meaningful" (see Table 39).

I believe these elements come together to form the outlines of a coherent picture. We noted that although the seminarians strongly asserted their belief that human nature is sinful and corrupt, they were less convinced that their society and culture are similarly corrupt, and they expressed very little concern that they might become morally and spiritually contaminated by the world. Reinhold Niebuhr wrote *Moral Man and Immoral Society,* but the students seem to want to turn it around and speak of immoral man and moral society — or, perhaps more accurately, *neutral* society. And I believe it is the students' belief in the relative innocence of culture that sets the stage for their acceptance — indeed, their overwhelmingly acceptance — of divine immanence. They indicate not only a belief that God provides shape and meaning to life through his presence in it but also that they can gain access to this meaning through the self. It appears that however corrupt and sinful they belief human beings to be, they nonetheless assume that they are sufficiently innocent to be capable of discerning the meaning of life and simultaneously achieving self-fulfillment through a process of looking within themselves.

In this unusual confluence of ideas, seeds have been sown that may change the shape of evangelical faith very significantly in the years to come. The seminarians who participated in the survey appear to have adopted an evangelical piety with both theological and religious dimensions, the one defined more by a sense of divine transcendence and the other more by a sense of divine immanence. From the first come their beliefs about God's holiness, human corruption, the person of Christ, about the need for his death. From the second come practices associated with their regard for the self, their understanding of the presence of God in society (a more liberal understanding than that expressed by the sampling of those in the larger secular society), and their belief that their experience in society will help them to determine God's meaning for them as individuals. Exactly how these different models of relating Christ and culture will work out has yet to be seen, but it seems clear to me that this is an unstable mix. In time it will either come apart or mutate into something different.

The Sum of It All

It is now a truism among most social scientists who have analyzed modern culture that it is characterized by a deep and profound bifurcation between public and private life. The public square has come to be dominated by large corporations, bureaucracies, and institutions that, in the denseness of their interconnections and the anonymity of the ethos they create, have rendered private interests and values largely irrelevant to public discourse. Individuals are fit into this context like small cogs in a mammoth machine — a machine that is not at all responsive to, or even knowledgeable about, the content of their private consciousness. And, on the other side of this divide, individuals now think of life in terms of internal attitudes, private perceptions, and the interests associated with any of a number of isolated worlds — family, church, friends, colleagues, and the like. They are likely to function with one set of values and expectations in the public arena and an entirely different set in the private arena.

This state of affairs typically produces an enfeebling sense of having been dislodged from much of life, a sense of overwhelming powerlessness that undermines personal security and fulfillment in the public world. This sense of dislocation and alienation has produced many different forms of protest ranging from cultural and political movements that are seeking to "take back" portions of public life to new religious movements that are challenging the nature of public rationality and purpose. The invincibility of these powerful and deeply entrenched processes of modernization, however, virtually ensures that these protests will eventually have to be internalized and their advocates have to be content to settle for privatized meaning.

The results of our survey appear to offer fairly clear evidence of this process. It is there in a heightened sense of civility toward other religions, a tolerance that sometimes carries with it a willingness to accord those teachings some truth and, in a few cases, a lot of truth. It is there in a heightened concern to avoid offending people with the claims of an exclusive gospel. It is there in the rise of the therapeutic impulse within the evangelical faith, a growing sense that the constraints placed on believers by the world — its daily routines and its work demands — are largely incidental to the discovery of what life is *really* about. And it is very significantly there in the new and growing emphasis on the self. Indeed, the survey participants seemed disinclined to attach any biblical inhibitions to the cultivation of the self because they apparently assume that while human nature may be corrupt, the self is not.

I believe that the anomaly of the seminarians' theological affirmation of the concept of human depravity and simultaneous psychological endorsement of the essential innocence of the self is best explained by the fact that these students adopt alternate worldviews as they move from one context to another. A theistic worldview that is significantly defined by a sense of divine transcendence will typically drive those who hold it to view human nature and modern culture as perverse and corrupt; a theistic worldview that is significantly defined by a sense of divine immanence, on the other hand, will not. In contexts where they actually engage the world, the seminarians who took part in the survey gave evidence of moving away from a transcendence-oriented theistic worldview toward a more immanence-oriented theistic worldview, which more naturally assumes that God ensures the essential innocence of life's experiences. In contexts where they become more specifically involved with matters of the self, the majority of seminarians gave evidence of shifting away from a theistic worldview altogether, toward individualistic or mystical worldviews. They appear to assume that the self provides a vantage point from which the world can accurately be viewed and that the world intrudes few of its discordant realities upon the self. More than this, a significant number of the respondents to the survey appear to believe that the self is the locus within which the divine can be found through peak experiences that are grasped intuitively.

As we have seen, the 1993 survey uncovered some large inconsistencies in the respondents' perspectives. These inconsistencies are rooted in two facts. First, the Word of God, which a substantial majority of the seminarians consider divinely inspired in a stringent sense, is not engaging their inner lives very completely. Two decades ago, the debate was over the *nature* of Scripture; today the debate should be over its *function*. The students affirm biblical authority, but in practice they greatly circumscribe it. When it comes to the way they view the world and the place they accord to the self, they are guided less by a biblical worldview than by contemporary assumptions derived from the culture. Second, the students' perspective on God is also a blend of what is biblical and what is cultural. Some internal cognitive bartering has taken place, probably inadvertently, that has produced an understanding of God that is partly biblical (and typically defined in orthodox theological terms) and partly indebted to the presumptions of modernity, subordinating a sense of divine transcendence to a sense of divine immanence that is not far removed from what once prevailed in older Protestant liberalism.

Our respondents seemed to be aware of the changing shape of evangelical faith today, though they were less certain about the direction in which it might be headed. It is significant that as they looked to the future, roughly a third (31.4%) believed evangelicalism would stay the same as it is today, but nearly the majority (46.6%) believed it would polarize, producing a split between those who were more liberal and those who were more conservative (see Table 40). Those who predicted change were uncertain whether the new developments would be good or bad. In any event, the fact that most of the coming generation is expecting potentially explosive changes in the evangelical world has to be disquieting for the leaders who are currently presiding over this world.

But the 1993 survey also offered three encouraging findings to balance this uncertainty. First, the participating seminarians do take Scripture seriously, and this has always been a *sine qua non* for any successful reform of the church. There is at least the potential for the renewal of the church in their commitment.

Second, these students affirm that theology should be central in the life of the church. If they carry through on this, they may be able to prevent the church from being absorbed into modernity. It is theology as we defined it for the purposes of the 1993 survey that provides the reason for the "vivid otherworldliness" of the sort that preserves the church in the midst of the world and fuels the church's desire to change its world morally and spiritually. Genuine theology is other-worldly in the sense that it grounds our understanding of God in divine revelation rather than human intuition or reason, and this grounding confers the power and authority to transform the world. Without theology, the church will inevitably become "this-worldly." To value theology, then, is to value the means by which the church can become more faithful and more effective in this world.

Third, these students are dissatisfied with the current status of the church. They believe it has lost its vision, and they want more from it than it is giving them. Neither their desire nor their judgment in this regard is necessarily amiss. Indeed, it is not until we experience a holy dissatisfaction with things as they are that we can plant the seeds of reform. Of course, dissatisfaction alone is not enough. It remains uncertain whether these particular students, inwardly burdened as they seem to be with the traumas and pains of dysfunctional families, will actually be able to provide the *kind* of leadership that the church needs today. But God's grace is bigger than our biggest needs, deeper than our deepest cuts and wounds, and greater than even our greatest hopes. Those whom God has used to move the church in the past have not always come from perfect families, have not been without their inadequacies, fears, and insecurities. In spite of these frailties and wounds, however, God has used them; sometimes, it seems, he has used them to special effect *because* of these frailties and wounds. There is nothing in modern experience that is so overwhelming that God cannot again actualize his truth in the life of his people, nothing so deafening in modernity as to drown out the voice of grace, and nothing in our contemporary world that need lead us to think that God does not intend to reform, strengthen, and renew his people once again.

CHAPTER 9

Speaking with a Different Voice

I have been on my guard
not to condemn the unfamiliar.
For it is easy to miss Him
at the turn of a civilization.

David Jones

I have written this book because, like the students who participated in our survey, I believe the vision of the evangelical church is now clouded, its internal life greatly weakened, its future very uncertain, and I want something better for it. I want the evangelical church to be *the church*. I want it to embody a vibrant spirituality. I want the church to be an alternative to post-modern culture, not a mere echo of it. I want a church that is bold to be different and unafraid to be faithful, a church that is interested in something better than using slick marketing techniques to swell the numbers of warm bodies occupying sanctuaries, a church that reflects an integral and undiminished confidence in the power of God's Word, a church that can find in the midst of our present cultural breakdown the opportunity to be God's people in a world that has abandoned God.

To be the church in this way, it is also going to have to find in the coming generation leaders who exemplify this hope for its future and who will devote themselves to seeing it realized. To lead the church in the way that it needs to be led, they will have to rise above the internal politics of the evangelical world and refuse to accept the status quo where that no longer serves the vital interests of the kingdom of

God. They will have to decline to spend themselves in the building of their own private kingdoms and refuse to be intimidated into giving the church less and other than what it needs. Instead, they will have to begin to build afresh, in cogently biblical ways, among the decaying structures that now clutter the evangelical landscape. To succeed, they will have to be people of large vision, people of courage, people who have learned again what it means to live by the Word of God, and, most importantly, what it means to live before the holy God of that Word.

Can this happen? I believe it can, but not until these leaders have successfully accomplished two major projects. First, the church is going to have to learn how to detect worldliness and make a clear decision to be weaned from it. Around us today there looms a post-modern world that is bringing about many ominous breaks from our cultural past. These dislocations are reshaping the entire way in which the world is experienced, and that experience, with growing frequency and intensity, is blatantly pagan and injurious. It is to address this new situation, this new cross-cultural missionary situation, that the evangelical church needs to be reshaped, reformed, and filled with the fullness of God. Our post-modern world, in its own unique way, is enacting what the Bible refers to as "the world." It is an enchanted reality that has the power to extinguish the reality of God when it intrudes on the mind and heart. Unless we understand this, unless we recognize the ways in which the world has insinuated its tentacles into the life of the church, unless we unmask its deceits, the church will continue to wander in the wasteland, weakened and bewildered.

Second, the church is going to have to get much more serious about itself, cease trying to be a supermarket serving the needs of religious consumers, and become instead a force of countercultural spirituality that draws from the interconnected lives of its members and is expressed through their love, service, worship, understanding, and proclamation. That is a tall order, for the tempo and organization of the modern world, which exact a heavy toll on all who attempt to keep pace with it, clearly mitigate against this happening. But it can happen. It is a question, as I have already suggested, of Jesus and McGuire, and it can and must be resolved in favor of Jesus and at considerable cost to McGuire.

An Embarrassment of Being

Post-modern Pomp

What is the worldliness of which I speak? What particular form does it take in its post-modern context? To answer these questions I want to begin by exploring two senses in which I question whether the world in which we now live is in fact post-modern. In doing so, I hope to uncover some of the important ways in which our world's unique brand of modernity is beginning to remake the evangelical church after its own image, to produce a worldly Christianity.

Post-modern writers, artists, and philosophers have contended that modernity was dead by 1960 or soon thereafter and that it is now in the process of being replaced by the products of their fertile collective imagination. It is thus that they differentiate themselves from the past: that was modern; they are *post*-modern. The progeny has arisen to take revenge on the fathers and mothers as they lie dead or dying from fraud and old age. These parents were once the celebrated visionaries of the brave new Enlightenment world, but now they are worthless. Upon them has fallen the most feared and damning judgment of Our Time: they have been declared passé; they are obsolete.

I would scarcely dispute the assertion that we are in the midst of a cultural disjunction, a rending of the fabric of consensual meaning, and a deep and radical displacement of the values, norms, and expectations that have been in place for a long time in America. But I am inclined to think that post-modernity is actually bringing forth a variant of modernity rather than a radical break from it. Post-modernity is really just modernity stripped of the false hopes that were once supported by the straw pillars of Enlightenment ideology, the illusions that once rendered modernity at least tolerable for many people. Their faith in the idea of progress proved to be the last Western superstition, and now it has died. But the essential impulses that brought modernity into being still remain. Post-modernity is proving to be the unfolding of the final stages in modernity, in which, as it were, the beast, now sickened and deranged, has fallen and begun to consume its own innards.

Taking issue with post-modern pomp in this way is no mere academic quibble, for it entails the assertion that the post-modern person — this pastiche personality, this eclectic gatherer of styles, habits, and bits of worldviews — has not sprung fully developed during the 1980s but has, in fact, been long in the making. Its genesis lies much farther back than the 1960s, when the post-moderns claim to have buried modernity and started to bring forth their own world.

Indeed, if Christopher Lasch is correct, the development of this post-modern personality is actually rooted in the slow disintegration of the family that began at least a hundred years ago. It was already at this point that the conduit by which values were formerly transmitted from generation to generation first began to clog. The problem has progressed to the point that in Our Time the young gather most of their values elsewhere, most commonly from peers and the cinematic and video fantasies with which their inner world is randomly festooned. Over time, other agencies have moved in or been forced in to make good the deficit. Added to peer groups and the mass media, perhaps at a second level of importance in this new mode of parenting, are the schools and the "helping professions." This coalition of parental surrogates, cobbled together in a blind attempt to preserve the social order, has ironically had the effect of further diminishing the remaining parental authority.

Lasch reasons that this new arrangement will have far-reaching consequences, because child-raising patterns are directly related to the personality of a generation. He asserts that it is already responsible for producing what he calls the "narcissistic" personality, by which he means a person who has been hollowed out, deprived of the internal gyroscope of character that a former generation sought to develop, and endowed instead with an exaggerated interest in image as opposed to substance. Efforts to build character have been replaced by efforts to manage the impression we make on others. Behind this constant game of charades, this shifting of cultural guises, is a personality that is typically shallow, self-absorbed, elusive, leery of commitments, unattached to people or place, dedicated to keeping all options open, and frequently incapable of either loyalty or gratitude. This, in turn, produces a strange psychological contradiction. On the one hand, wracked by insecurity, this personality is driven by a strong desire for total control over life. This accounts for the modern mania for technology, which is one of the principal means by which the people of Our Time seek to secure this sort of control. On the other hand, this kind of person often proves unwilling to accept the limitations of life and hence is inclined to believe in what is deeply irrational. Thus primitive myths and superstitions are now making their appearance side by side with computer wizardry and rampant secularization. Witchcraft and astrology, crystals and channelers are as popular as computer-designed drugs, space probes, and the information superhighway. Our unwillingness to be tamed by reality, of which this irrationality is the symptom, has also led us to deny or ignore the reality of sorrow, pain, aging, disease, violence, death, and all of the other accompaniments of our fallenness.

From this angle, then, what we think of as post-modern is in fact not of very recent vintage. Its roots reach far back and are associated with the breakdown of the family. Thus there is a significant sense in which post-modernity is deeply modern, which means that the rhetoric of the architects of the post-modern world needs to be taken with a pinch of salt. Their world is less a fresh creation than a new episode in a work in progress.

There is a second sense in which I question whether the world in which we live is truly post-modern in the sense indicated by the proponents of post-modernity. Some authors, such as Thomas Oden and Diogenes Allen, understand modernity in exclusively intellectual ways — what, in shorthand, we have in mind when we speak of "the Enlightenment project" — and they overlook the enormously powerful social realities that have created a world in which Enlightenment humanism seems so plausible. These include urbanization, technology, telecommunications, and capitalism — realities that have intersected and developed to reshape our world. These are the forces that are principally responsible for reorganizing the modern world around the processes of production and consumption and have established the prevailing psychological environment. This is the process sociologists refer to as *modernization,* and the cultural habitat it creates, the kind of values, interests, and appetites that cohere with it, is *modernity.*

It is true that the Enlightenment ideals of truth, justice, and progress that contributed to the making of the modern world have now largely passed from the scene — that is why Oden argues that modernity has died. What remains, he reasons, must be post-modernity. But I believe we can reach a different conclusion by approaching the matter from a different angle. Given the fact that the social forces that have redrawn our social world, our public square, and the terrain of our inner lives are now stronger than ever, it could as easily be argued that we are living not after the demise of modernity but at the peak of its ascendancy. Nor is this an inconsequential point. The dominance of these social processes is really the key to understanding one of the chief characteristics of the post-modern person. This person, fashioned by modernity, is a *consumer.*

A new generation has learned the art of consumption in the midst of an unprecedented flood of sleek and shiny trinkets. Every year twelve billion catalogues are mailed in the United States and the average American child sees twenty thousand advertisements on television. Our culture has become so oriented toward consumption that we consume not just the artifacts of capitalism but virtually everything else as well. Everything is marketed as a product to settle some internal dissatisfaction — sex, convenience, comfort, security. We use other people as quarries from which to mine whatever materials we think will satisfy our desires and fill our emptiness. Our relationships are often as impersonal and disconnected as the transactions in a shopping mall. Even knowledge has become a commodity in our culture. The manufacture, dissemination, and consumption of information are now a sizable part of our national economy. The acquisition of knowledge, even if only at the level of TV talk shows, is perceived to satisfy an internal need. The selling of image, too, is now big business, because image sells everything else, from pet food to public office. Our commerce, it has been said, has become our culture, and advertising is the art form that weaves them together. It plays the role in our world that Michelangelo once played in his.

While the Enlightenment ideals were still intact, all these forms of consumption took place under the umbrella of humanistic ideas about human autonomy, progress, morality, justice, and rationality. It has become increasingly evident, however, that these universal values, these "metanarratives," have vanished. We can no longer appeal to objective criteria of this sort in adjudicating truth claims or in determining how life should be lived. In the West, the Enlightenment severed these norms from the reality and revelation of God, and once cut loose, they could not be sustained as naked, ungrounded values. We are left to ask with Alasdair MacIntyre, whose justice, which rationality? Any number of schemes of justice and forms of rationality now serve as warrants for a multitude of beliefs and practices; there is no longer any firm consensus as to what constitutes an absolute. Indeed, nearly seven out of ten Americans no longer believe there are any absolutes at all.

The collapse of these Enlightenment ideals has mightily hastened the torrent of diversity. In today's architecture, for example, the style is thoroughly eclectic. Bits and pieces from past styles are randomly grafted onto radically innovative building designs. Today's literature is characterized by jarring juxtapositions of events and references that defy logic and order, the intent being to show that there is no longer an external world of meaning beyond the page, that the words point to nothing beyond themselves, that they can mean what the reader wants them to mean, for style and sensation are all that remain. Indifferent to consistency, post-modern movies blur all the old distinctions, including the line between fiction and nonfiction, serving up stunning contradictions of mood — scenes that are simultaneously comic and tragic, tender and violent, wanton and demure, broad and refined. And on MTV, this demise of narrative, of the meaningful connections between events, is taken to new heights, producing a complete triumph of the sensate over the cognitive. Nobody can say what the lightning pace of disjointed hallucinatory images in most music videos means, but it does the job it's supposed to. The post-modern mood is essentially nihilistic. It wanders the world blankly, no longer looking for meaning. That is why its art is, in the deepest sense, superficial: it lives for the surface and abjures what lies beneath. It views the search for depth and meaning as nostalgic, a longing for a world now lost forever.

The external world in which meaning and morality were once rooted has collapsed. Only the inner world of need and experience remains. Meaning has become a matter of psychological connectedness to various communities — street gangs, substance abuse recovery groups, macrobiotic food collectives, off-road vehicle associations. We come as consumers to buy into one or another of these communities, often finding little more than a momentary sense of belonging some-where.

I will grant that we can locate a cultural disjunction between the Enlightenment world and our own post-1960s world, but I think the proponents of post-modernity are grossly overstating the case when they say that the post-modern world owes nothing to modernity. Indeed, as I have suggested, there is an ironic sense in which the proponents of post-modernity can be viewed as the purest exponents of Enlightenment humanism, having taken its essential principles to their logical extremes. They have denounced the false values of mod-ernity, pushing on to a point where they are no longer restrained by any moral or religious values — but this process is itself quintessentially modern. The program they are advocating cannot be understood apart from the modernity from which they claim to be emancipated. Having said this, I will for the sake of convenience continue to use the language of post-modernity as I proceed to ask what, in this new world, is especially to be asked of the church.

The Disguise of Faith

What is the church to do in a culture that champions truths but not truth? More specifically, what is the church to do in a culture that recognizes only personal preferences and in which proponents of the various preferences are so insecure about their status that they typically demand that they be considered beyond critique or question? How is the church to confront the one god who now holds sway — the god of personal choice? How is the church to chart a course in a culture cut loose from the past, a culture defined only by the present, a world without a center, and a world in which time and space have been rendered relative by the advent of supersonic travel and instantaneous communication? What is the church to do when old patterns of reasoning appear to have gone the way of the dinosaur, when the ability to read has faded or departed altogether, when the *illuminati* announce that words point to nothing outside of themselves even for those who are still able to read them? What is the church to do in a world that places a higher value on style than substance and on experience than truth? What is the church to do in a world that refuses to tolerate any worldview that makes exclusive claims on personal allegiance?

The answer coming from the architects and devotees of the megachurches is that the church should lighten its load. It is time, they say, to relegate its traditional framework of beliefs to the background, to more or less bury its traditional worldview altogether, and to abandon the conventions that once produced predictable routines in its life. They seem to be saying that in order to thrive in this new world, the church will have to disguise itself. Sentiments such as these are in fact driving the far-ranging experimentation on which many evangelicals have embarked in an effort to meet post-moderns on their own turf. The key point of contact between the two camps is *marketing*.

What's the connection? Evangelism without a worldview is simply marketing with no purpose other than a desire for success and no criteria by which to judge the results other than mounting numbers of warm bodies. In this sense, marketing is the most purely pragmatic of all our undertakings — a characteristic that makes it quite at home in the post-modern world. Even when the machinery is hooked up to market specifically religious claims, it provokes little angst in post-modern quarters, for the machinery itself is perceived to render the marketed object harmless: it's just one more commodity in a crowded marketplace. And that feature is appealing to the brave new megachurches as well. Post-moderns of all stripes are into marketing. They happily sport vanity plates on their autos because the unashamed promotion of self is what their world is all about. For many of our brashly experimental churches, consumer interest is the Wicket Gate through which they enter the post-modern world just as John Bunyan's

Pilgrim entered his. But what will the end product be? I believe that today's churches are simply in a transitional period and that if they fail to repudiate their experimentation and repent of its outworkings, the day will shortly be upon us when evangelical spirituality will become indistinguishable from New Age spirituality.

No group has more effectively exploited the post-modern ethos than the proponents of New Age spirituality. Their appeal — and increasingly the appeal of parts of the evangelical world as well — is that they are willing to negotiate on post-modern terms. If this is an irreligious age, New Agers offer a spirituality that is not at odds with irreligious sentiment, a spirituality that is really about self-realization. Evangelicalism has often proved willing to follow suit. New Agers characterize conversion in terms of heightened inner consciousness, and evangelicals now speak in terms of looking to greater self-discovery. New Agers seek to fulfill a desire for connectedness through appeals to a hazy pantheism. Evangelicalism moves in much the same directions, however inadvertently, by diminishing its emphasis on divine transcendence and recasting the meaning of faith very largely in terms of divine immanence. New Agers are very eclectic in gathering bits and pieces of worldviews according to personal preference, and so too are many of the baby boomers fished into evangelical churches by marketing techniques. New Age spirituality is not burdened by moral absolutes, and many evangelical churches appear to be drifting toward a deemphasis of such absolutes as well, at least in their initial attempts to attract seekers into their midst. New Agers tend to gloss over the realities of sorrow, pain, aging, disease, and death out of a constitutional idealism that disparages the importance of the material world, whereas evangelicalism is increasingly glossing over these realities because they're difficult to deal with in the context of an essentially therapeutic worldview. In post-modern culture, evangelism unconnected to the orthodox Christian worldview will inevitably produce a New Age kind of spirituality, even if it retains the patina of evangelical rhetoric.

The children who have grown up or are growing up in the post-modern world bear its mark. They are cut loose from everything, hollowed out, eclectic, patched together from scraps of personality picked up here and there, leery of commitments, empty of all passions except that of sex, devoid of the capacity for commitment, fixated on image rather than substance, operating on the seductive elixir of unrestricted personal preference, and informed only by personal intuition. They are sophisticates haunted by ominous superstitions, brittle rationalists living in the grip of outrageous myths, shifting, aching beings who gaze on the world as voyeurs and whose vision of salvation has dwindled to nothing more than hope for a fleeting sense of personal well-being. When these children shape a faith after their own habits, as they are doing in some evangelical churches, it does not much resemble the classic contours of historic Christianity.

When the church abandons the biblical worldview, when it fails to confront its culture with this worldview in a cogent fashion, it has lost its nerve, its soul, and its *raison d'être*. It becomes like an English teacher who goes to China but makes only a feeble attempt to teach the language and then, out of a desperate sense of loneliness, learns Cantonese so that no one will have to speak English again.

The church has no future if it chooses from weakness not to speak its own language, the language of truth and understanding, in the post-modern world. The days when the church could bumble along in the context of an essentially civil culture are gone. The choices now are sharp and clear. Which of these two competing and antagonistic loves will hold the evangelical heart: love for God or love for the world?

A Strange Confidence

The choice for God now has to become one in which the church begins to form itself, by his grace and truth, into an outcropping of counter-cultural spirituality. It must first recover the sense of antithesis between Christ and culture and then find ways to sustain that antithesis. It is, after all, only when we see what the church is willing to give up by developing this antithesis that we see what it is actually for. If it is for God, for his truth, for his people, for the alienated and trampled in life, then it must give up what the the post-modern world holds most dear: it must give up the freedom to do anything it happens to desire. It must give up self-cultivation for self-surrender, entertainment for worship, intuition for truth, slick marketing for authentic witness, success for faithfulness, power for humility, a God bought on cheap terms for the God who calls us to a costly obedience. It must, in short, be willing to do God's business on God's terms. As it happens, that idea is actually quite old, as old as the New Testament itself, but in today's world it is novel all over again.

There are ironies here. For one thing, the legacy that the church has left behind in its efforts to appeal to the modern world itself holds the secret to engaging that world in ways that it can understand. The legacy abandoned as irrelevant has the potential to provide the sort of success in attracting people that the evangelical church yearns for — and this despite the fact that it has no interest in this sort of number-tallying success. Indeed, the path it calls God's people to walk would seem by post-modern standards virtually to ensure the ruination of the church. But the fact is that when the church is authentic, when it is true to its nature as a possession of God, its cultural irrelevance becomes a very real virtue. In the post-literate and post-rational world we are entering, the truth of Christian faith may no longer travel on the wings of logical argument as it has in the past, but it will be compelling nonetheless as churches reform their inner lives to embody a fitting countercultural spirituality centered in a serious, worshipful recognition of the presence of God, an obedient submission to his Word, and a compassionate outworking of his grace in loving service of the stricken of this world.

In too many quarters today, evangelicals are inadvertently advertising the fact that God rests only lightly upon the church. That much is evident in the pervasive *Reader's Digest* spirituality that has now become more or less synonymous with the term *evangelical* — a spirituality that is light, bouncy, simple, fun, engaging, and uplifting. The church has adopted a sort of cocktail party atmosphere, serving up pleasantries and trying to avoid unpleasantness. The celebration proceeds apace because the church is free from any worries about enemies. This is not to say that no one opposes it or wishes it harm: it is simply the case that it tends to view very few others with any degree of moral alarm. Sunday by Sunday, sin may be confessed, but it is not much connected with anything that happens in the real world. The church has become adept at distributing Band-Aids for a lot of little cuts and scrapes. It fills harmless little prescriptions for the anxious, the lonely, the disconnected. It offers bright techniques for better self-management. And in the midst of the bonhomie, the raised hands and fun in the sanctuary, the church pays scant attention to the gaunt figure of Death stalking the post-modern world. The truth is that too many evangelical churches are simply not on the same moral scale as the offenders who fill our world; they flitter about like children at the feet of ominous giants. The profane spirituality of the post-modern culture is diminishing the church. The church will not regain its status as true church again until this ersatz spirituality dies. More to the point, the church itself will have to put it to death, for as long as it is indulged, the reality of God will remain remote and inconsequential.

Recent proposals for church reform have rarely amounted to

anything more than diversions. They tend, in fact, to lead the church away from what it needs most to confront. They suggest that its weakness lies in the fact that its routines are too old, its music is too dull, its programs too few, its parking lots too small, its sermons too sermonic. They suggest that the problems are all administrative or organizational, matters of style or comfort. That is precisely what one would expect to surface in an age that is deeply pragmatic and fixated on image rather than substance. Real reform will have to look beneath the surface to see the poverty of spirit in the evangelical world, its lack of seriousness, its tendency to engage in superficial rather than penetrating analyses, its childish inability to withstand the diversions of flash, fun, and glamor. God now rests too inconsequentially upon the church. His Word, if it is preached at all, does not summon enough. His Christ, if he is seen at all, is impoverished, thin, pale, and scarcely capable of inspiring awe, and his riches are entirely searchable. If God is at the center of the worship, one has to wonder why there is so much surrounding the center that is superfluous to true worship — indeed, counterproductive to it. It is God that the church needs most — God in his grace and truth, God in his awesome and holy presence, not a folder full of hot ideas for reviving the church's flagging programs. But this is what makes the reform of the church so profoundly difficult. Church facilities, landscaping, programs, and liturgies can all be changed — changed overnight and changed over and over again. The human heart cannot be so easily changed.

But the very fact that it is beyond our capacity to solve the problem we are facing points us back to what the church most deeply needs to rediscover: it needs to rediscover what it means to be the church.

Of course it is the case that only God can change human nature. Only God can incite the human heart to rebellion against the world, overturning worldly assumptions about what is morally and spiritually normative and exposing them as contradictory to his Word. Only God can invigorate a hardened human heart to love him with a robust and righteous passion. Only God can resuscitate a lost appetite for his truth. Only God can enable families to recover their order and connectedness. Only God can make known in new measure the sweetness of his grace in the life of the church.

By this late date, evangelicals should be hungering for a genuine revival of the church, aching to see it once again become a place of seriousness where a vivid other-worldliness is cultivated because the world is understood in deeper and truer ways, where worship is stripped of everything extraneous, where God's Word is heard afresh, where the desolate and broken can find sanctuary. Why, then, are they not more serious in their efforts to recover the true church? It is because virtually everything within them and around them militates against it. Cultural pressures and influences are so intrusive and inwardly destabilizing that Christian spirituality becomes a forlorn pursuit unless the individual is embodied in a structure that gives corporate expression to private spirituality, in which the lone thread is woven into a fabric. In this sense, the local church creates its own Christian culture, its own set of values and ways of looking at the world, its own hopes and dreams, which, because they are corporately held and practiced, become normative. Unfortunately, too much church experience is not like this at all. Too often it amounts to little more than a glancing encounter with others, for a brief period of time, in which some inspirational stories are shared and hands are shaken. If members cannot give more of themselves to the churches than this, however difficult this may be, and if churches will ask for nothing more than this, then Christian spirituality will be that much more easily eroded by the torrents of modernity. The truth is that the lot of the cognitive dissident in today's world is extremely hard, and especially where dissent is registered against all the most cherished maxims of modernity. Unless the dissident can return to a center and receive a fresh confirmation of his or her biblical worldview, a fresh understanding of the world and human life, fresh nourishment in believing, and a renewed connectedness with the people of God, failure is as predictable as the rising of the sun.

Many churches have not learned the lessons that most parents stumble on sooner or later. Churches imagine that the less they ask or expect of believers, the more popular they will become and the more contented the worshipers will be. The reverse is true. Those who ask little find that the little they ask is resented or resisted; those who ask much find that they are given much and strengthened by the giving. For it is only as lives begin to intersect in sacrificial ways that the church starts to develop its own internal culture, and it is only in this context that the reality of God will both weigh heavily on the church and be preserved in its life.

Evangelicals profess a deep yearning for greater spiritual authenticity. This yearning has led some into Catholic churches and others into Greek Orthodoxy in a desperate search for a home. It is true that some pockets of Catholicism are less tainted by modernity than is evangelicalism, and Greek Orthodoxy is even less tainted than Catholicism, but a flight from modernity will not in itself guarantee spiritual renewal. It may lead to places where consumption is less rampant, where unrestrained individualism is more frowned on, where faith is less privatized, where there is still some mystery and decorum in worship. To scrape away what is ugly, though, is not necessarily to uncover what is beautiful.

We will know that the evangelical world is being reformed when it not merely escapes modernity but pointedly casts it out of its life, once again making room for the presence of God in his truth and grace. Evangelicals must formulate anew their answer to the question of what constitutes the chief end of man. Can the wisdom of the Westminster divines in this regard once again become ours? I believe it can. It will be the task of the coming generation of leadership to see that it does.

Appendix

TABLE 1

Theological/doctrinal preference: In percentages

Theological/doctrinal preference — first choice	1993 (N = 723)	1982 (N = 836)
Evangelical	68.3	73.9
Traditional/confessional	10.0	6.0
Charismatic	8.4	8.4
Fundamental	4.8	4.3
Pentecostal	3.7	NA
Neo-orthodox	1.5	1.0
Liberal	1.4	0.7
Other	5.3	5.7

Theological/doctrinal preference — second choice	1993 (N = 723)
Evangelical	16.6
Traditional/confessional	15.1
Charismatic	12.2
Fundamental	9.4
Pentecostal	4.0
Neo-orthodox	2.5
Liberal	1.5
Other	3.3

TABLE 1 (cont.)

Theological/doctrinal preference — first and second choice	1993 (N = 723)
Evangelical	83.5
Traditional/confessional	22.1
Charismatic	23.4
Fundamental	14.0
Pentecostal	7.6
Neo-orthodox	4.0
Liberal	2.9
Other	8.7

TABLE 2

Denominational affiliation grouped by major religious and theological traditions in Evangelicalism: In percentages

	1993 (N = 719)	1982 (N = 810)
Baptist	55.5	56.5
Reformed-Confessional	22.9	28.9
Holiness-Pentecostal	16.8	11.5
Anabaptist	1.8	3.1
Traditions outside Evangelicalism	0.6	NA
No affiliation	2.4	NA

TABLE 3

Denominational affiliation classified by family group:
In percentages

	(N = 719)
Pietist-Methodist	29.2
Reformed-Presbyterian	18.6
Baptist	16.4
Independent Fundamentalist	10.3
Holiness	9.9
Pentecostal	8.1
Liturgical	2.1
European Free-Church	1.5
Lutheran	0.8
Adventist	0.7
No affiliation	2.4

TABLE 4

Denominational affiliation classified liberal to conservative:
In percentages

	(N = 719)
Liberal Protestant	8.5
Moderate Protestant	45.5
Conservative Protestant	41.9
Others	1.8
No affiliation	2.4

TABLE 5

Extent of agreement with the study's definition of theology:
In percentages

Theology is reflection on the truth of God's word and application of that truth to ourselves and our world	(N = 717)
Strongly agree	47.3
Agree	43.9
Disagree	2.8
Strongly disagree	0.4

TABLE 6

Theology and meaning of life: In percentages

Without theology, the rest of my life would not have much meaning to it	(N = 725)
Strongly agree	22.5
Agree	43.9
Uncertain	18.1
Disagree	13.9
Strongly disagree	1.7

TABLE 7

Theological beliefs as basis for important life decisions:
In percentages

Extent to which important decisions of life are based on my theological beliefs	(N = 725)
I seldom if ever base such decisions on theological beliefs.	1.0
I sometimes base such decisions on my theological beliefs but definitely not most of the time.	1.0
I feel that most of my important decisions are based on my theological beliefs, but usually in a general, unconscious way.	23.2
I feel that most of my important decisions are based on my theological beliefs, and I usually consciously attempt to make them so.	74.9

TABLE 8

Views of the Bible held by seminarians, 1982:
In percentages

	(N = 833)
The Bible is the inspired Word of God, not mistaken in its statements and teachings and is to be taken literally, word for word.	43.3
The Bible is the inspired Word of God, not mistaken in its teachings, but it is not always to be taken literally in its statements concerning matters of science, historical reporting, etc.	53.8
The Bible becomes the Word of God for a person when he reads it in faith.	2.3
The Bible is an ancient book of legends, history, and moral precepts recorded by men.	0.1
Don't know	0.5

TABLE 9

Views of the Bible held by seminarians, 1993:
In percentages

	(N = 727)
The Bible is the inspired Word of God, not mistaken in its statements, and therefore what it teaches is authoritative and is to be followed without question.	54.9
The Bible is the inspired Word of God, not mistaken in its statements, but it is not always to be taken as speaking factually in matters of science, details of history, etc.	41.8
The Bible becomes the Word of God when a person reads it in faith.	2.2
The Bible is important to Christian faith, and should be read respectfully, but there are other writings which should also be read as a basis for one's faith.	0.8
The Bible is an ancient book of legends, history, and moral precepts.	0.0
Don't know.	0.3

TABLE 10

View of the Bible by three theological traditions in evangelicalism:
In percentages

Which statement is closest to your feeling about the Bible?	Baptist (N = 394)	Holiness-Pentecostal (N = 121)	Reformed-Confessional (N = 164)
Inerrantist[a]	59.9	47.9	48.8
Infallibility[b]	36.5	50.4	48.8
Other statements	3.6	1.7	2.4

[a]Inerrantist statement = "The Bible is the inspired Word of God, not mistaken in its statements, and therefore what it teaches is authoritative and is to be followed without question."

[b]Infallibility statement = "The Bible is the inspired Word of God, not mistaken in its statements, but it is not always to be taken as speaking factually in matters of science, details of history, etc."

TABLE 11

Worship-service attendance and Bible study: In percentages

Frequency of worship service attendance	(N = 730)
More than once a week	55.1
Once a week	42.5
Less than once a week	2.5
Frequency of Bible study	(N = 713)
2 days or fewer per week	12.8
3-4 days per week	25.8
5-6 days per week	33.4
7 days per week	28.1
Mean number of days per week	4.9 days
Standard deviation	1.9 days
Median	5.0 days
Mode	7.0 days
Length of Bible study on average day	(N = 703)
1 hour or more	17.1
30-59 minutes	30.9
15-29 minutes	39.3
Less than 15 minutes	12.8
Most significant expected gain from Bible study	(N = 702)
Instructs about God and His will for His people	58.0
Helps discern God's speaking to me within	32.1
Helps me to be more knowledgeable about my faith	9.3
Helps get in touch with myself or my feelings	1.0

TABLE 12

Most churches today have lost a clear sense of the real spiritual
nature of religion: In percentages

	(N = 728)
Strongly Agree	20.1
Agree	51.5
Uncertain	28.4
Disagree	10.7
Strongly Disagree	0.7

TABLE 13

Attitudes toward denominationalism: In percentages

Positive statements about denominationalism:	Agree	Uncertain	Disagree	(N=)
The purpose of denomination-wide departments and offices should be to promote co-operation between churches of different denominations.	57.5	24.0	18.5	(725)
Merging denominations tends to muddy religious conviction by choosing the lowest common denominator.	36.4	37.2	26.4	(726)
The variety of denominations in the U.S. is more a positive good than a problem.	29.3	28.3	42.4	(727)
I need to work harder to make my own denomination more distinct from others.	4.3	13.6	82.1	(725)
Negative statements about denominationalism:				
Protestant denominations should be encouraged to lessen their doctrinal differences.	47.5	19.0	33.5	(728)
I would feel comfortable switching my membership from one denomination to another.	46.0	20.6	33.3	(728)
Doctrinal differences among denominations are no longer clear enough to keep members from switching their membership to other denominations.	36.9	22.1	41.0	(724)
Ecumenism should be a priority for my denomination.	34.3	27.5	38.2	(720)
Most differences among denominations stem from outdated historical and cultural disputes.	30.5	21.4	48.1	(728)

TABLE 14

Most churches today are not concerned enough with social justice:
In percentages

	(N = 728)
Strongly Agree	10.7
Agree	38.9
Uncertain	19.5
Disagree	18.8
Strongly Disagree	2.1

TABLE 15

Extent of influence of church's theology on life: In percentages

How much is your life influenced by your church's theology	(N = 724)
Determines my life almost entirely	3.3
Strong influence on my life	56.8
Small influence on my life	36.3
No influence on my life	3.6

TABLE 16

Church doctrines as guide for knowing ultimate religious truth:
In percentages

Long-standing church doctrines are the surest guide for knowing ultimate religious truth	(N = 729)
Strongly agree	3.7
Agree	22.9
Uncertain	18.2
Disagree	44.0
Strongly disagree	11.1

TABLE 17

Theology of my own denomination is truest: In percentages

The theology taught by my denomination is the truest *of all Christian religions*	(N = 723)
Strongly agree	2.3
Agree	21.4
Uncertain	28.3
Disagree	34.8
Strongly disagree	13.0

TABLE 18

Contrasting images of the goodness and perverseness of human nature: In percentages

	ESS1993[a] (N = 725)	GSS1983-88[b] (N = 4745)
1. Human nature is basically good.	2.3	23.6
2.	2.3	19.6
3.	4.4	17.8
4. [midpoint]	11.4	22.4
5.	12.1	6.7
6.	27.6	2.9
7. Human nature is fundamentally perverse and corrupt.	39.7	7.0

[a]ESS1993: Evangelical Seminary Survey, 1993, conducted by Social Research Center, Calvin College.

[b]GSS1983-88: General Social Surveys, 1983-88, conducted by National Opinion Research Center, University of Chicago.

TABLE 19

Contrasting images of sin and goodness in the world: In percentages

	ESS1993[a] (N = 725)	GSS1983-88[b] (N = 4748)
1. The world is basically filled with evil and sin.	4.6	7.3
2.	11.7	3.4
3.	22.1	7.8
4. [midpoint]	33.7	28.1
5.	17.5	22.9
6.	7.3	12.6
7. There is much goodness in the world which hints at God's goodness.	3.2	17.8

[a]ESS1993: Evangelical Seminary Survey, 1993, conducted by Social Research Center, Calvin College.

[b]GSS1983-88: General Social Surveys, 1983-88, conducted by National Opinion Research Center, University of Chicago.

TABLE 20

Contrasting images of the nature of the world: In percentages

	ESS1993[a] (N = 726)	GSS1983-88[b] (N = 1498)
1. The world is a place of strife and disorder.	16.5	10.9
2.	37.9	8.5
3.	25.1	14.4
4. [midpoint]	13.6	37.7
5.	4.4	16.2
6.	1.7	5.5
7. Harmony and cooperation prevail in the world.	0.8	6.8

[a]ESS1993: Evangelical Seminary Survey, 1993, conducted by Social Research Center, Calvin College.

[b]GSS1983-88: General Social Surveys, 1983-88, conducted by National Opinion Research Center, University of Chicago.

TABLE 21

Contrasting images of human activity: In percentages

	ESS1993[a] (N = 724)	GSS1983-88[b] (N = 1478)
1. Human achievement helps to reveal God in the world.	4.0	27.1
2.	13.3	19.8
3.	20.2	42.4
4. [midpoint]	25.4	20.3
5.	17.0	5.8
6.	14.9	2.8
7. Most human activity is vain and foolish.	5.2	4.1

[a]ESS1993: Evangelical Seminary Survey, 1993, conducted by Social Research Center, Calvin College.

[b]GSS1983-88: General Social Surveys, 1983-88, conducted by National Opinion Research Center, University of Chicago.

TABLE 22

Contrasting images of the good person's involvement in and avoidance of the world: In percentages

	ESS1993[a] (N = 726)	GSS1983-88[b] (N = 1505)
1. Good person must be deeply involved in problems and activities of world.	16.9	22.7
2.	35.7	13.1
3.	19.4	16.1
4. [midpoint]	19.6	27.6
5.	4.8	8.0
6.	2.6	4.1
7. Good person must avoid contamination by the corruption of the world.	1.0	8.4

[a]ESS1993: Evangelical Seminary Survey, 1993, conducted by Social Research Center, Calvin College.

[b]GSS1983-88: General Social Surveys, 1983-88, conducted by National Opinion Research Center, University of Chicago.

TABLE 23

The only absolute Truth for humankind is Jesus Christ:
In percentages

	(N = 728)
Strongly agree	74.2
Agree	15.9
Uncertain	4.0
Disagree	4.7
Strongly disagree	1.2

TABLE 24

Which of these statements comes closest to expressing your views
on religions other than Christianity: In percentages

	(N = 725)
Other religions are merely human attempts at understanding God and are untrue.	50.6
Other religions contain some truth and should not be seen as completely wrong.	40.4
Different religions are the different ways in which people approach God and they should be treated with respect.	8.0
God meets people through other religions and so each religion is true to those who find God through it.	1.0

TABLE 25

View of whether it is in poor taste when sharing the gospel to
emphasize damnation and repentance, 1993 and 1982: In
percentages

	1993 (N = 724)	1982 (N = 803)
Yes, always	4.1	2.7
Yes, under most circumstances	37.8	44.3
No, not under most circumstances	49.9	46.1
No, never	8.4	6.8

TABLE 26

View of self and self-fulfillment: In percentages

	1993		1982	
	Agree	(N =)	Agree	(N =)
Self improvement is important to me and I work hard at it.	86.7	(729)	81.5	(837)
A good Christian will strive to be a "well-rounded person."	74.5	(726)	79.5	(831)
I feel a strong need for new experiences.	64.6	(727)	51.8	(839)
As a Christian, realizing my full potential as a human being is just as important as putting others before myself.	40.2	(729)	46.3	(832)
I spend a great deal of time thinking about myself.	52.3	(728)	NA	(NA)
I often use intuition as a basis for decision-making or action.	52.3	(728)	NA	(NA)
I have experienced the feeling that I was in harmony with the universe	28.2	(726)	NA	(NA)
It is good to live in a fantasy world every now and then.	27.3	(728)	NA	(NA)
I grasp the meaning of life best through intense peak experience	14.8	(729)	NA	(NA)

TABLE 27

View of work: In percentages

	1993 Agree	(N =)	1982 Agree	(N =)
Hard work is a good builder of character.	89.3	(729)	74.9	(838)
I prefer a more creative life to financial well-being.	70.5	(729)	74.8	(837)
Competition encourages excellence	49.4	(729)	36.0	(833)
I get more satisfaction in life from my friends, family, and hobbies than from my work.	47.2	(724)	36.0	(833)
Hard work always pays off.	40.9	(728)	39.4	(839)
Being productive in life and making constant effort in a chosen field are among the most important qualities of life.	39.5	(729)	37.0	(834)
If one works hard enough, he or she can do anything he or she wants to.	40.3	(727)	NA	(NA)

TABLE 28

Which of these beliefs of God's salvation is most important to you:
In percentages

	(N = 722)
I have been and will be spared His judgment because of Christ.	41.6
He guides my life every day.	19.8
I can experience inner peace.	13.3
I can experience His power in my life.	12.2
He enables me to love others.	10.2
He has given me a community to which to belong, the church.	4.3

TABLE 29

Index of a social-scientific worldview: In percentages

Index categories and score ranges[a]	(N = 720)
Highest (5-12)	20.3
Next highest (2-4)	69.3
All others (0-1)	10.4

[a]Index scores produced by summing values of four items:
  Humans evolved from lower animals.
  Science, rather than religion, will give a better understanding of the origin of human life.
  Suffering is caused by social arrangements that make people greedy for riches and power.
  Suffering comes about because people at the top keep those at the bottom from getting their share.

TABLE 30

Index of a theistic worldview: In percentages

Index categories and score ranges[a]	(N = 724)
Highest (11)	61.2
Next highest (10)	29.1
All others (1-9)	9.7

[a]Index scores produced by summing values of three items:
  I definitely believe God
  God is the chief agent who constructs reality and makes life meaningful
  How much of your life is influenced by God

TABLE 31

Index of an individualistic worldview: In percentages

Index categories and score ranges[a]	(N = 711)
Highest (25-40)	17.3
Next highest (21-24)	31.5
Lower middle (16-20)	34.7
Lowest (0-15)	16.5

[a]Index scores produced by summing values of ten items:
> If one works hard enough, he or she can do anything he or she wants to.
> Whenever I fail, I have no one to blame but myself.
> Self improvement is important to me and I work hard at it.
> Hard work always pays off.
> If someone is poor, then it is probably his/her own fault.
> Hard work is a good builder of character.
> People should be responsible for supporting themselves in retirement and not be totally dependent on government agencies like social security.
> Social problems, like crime and poverty, can be attributed ultimately to the faults of individual character.
> I am primarily in charge of my own destiny.
> How much my life is influenced by my own power.

TABLE 32

Index of a mystical worldview: In percentages

Index categories and score ranges[a]	(N = 719)
Highest (12-19)	15.2
Higher middle (9-11)	36.4
Lower middle (6-8)	35.2
Lowest (0-5)	13.2

[a]Index scores produced by summing values of five items:
> It is good to live in a fantasy world every now and then.
> I have experienced the feeling that I was in harmony with the universe.
> I grasp the meaning of life best through intense peak experiences.
> I often use intuition as a basis for decision-making or action.
> How much my life is influenced by new insights about myself.

TABLE 33

View of Evangelical theology in America held by 1993 seminarians:
In percentages

Coded responses to the open-ended statement:
"While evangelical theology is still professed,
it is losing its power to define what being an
evangelical means and how evangelicalism
is practiced." (N = 618)

Response expressed:

agreement with statement	61.2
disagreement with statement	14.2
uncertainty about the statement	8.6
was indeterminate	16.0

TABLE 34

Index of theological saliency: In percentages

Index categories and score ranges[a]	(N = 708)
Highest (18-23)	17.0
Higher middle (15-17)	38.3
Lower middle (12-14)	30.8
Lowest (1-11)	13.0

[a]Index scores produced by summing values of four items:
  Extent to which important decisions of life are based on your theological beliefs
  Without theology, the rest of my life would not have much meaning to it
  The theology taught by my denomination is the truest of all Christian religions
  How much your life is influenced by your church's theology

Break point for lowest and highest scores is one standard deviation from the group
point. Midpoint = 11.0; mean = 14.9; s.d. = 2.7.

TABLE 35

How much your life is influenced by God: In percentages

	(N = 726)
Determines my life almost entirely	69.0
Strong influence on my life	30.6
Small influence on my life	0.4

TABLE 36

Without my religious faith, the rest of my life would not have much meaning to it: In percentages

	(N = 729)
Strongly agree	69.4
Agree	25.4
Uncertain	2.6
Disagree	2.3
Strongly disagree	0.3

TABLE 37

Contrasting images of God's presence in the world [respondent's position on seven-point scale]: In percentages

	ESS1993[a] (N = 721)	GSS1983-87[b] (N = 1476)
1. God is almost totally removed from the sinfulness of the world.	1.2	4.1
2.	1.8	2.2
3.	4.3	2.6
4. [midpoint]	13.6	20.1
5.	16.4	18.9
6.	29.5	16.1
7. God reveals Himself in and through the world.	33.1	35.9

[a]GSS1983-87: General Social Surveys, 1983-87, conducted by National Opinion Research Center, University of Chicago

[b]ESS1993: Evangelical Seminary Survey, 1993, conducted by Social Research Center, Calvin College

TABLE 38

Which of two statements about God is closest to your feeling:
In percentage

	(N =712)
God's love includes all people; His desire is that all should know Him.	80.3
God is holy; evil will not finally triumph.	18.5
Both are closest to my feeling about God.	1.1

TABLE 39

God is the chief agent who constructs reality and makes life
meaningful: In percentages

	(N = 729)
Strongly agree	84.4
Agree	13.3
Uncertain	1.9
Disagree or strongly disagree	0.4

TABLE 40

View of Evangelical movement in America in the next few decades
held by 1982 seminarians: In percentages

View of Evangelical movement pertaining to theology:	(N = 809)
On whole, Evangelicals will become increasingly liberal.	6.6
On whole, Evangelicals will become increasingly conservative.	12.0
Some factions of Evangelicals will become more liberal while other factions will become more conservative.	46.6
On whole, Evangelical movement will remain basically as it is now.	31.4
None of those above.	3.5
View of Evangelical movement pertaining to social issues:	(N = 806)
On whole, Evangelicals will become increasingly liberal.	28.2
On whole, Evangelicals will become increasingly conservative.	9.1
Some factions of Evangelicals will become more liberal while other factions will become more conservative. May ultimately result in major split in movement.	42.8
On whole, Evangelical movement will remain basically as it is now.	17.0
None of those above.	3.0
View as to whether these are good or bad trends:	(N = 767)
Good	31.2
Bad	30.5
Neither good nor bad	38.3

TABLE 41

Results of Survey Procedures by Seminary

Seminary	1993 FTE Master's Enrollment	Total Questionnaires Distributed	Total Questionnaires Returned	Response Rate
Asbury	737	357	250	70.0%
Bethel	350	175	71	40.6
Calvin	167	83	47	56.6
Denver	420	207	71	34.3
Fuller	630	323	115	35.6
Gordon-Conwell	476	236	129	54.7
Talbot	475	210	47	22.4
Totals	3,255	1,591	730	45.9%

TABLE 42

Comparison of Survey Sample with Enrollment by Seminary

Seminary	1993 FTE Enrollment Number	Percent	Total Questionnaires: Distributed Number	Percent	Returned Number	Percent
Asbury	737	22.6	357	22.4	250	34.2
Bethel	350	10.8	175	11.0	71	9.7
Calvin	167	5.1	83	5.2	47	6.4
Denver	420	12.9	207	13.0	71	9.7
Fuller	630	19.4	323	20.3	115	15.8
Gordon-Conwell	476	14.6	236	14.8	129	17.8
Talbot	475	14.6	210	13.2	47	6.4
Totals	3,255	100.0	1,591	100.0	730	100.0

TABLE 43

Comparison of the Sample of Respondents to Wells's 1993 Survey
and to Hunter's 1982 Survey by Seminary

Seminary	Included in: Wells 1993	Included in: Hunter 1982	Sample of respondents to: Wells 1993 Number	Sample of respondents to: Wells 1993 Percent	Sample of respondents to: Hunter 1982 Number	Sample of respondents to: Hunter 1982 Percent
Asbury	Yes	Yes	250	34.2[a]	194	22.9[a]
Bethel	Yes	No	71	9.7	NA[b]	NA
Calvin	Yes	No	47	6.4	NA	NA
Denver	Yes	Yes	71	9.7	89	10.5
Fuller	Yes	Yes	115	15.8[a]	183	21.6[a]
Gordon-Conwell	Yes	Yes	129	17.8	157	18.5
Talbot	Yes	Yes	47	6.4	69	8.1
Westminster	No	Yes	NA	NA	85	10.0
Wheaton	No	Yes	NA	NA	70	8.3
Totals			730	100.0	847	100.0

[a]Percentage difference between the surveys is statistically significant to the .05 level.
[b]NA means not applicable.

TABLE 44

Years attended seminary, degree program, and full-time or
part-time status: In percentages

Number years attended this seminary	1993 (N = 727)	1982 (N = 840)
Less than one year	15.4	17.4
One year	37.0	40.5
Two years	22.4	20.4
Three or more years	25.2	21.8
Mean	1.7 years	1.6 years
Standard deviation	1.4 years	1.4 years
Median	1.0 years	0.8 years
Mode	1.0 years	1.0 years

Degree program enrolled in	1993 (N = 726)	1982 (N = 796)
M. Div.	68.0	63.9
M. A.	31.0	30.7
Th. M.	1.5	5.4

Full-time or Part-time	1993 (N = 727)
Full-time	79.8
Part-time	20.2

TABLE 45

Type of school for undergraduate studies: In percentages

Type of undergraduate school:	1993 (N = 728)	1982 (N = 808)
Research/public state university	52.1	40.6
Private non-church-related college	11.4	14.7
Private church-related college	44.5	31.8
Bible college or institute	13.6	12.9

TABLE 46

Gender of seminarians: In Percentages

	1993 (N = 727)	1982 (N = 844)
Female	25.7	18.6
Male	74.3	81.4

TABLE 47

Ethnicity: In percentages

	1993 (N = 727)	1982 (N = 840)
American Indian/Canadian Indian/ Native American	2.1	NA[a]
Asian/Oriental/Pacific Islander	8.7	4.6
Black/African-American	1.9	2.6
Hispanic/Spanish origin/Latino	2.1	1.0
White/Caucasian	85.8	91.8

[a]NA, in this and subsequent tables, means not applicable or not available.

TABLE 48

Age: In percentages

	1993 (N = 725)	1982 (N = 840)
Under 25 years old	17.8	26.7
25-29 years old	32.6	45.7
30-39 years old	32.1	22.3
40 and older	17.5	5.4
Mean	32.3 years	28.1 years
Standard deviation	9.9 years	5.6 years
Median	29.5 years	26.1 years
Mode	26.0 years	26.0 years

TABLE 49

Marital and parental status: In percentages

Marital Status	1993 (N = 727)	1982 (N = 844)
Single, never married	34.9	38.3
Married	61.6	60.1
Divorced, separated, or widowed	3.4	1.7
Children	(N = 727)	(N = 844)
Yes	39.2	60.8
No	30.5	69.5

TABLE 50

Community Size: In percentages

Community Size where lived before college:	1993 (N = 720)	1982 (N = 842)
Metropolis or suburb (1+ million)	24.8	23.3
Large city or suburb (250K to 1 million)	18.4	17.3
Medium city or suburb (50K to 250K)	15.8	19.1
Small city or suburb (10K to 50K)	15.5	15.3
Town (less than 10K)	13.7	14.6
Rural	11.9	10.3

TABLE 51

U.S. regional location of home state or country: In percentages

Home state's region:	1993 (N = 645)	1982 (N = 830)
U.S. — East	12.6	26.4
U.S. — South	21.1	15.9
U.S. — Midwest	29.6	23.4
U.S. — West	21.2	28.3
U.S. — Territory or region unknown	3.6	NA
Outside U.S. (international)	11.9	6.0

TABLE 52

Highest education level of family's chief wage-earner:[a]
In percentages

Highest education level:	1993 (N = 724)	1982 (N = 830)
Some high school or less	11.6	15.7
Completed high school or trade school	21.1	25.3
Some college	16.7	14.5
Completed college (4-year degree)	21.0	18.2
Post-graduate education	29.6	23.2

[a]The 1993 question asked, "What was the highest level of education achieved by the chief wage-earner in your family when you were 16 years old?" The 1982 question was "What is your father's highest level of education? (If the chief wage earner in your family is other than you father, please specify that person's highest level of educational attainment.)"

TABLE 53

Ever spoken in tongues: In percentages

Ever spoken in tongues:	1993 (N = 724)	1982 (N = 836)
Yes	33.3	34.2
No	66.7	65.8

TABLE 54

Ever spoken in tongues by denominational affiliation grouped by major religious and theological traditions in Evangelicalism: In percentages

	% spoken	(N =)
Holiness-Pentecostal	53.7	(121)
Baptist	31.7	(397)
Anabaptist	30.8	(13)
Reformed-Confessional	22.0	(164)

TABLE 55

Ever spoken in tongues by denominational family group:
In percentages

	% spoken	(N =)
Pentecostal	84.2	(57)
Independent Fundamentalist	47.3	(74)
Pietist-Methodist	30.1	(209)
Holiness	25.4	(71)
Baptist	23.7	(118)
Reformed-Presbyterian	20.3	(133)

TABLE 56

Ever spoken in tongues by denominational affiliation classified
liberal to conservative: In percentages

	% spoken	(N =)
Liberal Protestant	35.0	(60)
Moderate Protestant	27.9	(326)
Conservative Protestant	38.7	(300)

TABLE 57

Ever spoken in tongues by theological/doctrinal preference:
In percentages

Theological/doctrinal preference — first choice	% spoken	(N =)
Charismatic	86.9	(61)
Pentecostal	81.5	(27)
Neo-orthodox	36.4	(11)
Evangelical	28.9	(492)
Fundamental	29.4	(34)
Traditional/confessional	12.5	(72)
Liberal	11.1	(9)

Theological/doctrinal preference — second choice	% spoken	(N =)
Pentecostal	81.8	(55)
Charismatic	73.4	(169)
Neo-orthodox	39.3	(28)
Evangelical	30.2	(602)
Liberal	25.0	(20)
Fundamental	23.0	(100)
Traditional/confessional	19.0	(158)

Bibliography

Acquaviva, S. S. *The Decline of the Sacred in Industrial Society.* Translated by Patricia Lipscomb. Oxford: Basil Blackwell, 1979.

Allen, Diogenes. *Christian Belief in a Postmodern World: The Full Wealth of Conviction.* Louisville: Westminster/John Knox Press, 1989.

Aquinas, Thomas. *Providence and Predestination.* Translated by Robert W. Mulligan. Chicago: Henry Regnery, 1953.

Aulén, Gustav. *Christus Victor: An Historical Study of the Three Main Types of the Idea of the Atonement.* Translated by A. G. Hebert. New York: Macmillan, 1969.

_____. *The Faith of the Christian Church.* Translated by Eric H. Wahlstrom and G. Everett Arden. Philadelphia: Muhlenberg Press, 1948.

Baillie, John. *The Sense of the Presence of God.* New York: Scribner's, 1962.

Barfield, Owen. *Saving the Appearances: A Study in Idolatry.* New York: Harcourt Brace Jovanovich, 1965.

Barna, George. *The Frog in the Kettle: What Christians Need to Know about Life in the Year 2000.* Ed. Ron Durham. Ventura, Cal.: Regal Books, 1990.

_____. *Marketing the Church: What They Never Taught You about Church Growth.* Colorado Springs: Navpress, 1988.

_____. *The Power of Vision: How You Can Capture and Apply God's Vision for Your Ministry.* Ed. Duncan Kyle. Ventura, Cal.: Regal Books, 1992.

_____. *A Step-by-Step Guide to Church Marketing: Breaking Ground for the Harvest.* Ed. Virginia Woodward. Ventura, Cal.: Regal Books, 1992.

_____. *User Friendly Churches: What Successful Churches Have in Common and Why Their Ideas Work.* Ed. Ron Durham. Ventura, Cal.: Regal Books, 1991.

_____. *What Americans Believe: An Annual Survey of Values and Religious Views in the United States.* Ed. Ron Durham. Ventura, Cal.: Regal Books, 1992.

_____ and William Paul McKay. *Vital Signs: Emerging Social Trends and the Future of American Christianity*. Westchester, Conn.: Crossway Books, 1984.

Barrett, William. *Time of Need: Forms of Imagination in the Twentieth Century*. New York: Harper Colophon Books, 1972.

Barth, Karl. *Church Dogmatics*. 5 vols. Edited by Thomas F. Torrance, translated by Geoffrey W. Bromiley. Edinburgh: T. & T. Clark, 1936-77.

_____. *Evangelical Theology: An Introduction*. Translated by Grover Foley. London: Weidenfeld & Nicolson, 1963.

_____. *The Theology of Schleiermacher: Lectures at Göttingen, Winter Semester of 1923/24*. Translated by Geoffrey W. Bromiley, edited by Dietrich Ritschl. Grand Rapids: William B. Eerdmans, 1982.

Barzun, Jacques. *A Stroll With William James*. New York: Harper & Row, 1983.

Bellah, Robert, et al. *Habits of the Heart: Individualism and Commitment in America*. Berkeley and Los Angeles: University of California Press, 1985.

Berdyaev, Nicolas. *The Fate of Man in the Modern World*. Translated by Donald A. Lowrie. Ann Arbor: University of Michigan Press, 1961.

Berger, Peter L. *A Far Glory: The Quest for Faith in an Age of Credulity*. New York: Free Press, 1992.

_____. *The Precarious Vision: A Sociologist Looks at Social Fictions and Christian Faith*. Garden City, N.Y.: Doubleday, 1961.

_____. *A Rumor of Angels: Modern Society and the Rediscovery of the Supernatural*. Garden City, N.Y.: Doubleday, 1969.

_____. *The Sacred Canopy: Elements of a Sociological Theory of Religion*. Garden City, N.Y.: Doubleday, 1969.

_____, ed. *The Other Side of God: A Polarity in World Religions*. Garden City, N.Y.: Doubleday-Anchor, 1981.

_____ and Richard John Neuhaus, eds. *Against the World for the World*. New York: Seabury Press, 1976.

Berman, Marshall. *All That Is Solid Melts into Air: The Experience of Modernity*. New York: Simon & Schuster, 1982.

Blau, Herbert. *The Eye of the Prey: Subversions of the Postmodern*. Bloomington, Ind.: Indiana University Press, 1987.

Bloesch, Donald G. *The Evangelical Renaissance*. Grand Rapids: William B. Eerdmans, 1973.

_____. *The Future of Evangelical Christianity: A Call for Unity amid Diversity*. Garden City, N.Y.: Doubleday, 1983.

Bloom, Harold. *The American Religion: The Emergence of the Post-Christian Nation*. New York: Simon & Schuster, 1992.

Bohn, Willard. *Apollinaire and the Faceless Man: The Creation and Evolution of a Modern Motif*. Toronto: Associated University Presses, 1991.

Bonino, José Míguez, ed. *Faces of Jesus: Latin American Christologies.* Translated by Robert R. Burr. Maryknoll, N.Y.: Orbis Books, 1977.

Boorstin, Daniel. *The Americans: The Democratic Experience.* New York: Random House, 1973.

Bornkamm, Gunther. *Early Christian Experience.* Translated by Paul L. Hammer. New York: Harper & Row, 1969.

Boubaker, Rogers. *The Limits of Rationality.* London: Allen & Unwin, 1984.

Boulding, Kenneth E. *The Meaning of the Twentieth Century: The Great Transition.* New York: Harper & Row, 1965.

Braaten, Carl E. *No Other Gospel: Christianity among the World's Religions.* Minneapolis: Fortress Press, 1992.

Brown, James, *Subject and Object in Modern Theology.* London: SCM Press, 1953.

Bruce, A. B. *The Moral Order of the World in Ancient and Modern Thought.* New York: Scribner's, 1899.

_____. *The Providential Order of the World.* New York: Scribner's, 1899.

Brunner, Emil. *The Christian Doctrine of Creation and Redemption.* Dogmatics series, vol. 2. Translated by Olive Wyon. Philadelphia: Westminster Press, 1952.

_____. *The Mediator: A Study of the Central Doctrine of Christian Faith.* Translated by Olive Wyon. New York: Macmillan, 1934.

Bultmann, Rudolf. *Essays: Philosophical and Theological.* Translated by James C. G. Grieg. New York: Macmillan, 1955.

_____. *Theology of the New Testament.* 2 vols. Translated by Kendrick Grobel. New York: Scribner's, 1955.

Burke, Patrick. *The Fragile Universe: An Essay in the Philosophy of Religions.* New York: Barnes & Noble, 1979.

Burrell, David B. *Exercises in Religious Understanding.* Notre Dame, Ind.: University of Notre Dame Press, 1974.

Campbell, Angus. *The Sense of Well-Being in America: Recent Patterns and Trends.* New York: McGraw-Hill, 1981.

Cantor, Norman F. *Twentieth Century Culture: Modernism to Deconstruction.* New York: Peter Lang, 1988.

Carroll, Jackson W., Carl S. Dudley, and William McKinney, eds. *Handbook of Congregational Studies.* Nashville: Abingdon Press, 1990.

Carter, Paul A. *The Decline and Revival of the Social Gospel: Social and Political Liberalism in American Protestant Churches, 1920-40.* Ithaca, N.Y.: Cornell University Press, 1954.

Carter, Stephen L. *The Culture of Disbelief: How American Law and Politics Trivialize Religious Devotion.* New York: Basic Books, 1993.

Cauthen, Kenneth. *Systematic Theology: A Modern Protestant Approach.* Lewiston, N.Y.: Edwin Mellen Press, 1986.

Coalter, Milton J., John M. Mulder, and Louis B. Weeks. *The Organizational*

Revolution: Presbyterians and American Denominationalism. Louisville: Westminster Press, 1992.

Conn, Harvey, ed. *Theological Perspectives on Church Growth.* Nutley, N.J.: Presbyterian & Reformed, 1976.

Copleston, Frederick. *History of Philosophy.* Vol. 8: *Bentham to Russell.* London: Burnes & Oates, 1966.

Cromartie, Michael, ed. *No Longer Exiles: The Religious Right in American Politics.* Washington: Ethics and Public Policy Center, 1993.

Cullmann, Oscar. *Christ and Time: The Primitive Christian Conception of Time and History.* Rev. ed. Translated by Floyd V. Filson. Philadelphia: Westminster Press, 1964.

Davidson, A. B. *The Theology of the Old Testament.* Edinburgh: T. & T. Clark, 1911.

Day, Heather F. *Protestant Theological Education in America: A Bibliography.* Metuchen, N.J.: Scarecrow Press, 1985.

Demerath, N. J. *Social Class in American Protestantism.* Chicago: Rand McNally, 1965.

Dodd, C. H. *The Johannine Epistles.* New York: Harper, 1946.

Dolbeare, Kenneth M., and Patricia Dolbeare. *American Ideologies: The Competing Beliefs of the 1970s.* Chicago: Rand McNally, 1976.

Dooley, Patrick Kiaran. *Pragmatism as Humanism.* Chicago: Nelson-Hall, 1974.

Douglas, Ann. *The Feminization of American Culture.* New York: Alfred A. Knopf, 1977.

Douglas, Mary, and Steven M. Tipton, eds. *Religion and America: Spirituality in a Secular Age.* Boston: Beacon Press, 1983.

Dyrness, William A. *How Does America Hear the Gospel?* Grand Rapids: William B. Eerdmans, 1989.

Eichrodt, Walter. *Theology of the Old Testament.* 2 vols. Translated by J. A. Baker. Philadelphia: Westminster Press, 1961.

Ellul, Jacques. *The Technological Society.* Translated by John Wilkerson. New York: Alfred A. Knopf, 1965.

Erickson, Millard. *Christian Theology.* Grand Rapids: Baker Book House, 1983.

Evans, Donald. *Struggle and Fulfillment: The Inner Dynamics of Religion and Morality.* New York: Collins, 1979.

Farley, Wendy. *Tragic Vision and Divine Compassion: A Contemporary Theodicy.* Louisville: Westminster/John Knox Press, 1990.

Finke, Roger, and Rodney Stark. *The Churching of America, 1776-1990: Winners and Losers in Our Religious Economy.* New Brunswick, N.J.: Rutgers University Press, 1992.

Fish, Stanley. *Is There a Text in This Class? The Authority of Interpretive Communities.* Cambridge: Harvard University Press, 1980.

Forstmann, Jack. *A Romantic Triangle: Schleiermacher and Early German Romanticism.* Missoula, Mont.: Scholars Press, 1977.

Forsyth, Peter Taylor. *The Church, the Gospel and Society.* London: Independent Press, 1962.

_____. *The Cruciality of the Cross.* London: Independent Press, 1948.

_____. *God the Holy Father.* London: Independent Press, 1957.

_____. *The Justification of God: Lectures for War-Time on a Christian Theodicy.* London: Latimer House, 1917.

_____. *The Principle of Authority, in Relation to Certainty, Sanctity and Society: An Essay in the Philosophy of Experimental Religion.* London: Independent Press, 1952.

_____. *The Work of Christ.* London: Independent Press, 1910.

Foucault, Michel. *The Archaeology of Knowledge.* London: Tavistock, 1972.

Geach, P. T. *The Virtues.* Cambridge: Cambridge University Press, 1979.

Gergen, Kenneth J. *The Saturated Self: Dilemmas of Identity in Contemporary Life.* New York: Basic Books, 1991.

Gerrish, B. A. *A Prince in the Church: Schleiermacher and the Beginnings of Modern Theology.* Philadelphia: Fortress Press, 1984.

Gewirth, Alan. *Reason and Morality.* Chicago: University of Chicago Press, 1978.

Gibbs, Eddie. *I Believe in Church Growth.* Grand Rapids: William B. Eerdmans, 1981.

Giddens, Anthony. *The Consequences of Modernity.* Stanford: Stanford University Press, 1990.

_____. *Modernity and Self-Identity: Self and Society in the Late Modern Age.* Stanford: Stanford University Press, 1991.

Gilkey, Langdon. *Maker of Heaven and Earth: The Christian Doctrine of Creation in the Light of Modern Knowledge.* Garden City, N.Y.: Doubleday, 1965.

_____. *Naming the Whirlwind: The Renewal of God-Language.* Indianapolis: Bobbs-Merrill, 1969.

Goffman, Erving. *The Presentation of the Self in Everyday Life.* Garden City, N.Y.: Doubleday, 1959.

Gore, Al. *Earth in the Balance: Ecology and the Human Spirit.* New York: E. P. Dutton, 1992.

Grenz, Stanley J. *Revisioning Evangelical Theology: A Fresh Agenda for the Twenty-First Century.* Downers Grove, Ill.: InterVarsity Press, 1993.

_____ and Roger Olson. *Twentieth Century Theology: God and the World in Transition.* Downers Grove, Ill.: InterVarsity Press, 1992.

Guinness, Os. *Dining with the Devil: The Megachurch Movement Flirts with Modernity.* Grand Rapids: Baker Book House, 1993.

_____ and John Seel. *No God but God: Breaking with the Idols of Our Age.* Chicago: Moody Press, 1992.

Habermas, Jürgen. *Theory and Practice*. Translated by John Viertel. Boston: Beacon Press, 1974.

Halbertal, Moshe, and Avishai Margalit. *Idolatry*. Cambridge: Harvard University Press, 1992.

Harrison, Jonathan. *Our Knowledge of Right and Wrong*. New York: Humanities Press, 1971.

Harvey, David. *The Condition of Postmodernity: An Inquiry into the Conditions of Social Change*. Oxford: Basil Blackwell, 1989.

Hazlitt, Henry. *The Foundations of Morality*. Los Angeles: James H. Nash, 1972.

Heilbroner, Robert L. *An Inquiry into the Human Condition*. New York: W. W. Norton, 1974.

Heim, Karl. *God Transcendent: Foundation for a Christian Metaphysic*. Translated by Edgar Primrose Dickie. New York: Scribner's, 1936.

Heinecken, Martin J. *Beginning and End of the World*. Philadelphia: Muelenberg Press, 1965.

Henry, Carl F. H. *God, Revelation, and Authority*. 6 vols. Waco: Word Books, 1976-82.

Henry, Jules. *Culture against Man*. New York: Vintage, 1965.

Heppe, Heinrich. *Reformed Dogmatics: Set Out and Illustrated from the Sources*. Translated by G. T. Thomson, edited by Ernst Bizer. Grand Rapids: Baker Book House, 1978.

Hesselgrave, David J., and Edward Rommen. *Contextualization: Meanings, Methods, and Models*. Grand Rapids: Baker Book House, 1989.

Heyward, Carter. *Our Passion for Justice: Images of Power, Sexuality, and Liberation*. New York: Pilgrim Press, 1984.

_____. *Touching Our Strength: The Erotic as Power and the Love of God*. San Francisco: HarperCollins, 1989.

Hick, John. *God and the Universe of Faiths: Essays in the Philosophy of Religion*. New York: St. Martin's Press, 1973.

_____. *God Has Many Names*. Philadelphia: Westminster Press, 1982.

_____, ed. *The Myth of God Incarnate*. London: SCM Press, 1977.

Hick, John, and Paul Knitter, eds. *The Myth of Christian Uniqueness: Toward a Pluralistic Theology of Religions*. Maryknoll, N.Y.: Orbis Books, 1988.

Hirsch, E. D. *The Aims of Interpretation*. Chicago: University of Chicago Press, 1976.

_____. *Validity in Interpretation*. New Haven: Yale University Press, 1962.

Hoge, Dean R. *Division in the Protestant House: The Basic Reasons behind Intra-Protestant Conflicts*. Philadelphia: Westminster Press, 1976.

_____ and David A. Roozen. *Understanding Church Growth and Decline, 1950-1978*. New York: Pilgrim Press, 1979.

Hunter, James Davison. *Culture Wars: The Struggle to Define America*. New York: Basic Books, 1990.

_____. *Evangelicalism: The Coming Generation*. Chicago: University of Chicago Press, 1987.

Hutcheson, Richard G. *Mainline Churches and the Evangelicals: A Challenging Crisis?* Atlanta: John Knox Press, 1981.

Hutchison, William R. *The Modernist Impulse in American Protestantism.* Cambridge: Harvard University Press, 1976.

_____, ed. *Between the Times: The Travail of the Protestant Establishment in America, 1900-1960.* Cambridge: Cambridge University Press, 1989.

Huyssen, Andreas. *After the Great Divide: Modernism, Mass Culture, Postmodernism.* Bloomington, Ind.: Indiana University Press, 1986.

James, William. *The Meaning of Truth.* Cambridge: Harvard University Press, 1975.

_____. *Pragmatism: A New Name for Some Old Ways of Thinking.* Cambridge: Harvard University Press, 1975.

Jaspers, Karl, and Rudolf Bultmann. *Myth and Christianity: An Inquiry into the Possibility of Religion without Myth.* New York: Noonday Press, 1958.

Jencks, Charles. *The Language of Post-Modern Architecture.* London: Academie Editions, 1981.

Jenson, Robert W. *America's Theologian: A Recommendation of Jonathan Edwards.* New York: Oxford University Press, 1988.

Jewett, Paul K. *God, Creation and Revelation: A Neo-Evangelical Theology.* Grand Rapids: William B. Eerdmans, 1991.

Jüngel, Eberhard. *God as the Mystery of the World: On the Foundation of the Theology of the Crucified One in the Dispute between Theism and Atheism.* Translated by Darrell L. Guder. Grand Rapids: William B. Eerdmans, 1983.

Kaiser, Walter C. Jr. *Toward an Old Testament Theology.* Grand Rapids: Zondervan, 1978.

Kaminer, Wendy. *I'm Dysfunctional, You're Dysfunctional: The Recovery Movement and Other Self-Help Fashions.* Reading, Mass.: Addison-Wesley, 1991.

Kaplan, Anne. *Rocking around the Clock: Music Television, Post-Modernism, and Consumer Culture.* New York: Methuen, 1987.

Kaufman, Gordon. *God the Problem.* Cambridge: Harvard University Press, 1972.

Kelley, Dean M. *Why Conservative Churches Are Growing: A Study in Sociology of Religion.* New York: Harper & Row, 1972.

Klapp, Orrin. *Collective Search for Identity.* New York: Holt, Rinehart, & Winston, 1969.

Kraft, Charles. *Christianity and Culture.* Maryknoll, N.Y.: Orbis Books, 1979.

Kuhn, Thomas. *The Structure of Scientific Revolutions.* 2d ed. Chicago: University of Chicago Press, 1970.

Kuschel, Karl-Josef. *Born before All Time? The Dispute over Christ's Origin.* Translated by John Bowden. New York: Crossroad, 1992.

Lasch, Christopher. *The Culture of Narcissism: American Life in an Age of Diminishing Expectations.* New York: W. W. Norton, 1978.

_____. *Haven in a Heartless World: The Family Besieged.* New York: Basic Books, 1979.

_____. *The Minimal Self: Psychic Survival in Troubled Times.* New York: W. W. Norton, 1984.

_____. *The True and Only Heaven: Progress and Its Critics.* New York: W. W. Norton, 1990.

Lears, Jackson. *No Place of Grace: Antimodernism and the Transformation of American Culture, 1820-1920.* New York: Pantheon Books, 1981.

Lewis, Michael. *The Culture of Inequality.* Amherst: University of Massachusetts Press, 1978.

Lifton, Robert. *The Broken Connection: On Death and the Continuity of Life.* New York: Simon & Schuster, 1979.

Lindbeck, George. *The Nature of Doctrine: Religion and Theology in a Post-liberal Age.* Philadelphia: Westminster Press, 1984.

Luhman, Niklas. *Religious Dogmatics and the Evolution of Societies.* Lewiston, N.Y.: Edwin Mellen Press, 1984.

Lundin, Roger. *The Culture of Interpretation: Christian Faith and the Postmodern World.* Grand Rapids: William B. Eerdmans, 1993.

Lyotard, Jean-Françoise. *Just Gaming.* Translated by Wlad Godzich and Brian Wassumi. Minneapolis: University of Minneapolis Press, 1985.

_____. *The Postmodern Condition: A Report on Knowledge.* Translated by Geoff Bennington and Brian Wassumi. Minneapolis: University of Minneapolis Press, 1984.

McClendon, James W. *Biography as Theology: How Life Stories Can Remake Today's Theology.* Nashville: Abingdon Press, 1974.

McGavran, Donald. *Understanding Church Growth.* Grand Rapids: William B. Eerdmans, 1970.

MacIntyre, Alasdair. *After Virtue: A Study in Moral Theory.* Notre Dame, Ind.: University of Notre Dame Press, 1981.

_____. *The Religious Significance of Atheism.* New York: Columbia University Press,

_____. *Whose Justice? Which Rationality?* Notre Dame, Ind.: University of Notre Dame Press, 1988.

Mackintosh, H. R. *The Christian Apprehension of God.* London: SCM Press, 1929.

Macquarrie, John. *In Search of Deity: An Essay in Dialectical Theism.* New York: Crossroad, 1985.

_____. *Principles of Christian Theology.* New York: Scribner's, 1977.

Mannheim, Karl. *Ideology and Utopia.* New York: Harcourt, Brace & World, 1966.

Marty, Martin E. *A Nation of Behavers.* Chicago: University of Chicago Press, 1976.

_____. *Righteous Empire: The Protestant Experience in America*. New York: Harper Torchbooks, 1970.

Matczak, Sebastian A. *God in Contemporary Thought: A Philosophical Perspective*. New York: Learned Publications, 1977.

Miles, Rufus E. *Awakening from the American Dream: The Social and Political Limits to Growth*. New York: Universe Books, 1976.

Miller, Samuel H. *The Dilemma of Modern Belief*. New York: Harper & Row, 1963.

Moffatt, James. *Love in the New Testament*. London: Hodder & Stoughton, 1929.

Mol, Hans J. *Identity and the Sacred*. New York: Free Press, 1976.

Moltmann, Jürgen. *The Crucified God: The Cross of Christ as the Foundation and Criticism of Christian Theology*. Translated by R. A. Wilson and John Bowden. London: SCM Press, 1974.

_____. *The Theology of Play*. Translated by Reinhard Ulrich. New York: Harper & Row, 1972.

Moore, R. Lawrence. *Religious Outsiders and the Making of Americans*. New York: Oxford University Press, 1986.

Morris, Leon. *The Apostolic Preaching of the Cross*. Grand Rapids: William B. Eerdmans, 1955.

_____. *The Cross in the New Testament*. Grand Rapids: William B. Eerdmans, 1965.

_____. *New Testament Theology*. Grand Rapids: Academie Books, 1986.

_____. *Testaments of Love: A Study of Love in the Bible*. Grand Rapids: William B. Eerdmans, 1981.

Morris, Thomas, ed. *The Concept of God*. New York: Oxford University Press, 1987.

Moskin, J. Robert. *Morality in America*. New York: Random House, 1962.

Nash, Ronald H. *Faith and Reason: Searching for a Rational Faith*. Grand Rapids: Academie Books, 1988.

Netland, Harold A. *Dissonant Voices: Religious Pluralism and the Question of Truth*. Grand Rapids: William B. Eerdmans, 1991.

Neuhaus, Richard John, ed. *American Apostasy: The Triumph of "Other" Gospels*. Grand Rapids: William B. Eerdmans, 1989.

Niebuhr, H. Richard. *Christ and Culture*. New York: Harper, 1951.

_____. *The Kingdom of God in America*. New York: Harper and Row, 1937.

_____. *Schleiermacher on Christ and Religion*. New York: Scribner's, 1964.

Niebuhr, Reinhold. *Moral Man and Immoral Society*. New York: Scribner's, 1932.

Nygren, Anders. *The Essence of Christianity*. Translated by Philip S. Watson. Philadelphia: Muhlenberg Press, 1961.

Organ, Troy Wilson. *Philosophy and the Self: East and West*. Toronto: Associated University Presses, 1985.

Osborn, Lawrence. *Angels of Light: The Challenge of the New Age*. London: Darton, Longman, & Todd, 1992.

Pailin, David A. *The Anthropological Character of Theology: Conditioning Theological Understanding*. Cambridge: Cambridge University Press, 1990.

Pannenberg, Wolfhart. *Human Nature, Election, and History*. Philadelphia: Westminster Press, 1977.

_____. *Systematic Theology*. Translated by Geoffrey W. Bromiley. Grand Rapids: William B. Eerdmans, 1991.

Peck, M. Scott. *People of the Lie*. New York: Simon & Schuster, 1983.

Peters, George W. *A Theology of Church Growth*. Grand Rapids: Zondervan, 1981.

Phillips, D. Z. *Through a Darkening Glass: Philosophy, Literature and Cultural Change*. Notre Dame, Ind.: University of Notre Dame Press, 1982.

Piper, John. *The Justification of God: An Exegetical and Theological Study of Romans 9:1-23*. 2d ed. Grand Rapids: Baker Book House, 1993.

_____. *Let the Nations Be Glad: The Supremacy of God in Missions*. Grand Rapids: Baker Book House, 1993.

_____. *The Pleasures of God: Meditations on God's Delight in Being God*. Portland: Multnomah Press, 1991.

Pittinger, W. Norman. *The Christian Way in the Modern World*. Louisville: Cloister Press, 1944.

_____. *God's Way with Men: A Study of the Relationship between God and Man in Providence, Miracle and Prayer*. London: Hodder & Stoughton, 1965.

Plantinga, Alvin, and Nicholas Wolterstorff, eds. *Faith and Rationality: Reason and Belief in God*. Notre Dame, Ind.: University of Notre Dame, 1983.

Popper, Karl R. *The Open Society and Its Enemies*. Vol. 2: *The High Tide of Prophecy: Hegel, Marx, and the Aftermath*. London: Routledge & Kegan Paul, 1949.

Postman, Neil. *Technopoly: The Surrender of Culture to Technology*. New York: Alfred A. Knopf, 1992.

Prestige, G. L. *God in Patristic Thought*. London: S.P.C.K., 1959.

Rad, Gerhard von. *Old Testament Theology*. 2 vols. Translated by D. M. G. Stalker. New York: Harper & Row, 1965.

Reichley, A. James. *Religion in American Public Life*. Washington: Brookings Institution, 1985.

Reiff, Philip. *The Triumph of the Therapeutic: Uses of Faith after Freud*. New York: Harper & Row, 1968.

Reisman, David, et al. *The Lonely Crowd: A Study of Changing American Character*. Rev. ed. New Haven: Yale University Press, 1961.

Revel, Jean François. *Without Marx or Jesus: The New American Revolution Has Begun*. Garden City, N.Y.: Doubleday, 1970.

Reventlow, Henning Graf. *The Authority of the Bible and the Rise of the Modern*

World. Translated by John Bowden. Philadelphia: Fortress Press, 1985.

Richardson, Cyril C. *The Doctrine of the Trinity*. New York: Abingdon Press, 1958.

Ritschl, Albrecht. *The Christian Doctrine of Justification and Reconciliation*. Translated by H. R. Mackintosh and A. B. Macauley. Edinburgh: T. & T. Clark, 1902.

Ritzer, George. *The McDonaldization of Society: An Investigation into the Changing Character of Contemporary Social Life*. Newbury Park, Cal.: Sage Publications, 1992.

Roberts, Robert C. *Taking the Word to Heart: Self and Other in an Age of Therapies*. Grand Rapids: William B. Eerdmans, 1993.

Roof, Wade Clark. *Community and Commitment: Religious Plausibility in a Liberal Protestant Church*. New York: Pilgrim Press, 1983.

_____ and William McKinney. *American Mainline Religion: Its Changing Shape and Future*. New Brunswick, N.J.: Rutgers University Press, 1987.

Roozen, David A., William McKinney, and Jackson Carroll. *Varieties of Religious Presence: Mission in Public Life*. New York: Pilgrim Press, 1985.

Rorty, Richard. *Consequences of Pragmatism*. Minneapolis: University of Minnesota Press, 1982.

_____. *Philosophy and the Mirror of Nature*. Princeton: Princeton University Press, 1979.

Roszak, Theodore. *Unfinished Animal: The Aquarian Frontier and the Evolution of Consciousness*. London: Faber, 1976.

_____. *Where the Wasteland Ends: Politics and Transcendence in Post-Industrial Society*. Garden City, N.Y.: Doubleday, 1973.

Rouner, Leroy S., ed. *Foundations of Ethics*. Notre Dame, Ind.: University of Notre Dame Press, 1983.

Rupp, Gordon. *Luther's Progress to the Diet of Worms*. New York: Harper Torchbooks, 1964.

_____. *The Righteousness of God: Luther Studies*. London: Hodder & Stoughton, 1953.

Scheffler, Israel. *Four Pragmatists: A Critical Introduction to Peirce, James, Mead, and Dewey*. New York: Routledge & Kegan Paul, 1974.

Schleiermacher, Friedrich. *Brief Outline of the Study of Theology*. Translated by Terrence N. Tice. Richmond: John Knox Press, 1966.

_____. *The Christian Faith*. Edited and translated by H. R. Mackintosh and J. S. Stewart. Edinburgh: T. & T. Clark, 1928.

Schlesinger, Arthur A. *The Disuniting of America: Reflections on a Multicultural Society*. New York: W. W. Norton, 1993.

Schlier, Heinrich. *Principalities and Powers in the New Testament*. New York: Herder & Herder, 1964.

Shenk, Wilbert R., ed. *Exploring Church Growth*. Grand Rapids: William B. Eerdmans, 1983.

Silk, Leonard, and Mark Silk. *The American Establishment*. New York: Basic Books, 1980.

Silk, Mark. *Spiritual Politics: Religion and America since World War II*. New York: Simon & Schuster, 1988.

Silverman, Hugh J., ed. *Postmodernism: Philosophy and the Arts*. New York: Routledge, 1990.

Smart, Ninian. *Philosophers and Religious Truth*. London: SCM Press, 1964.

_____. *Worldviews: Crosscultural Explorations of Human Beliefs*. New York: Scribner's, 1983.

Smith, John E. *Reason and God: Encounters of Philosophy with Religion*. New Haven: Yale University Press, 1961.

Sokoloff, Boris. *The Permissive Society*. New Rochelle, N.Y.: Arlington House, 1972.

Sontag, Frederick. *How Philosophy Shapes Theology: Problems in the Philosophy of Religion*. New York: Harper & Row, 1971.

_____ and M. Farrol Bryant, eds. *God: The Contemporary Discussion*. New York: Rose of Sharon Press, 1982.

Sorel, Georges. *The Illusion of Progress*. Translated by John and Charlotte Stanley. Berkeley and Los Angeles: University of California Press, 1969.

Stevens, Edward. *The Religion Game: American Style*. New York: Paulist Press, 1976.

Stout, Jeffrey. *The Flight from Authority: Religion, Morality, and the Quest for Autonomy*. Notre Dame, Ind.: University of Notre Dame Press, 1981.

Sykes, Charles J. *A Nation of Victims: The Decay of the American Character*. New York: St. Martin's Press, 1992.

Terrien, Samuel. *The Elusive Presence: The Heart of Biblical Theology*. San Francisco: Harper & Row, 1978.

Thielicke, Helmut. *Being Human, Becoming Human: An Essay in Christian Anthropology*. Translated by Geoffrey W. Bromiley. Garden City, N.Y.: Doubleday, 1984.

_____. *The Evangelical Faith*. Translated and edited by Geoffrey W. Bromiley. Grand Rapids: William B. Eerdmans, 1974.

Tinder, Glenn. *Against Fate: An Essay on Personal Dignity*. Notre Dame, Ind.: University of Notre Dame Press, 1981.

Tippett, A. R. *Church Growth and the Word of God*. Grand Rapids: William B. Eerdmans, 1970.

Tipton, Steven M. *Getting Saved from the Sixties: Moral Meaning in Conversion and Cultural Change*. Berkeley and Los Angeles: University of California Press, 1982.

_____, ed. *God, Man and Church Growth*. Grand Rapids: William B. Eerdmans, 1973.

Torrance, Thomas F. *Theology in Reconstruction*. Grand Rapids: William B. Eerdmans, 1966.

Toynbee, Arnold J. *Christianity among the Religions of the World*. New York: Scribner's, 1957.

Turner, James. *Without God, without Creed: The Origins of Unbelief in America*. Baltimore: The Johns Hopkins University Press, 1985.

Van Engen, Charles. *The Growth of the True Church*. Amsterdam: Rodopi, 1981.

Von Laue, Theodore H. *The World Revolution of Westernization: The Twentieth Century in Global Perspective*. New York: Oxford University Press, 1987.

Wagner, C. Peter. *Church Growth and the Whole Gospel: A Biblical Mandate*. San Francisco: Harper & Row, 1981.

_____. *Leading Your Church to Growth*. Ventura, Cal.: Regal Books, 1984.

Walsh, James, and P. G. Walsh. *Message of the Fathers*. Vol. 17: *Divine Providence and Human Suffering*. Wilmington, Del.: Michael Glazier, 1985.

Ward, Keith. *The Concept of God*. New York: St. Martin's Press, 1974.

Weber, Max. *The Sociology of Religion*. Translated by Ephraim Fischoff. Boston: Beacon Press, 1963.

Webster, Douglas D. *Selling Jesus: What's Wrong with Marketing the Church*. Downers Grove, Ill.: InterVarsity Press, 1992.

Weiss, Michael J. *The Clustering of America*. New York: Harper & Row, 1988.

Weiss, Richard. *The American Myth of Success: From Horatio Alger to Norman Vincent Peale*. New York: Basic Books, 1969.

Wheeler, Barbara G., and Edward Farley, eds. *Shifting Boundaries: Contextual Approaches to the Structure of Theological Education*. Louisville: Westminster/John Knox Press, 1991.

White, Morton. *Pragmatism and the American Mind: Essays and Reviews in Philosophy and Intellectual History*. New York: Oxford University Press, 1973.

Whyte, William. *The Organization Man*. New York: Simon & Schuster, 1956.

Wingren, Gustav. *Creation and Gospel: The New Situation in European Theology*. Lewiston, N.Y.: Edwin Mellen Press, 1979.

_____. *Creation and Law*. Translated by Ross Mackenzie. London: Oliver & Boyd, 1961.

Wolterstorff, Nicholas. *On Universals: An Essay in Ontology*. Chicago: University of Chicago Press, 1971.

_____. *Reason within the Bounds of Religion*. Grand Rapids: William B. Eerdmans, 1971.

Wuthnow, Robert. *The Consciousness Reformation*. Berkeley and Los Angeles: University of California Press, 1976.

_____. *The Restructuring of American Religion: Society and Faith since World War II*. Princeton: Princeton University Press, 1988.

_____. *The Struggle for America's Soul: Evangelicals, Liberals, and Secularism.*
    Grand Rapids: William B. Eerdmans, 1989.
Wyschogrod, Edith. *Saints and Postmodernism: Revisioning Moral Philosophy.*
    Chicago: University of Chicago Press, 1990.
Yankelovich, Daniel. *New Rules: Searching for Self-Fulfillment in a World
    Turned Upside Down.* New York: Random House, 1981.

Index